DINGERS

DINGERS

The 101 MOST MEMORABLE HOME RUNS *in* BASEBALL HISTORY

JOSHUA SHIFRIN
and TOMMY SHEA

Sports Publishing books may be purchased in bulk at special discounts for sales promotion, corporate gifts, fund-raising, or educational purposes. Special editions can also be created to specifications. For details, contact the Special Sales Department, Sports Publishing, 307 West 36th Street, 11th Floor, New York, NY 10018 or sportspubbooks@skyhorsepublishing.com.

Sports Publishing® is a registered trademark of Skyhorse Publishing, Inc.®, a Delaware corporation.

Visit our website at www.sportspubbooks.com.

10 9 8 7 6 5 4 3 2 1

Library of Congress Cataloging-in-Publication Data is available on file.

Cover design by Tom Lau
Cover photo credit: AP Images

Papaerback ISBN: 978-1-68358-453-7
Ebook ISBN: 978-1-61321-832-7

Printed in the United States of America

Joshua:
This book is dedicated to my two amazing sons. I love you.

Tommy:
In memory of Paul Donoghue, Sister Patricia Feeley,
Jim Fox, and Garry Brown

CONTENTS

INTRODUCTION

Major League Baseball. The National Pastime. A piece of the world's sports fabric. Hundreds of millions of baseball fans span the globe. From Asia and South America to right here in the good ol' USA, the world loves its hardball.

From splitters to spitters, from a frozen rope to a suicide squeeze, from extra innings to no-hitters, baseball is truly a great game. But nothing gets the juices flowing like a home run, a round-tripper, a big bomb, the long ball.

A "dinger."

Baseball fans worldwide love the big hit. Some of the most iconic moments in all of sports have come via the home run. From a modern-day blast to the long shots of yesteryear, it's amazing how one mighty swat of the lumber can produce a moment that is remembered and revered for generations.

One of the many things that make this great sport so perfect is its very imperfect nature, its ability to spark conversation and debate. Who is the best player of all time? Which team was the greatest of them all? Which moments stand apart from the rest? And, of course, the argument over the greatest homer of all time. Was it Bobby Thomson's big hit that led to those immortal words, "The Giants Win the Pennant!"? Was it Hammerin' Hank Aaron's 715th blast that eclipsed the Babe's seemingly unreachable mark? Was it Kirk Gibson's walk-off blast in Game One of the 1988 World Series that ignited the Dodgers upset victory over the mighty A's? The deliberation will persist forever.

Now, Shifrin and Shea scour the chronicles of baseball history to choose the 101 most memorable home runs of all time. While this list may cause some disagreement, baseball fans everywhere will relish reliving these most memorable home run moments. Nothing—but *nothing*—creates more excitement than the classic long ball, the big bomb, the round-tripper, the homer.

The *DINGER!*

101 JOSE CANSECO: THAT'S USING YOUR HEAD!

On May 26, 1993, in a game between the Texas Rangers and Cleveland Indians, Jose Canseco became a part of one of the craziest home runs in history . . . but *not* with his bat. Like all castles filled with kings, there are always a couple of jesters around to keep things lively.

Canseco's mercurial career was filled with the highest of highs and the lowest of lows. After being drafted in the 15th round in 1982 by the Oakland A's, he eventually broke into the majors at the end of the 1985 season. The big man who carried a big bat and who had an ego to match quickly made a name for himself and, in 1986, he was named the American League Rookie of the Year. Two years later, in 1988, the multitalented Cuban-American became the first man to hit 40 home runs and steal 40 bases on his way to a unanimous American League Most Valuable Player title.

It wasn't all roses and rainbows for the superstar, however. After his retirement, Canseco admitted to using anabolic steroids during his career in a tell-all book entitled *Juiced: Wild Times, Rampant 'Roids, Smash Hits, and How Baseball Got Big*. Today, in addition to his exploits on the field, he is largely remembered for his financial woes, and the circus atmosphere that follows his unveiling the steroid era in baseball.

But in the middle of Canseco's career, there was one incident that qualifies as simply unique. Canseco was playing right field for the Rangers. When the Indians came to bat in the bottom of the fourth, the Tribe's utility infielder, Carlos Martinez, launched a shot toward the gap between right and center field. Canseco immediately sprinted toward the ball. He was about to glove it when he lost the ball in the sun. He found, or felt it, soon enough. It bounced off the top of his head and over the fence for a home run!

Martinez was credited with a dinger, both literally and figuratively, as the befuddled Canseco could only shake his throbbing head and smile. This wacky moment is widely remembered as one of the most unique four-baggers in the game's history.

100 DICK NEN: THE ONE THAT MATTERED

In September of 1963, the St. Louis Cardinals had won 19 of their previous 20 games.

They were within a game of the first-place Los Angeles Dodgers, whom they were hosting on September 18 as the end of the season was approaching.

The Cardinals had scored 120 runs in their 20-game sprint toward the National League pennant. It was also Hall of Famer Stan Musial's last season. There was definitely magic in the air.

That is, until the Cards faced Johnny Podres and Sandy Koufax.

The two Dodger lefties silenced the sizzling Cardinal bats, allowing one run and seven hits in the first two games of the series.

Game Three was close to a do-or-die one for the Redbirds. And they had future Hall of Famer Bob Gibson pitching for them.

Gibson was twenty-seven years old and just coming into his prime. He would go 18–8 that season—and only get better in the years that followed.

The Dodgers were starting Pete Richert, a lefty who had made his major-league debut a year earlier against the defending National League champion Cincinnati Reds and struck out the first six batters (Vada Pinson, Frank Robinson, Gordy Coleman, Wally Post, Johnny Edwards, and Tommy Hunter) he faced to start his career.

He would later be an All-Star with the Washington Senators and a key member of the great Baltimore Orioles teams of the 1960s and early '70s, but at this point in his career he couldn't crack the Dodger starting rotation that began with Koufax, Don Drysdale, and Podres.

Cardinals right fielder Charlie James hit a two-run homer off Richert in the second. In the third, center fielder Curt Flood doubled home two more.

The Cardinals owned a 5–1 lead in the top of the eighth, and Gibson had retired 10 straight Dodgers.

Bob Miller had kept the Dodgers in the game by spinning 4.2 innings of one-run ball in relief of Richert.

In the eighth, Dodger manager Walter Alston pinch-hit Dick Nen for Miller.

The night before, Nen had been playing for the Spokane Indians, the top farm team of the Dodgers, against the Oklahoma 89ers in Game Seven of the Pacific Coast League Championship.

Oklahoma City won the title, but Nen's consolation prize was a trip to the National League pennant race.

Gibson was the first pitcher he faced.

Nen, a first baseman with gap power, lined out to left center.

The Dodger lineup turned over.

Shortstop Maury Wills and second baseman Jim Gilliam hit consecutive singles following Nen's liner. Gibson, tiring, then walked Wally Moon. The bases were now loaded. Tommy Davis, en route to back-to-back National League batting titles, singled home Wills and Gilliam.

Cardinal manager Johnny Keane pulled Gibson and summoned southpaw Bobby Shantz to face Ron Fairly, who was hitting under .200 against southpaws.

Alston elected to go to his bench for Frank Howard. Howard was a 6-foot-7 former National League Rookie of the Year who would go on to lead the American League in home runs twice.[1] He finished his career with 382 dingers.

Howard walked to load the bases again.

Dodger center fielder Willie Davis followed with a sacrifice fly, bringing in another run. The Dodgers were now down 5–4.

Moose Skowron, whom the Dodgers had acquired from the New York Yankees in the off-season, was sent up to pinch-hit for catcher Johnny Roseboro. Cards manager Johnny Keane went to his bullpen again, this time for right-hander Ron Taylor. Taylor would later be a key bullpen cog for the 1969 "Miracle" New York Mets and the longtime team physician for the Toronto Blue Jays. He coaxed Skowron into ending the inning with a harmless groundball.

In the ninth, Taylor popped up Dodger third baseman Ken McMullen to open the inning.

Batting in the nine hole, Nen took strike one. Nen was a California kid signed by the Dodgers two years earlier at age twenty-one. He batted and threw left. While he had hit .288 and knocked in 84 runs for Spokane, he had hit only nine homers in 158 games.

---

1 Howard led the American League in home runs in 1968 and 1970, both times with 44 dingers.

His first major-league hit—his only hit as a Dodger—was a long drive over the pavilion at Busch Stadium to tie the score, 5–5, and send the game into extra innings.

In the 13th, Dodger Willie Davis led off with a single. Alston decided not to pinch-hit for Perranoski. The pitcher tried to sacrifice Davis to second, but struck out. Dick Tracewski hit a potential inning-ending grounder, but, thankfully for the Dodgers, the play was muffed. Davis went to third, Tracewski to second.

Up came Nen.

Keane decided to walk him to load the bases and set up a potential double-play opportunity with the speedy Maury Wills coming to bat. Wills hit a grounder, but Cardinal second baseman Julian Javier only had a play at first, which allowed Davis to score. Dodger reliever Ron Perranoski, who went 16–3 in 1963 out of the bullpen, pitched six shutout innings, escaping a bases-loaded jam in the 10th to secure the win.

The pennant race was over. The Dodgers would breeze to the National League pennant, winning by six games, and then sweep the Yankees in the World Series.

Dick Nen didn't play an inning for the Dodgers the following season. Instead, he spent the summer back in Spokane, where he hit 18 homers and batted .280. In December of 1964, Nen was traded along with Frank Howard, Ken McMullen, Pete Richert, and Phil Ortega to the Washington Senators for left-handed starting pitcher Claude Osteen and utility infielder John Kennedy.

Nen had his best year in the major leagues in 1965, his first full season, when he had six homers, 31 RBIs, and a .260 average. He spent six years in the bigs and hit a total of 21 homers, with a lifetime batting average of .224.

Nen played nine more years in the minors, retiring in 1972. While only having 21 dingers in the majors, he clubbed 103 in the minors with a .291 average.

When he retired, he returned to California. Dodger fans and Cardinal rooters never forgot him. Baseball fans remembered him, too, because of his palindromic last name.

He also instructed his son, Robb, in the finer points of the game.

* * *

Robb Nen started out as a third baseman, but was later shifted to the mound, and was drafted in 1987 by the Texas Rangers in the 32nd round. He made his major-league debut in 1993.

Robb Nen, a right-hander who could throw 98 miles an hour and had an out-of-this-world splitter, was one of the game's top relief pitchers, finishing his career with 314 saves and striking out 793 batters in 715 innings. He also helped the Florida (now Miami) Marlins to the 1997 World Series.[2] He would also help the San Francisco Giants to the Series in 2002.

"My father told me, it must have been a thousand times, 'Let everything you do show your respect for the game. Don't cheat yourself, and don't cheat your teammates.'"

Dick Nen would know. He had almost four times as many minor-league at-bats as he did big-league plate appearances.

Only one was famous, but he made them all count.

---

2 The 1997 Marlins were the quickest team to win a World Series after becoming a franchise (four years after entering the league in 1993), passing the 1969 "Miracle" Mets (seven years after entering the league in 1962).

99 JOHN LOWENSTEIN: THE TIME, LET IT BE LOWENSTEIN

For much of his 16-year career, John Lowenstein was a respected utility player.

He also was a character.

He had a quip for almost every occasion, including the effort he extended to being prepared for a long season. "I flush the john between innings to keep my wrists strong," Lowenstein once said.

Always available for a quote, he even shared his disdain of fan clubs. "What are they for? Does a player have to have one? I think they are a waste of people's time."

He then started the Lowenstein Apathy Club.

He couldn't keep up with the mail that promised no interest in his career.

Lowenstein loved it. He saw the intangibles in baseball.

"There are so many intangibles in victory," he noted. "I have always considered myself an intangible asset to a team. Perhaps because the tangible assets of my career are not so impressive."

Lowenstein led baseball in self-deprecation, although he was a lot better player than he would let on. Baltimore Orioles Hall of Fame manager Earl Weaver knew how good he was.

Weaver often said Lowenstein's acquisition was "the bargain of the decade."

* * *

Lowenstein was born in Montana in 1947, but grew up in California. Long and lean, he was a second-team All-American shortstop at the University of California at Riverside, where he hit .393 and earned a bachelor's degree in anthropology. The Indians selected the left-handed hitter in the 18th round of the 1968 draft.

He missed much of the 1969 minor-league season because of a Marine Reserve commitment. In his first full season as a pro, he hit .295 with 18 home runs for the Wichita Aeros.

"I honestly don't know what we would do without John," said Ken Aspromonte, former big-leaguer and Wichita manager. "He's playing short, third, all the outfield positions. He's hit the ball, made the plays, taken the extra base, everything anyone could ask."

That versatility earned Lowenstein a promotion to the Indians in September of 1970. He singled and knocked in a run in his first at-bat.

Lowenstein bounced between the Indians and Wichita in 1971. Along the way he picked up the nickname "Brother Lo" from teammates. He was in the big leagues for good by 1972. In 1974, the Indians traded right fielder Walt "No-Neck" Williams to the New York Yankees. That made Lowenstein the starting left fielder for the Tribe, although he would fill in for third baseman Buddy Bell when he was injured.

The difference between third and left field for Lowenstein?

"At third base I can hear the fans yelling at me when I miss a ball and I can pick out those fans and yell right back at them. In left field, you don't know who is yelling at you."

When the Indians lost designated hitter Rico Carty to the Toronto Blue Jays in the 1976 expansion draft, they realized their mistake in leaving him unprotected. Carty was still productive and popular. In December 1976, the Tribe sent Lowenstein and catcher Rick Cerone north to get him back.

Within days, the Indians shipped outfielder George Hendrick to the San Diego Padres for outfielder Johnny Grubb, infielder Hector Torres, and catcher Fred Kendall. When Grubb hurt his knee in spring training of 1977, the Indians swapped Torres to Toronto for none other than Lowenstein.

In Joseph Wancho's Lowenstein profile for the Society of American Baseball Research, he noted that Lowenstein considered the deal to be one of the great international trades of all time, and that the United Nations had to give their approval of the deal. "A Mexican (Torres) to a Canadian team (Toronto) for a Jewish gringo (me) to a tribe of Indians (Cleveland)," Lowenstein said. "Now figure that out. It's a three-nation deal at least. It involves money as well, pesos, Canadian, and American money. In fact, I'm the first Jewish Indian traded for a Mexican."

The amusing part of that comment was that the last sentence was more fiction than fact.

"The irony was that Lowenstein was not Jewish," Wancho wrote. "The Municipal Stadium organist would serenade him with 'Hava Nagila' when he came to bat until Lowenstein let the organist know he was actually a Roman Catholic. After that, the theme song for his at-bats was 'Jesus Christ Superstar.'"

No such details mattered in 1978. Lowenstein was traded to the Texas Rangers along with pitcher Tom Buskey for designated hitter Willie Horton, a one-time Detroit Tigers star, and left-handed pitcher David Clyde, the first pick in the 1973 draft.

After a season in Texas, Lowenstein was released, and later picked up on waivers by the Orioles for $20,000.

"We tried to get him for a long time from Cleveland but every time we talked to the Indians about him, they'd ask for one of our top pitchers, like Dave McNally or Mike Cuellar," Weaver said.

Weaver was already imagining platooning Lowenstein's left-handed bat with Gary Roenicke's right-handed stick in left field.

"I glance at the lineup card, I look for length," Lowenstein said that summer. "If I see a very long name, I know I am playing. I also see a misspelled name. Earl always puts the 'i' before the 'e.' Sometimes I'll correct it, but the next day it's still misspelled."

And in 1979, he was just one of the pieces that fit for the Birds as they stopped the Yankees three-year run and won the American League Eastern Division pennant.

Lowenstein, who favored aviator glasses and sported a droopy mustache and long dark hair, knocked 11 homers and 34 RBIs during the regular season. But he didn't become part of Oriole lore until the playoffs.

* * *

The Orioles were facing the California Angels in Game One at Baltimore's Memorial Stadium. The score was tied, 3–3, in the bottom of the 10th. The Birds had men on first and third with two outs.

Weaver decided to pinch-hit Lowenstein for the Orioles slick-fielding but light-hitting (.167) shortstop Mark Belanger. Weaver always had white index cards within reach. Each was filled with what hitters accomplished against pitchers and what pitchers did against hitters. The only thing he knew about California reliever John Montague was that Lowenstein was 3-for-4 with two home runs lifetime against the right-hander.

Montague got ahead of Lowenstein, 0–2. His third pitch, a forkball, was driven high and deep down the left field line.

Fair or foul? Deep enough?

Not only was it fair, but landed in the first row of seats. Lowenstein had secured his place in Oriole history. Municipal Stadium was bedlam.

The Orioles would beat the Angels, but lose in the World Series to the Pittsburgh Pirates.

Lowenstein's best season came in 1982, when he was thirty-five. He jacked 25 homers and batted .320. He retired in 1985 as an Oriole folk hero.

When asked what he remembered circling the bases on October 3, 1979, the date of his big home run, Lowenstein said he vividly recalled Weaver running toward him.

Weaver was a short man, built like a fire hydrant. He was thrown out of nearly 100 games in his Hall of Fame managerial career. It was strange to see Weaver so happy and so far from the dugout.

"I never saw such a little man in the baseline," Lowenstein joked.

98 HANK BLALOCK: A BOMB BY THE NEW BRETT

Hank Blalock was going to be the new George Brett.

That's what everybody—coaches, scouts, front-office decision-makers, and reporters—were saying about him.

Blalock was a high school third baseman from San Diego with a college scholarship in hand when the Texas Rangers took him in the third round of the 1999 amateur draft. He won the Gulf Coast League batting championship that summer with a .361 average.

John Sickels, a baseball writer who majors in the minors, wrote at the time: "I was impressed enough to put him in my 2000 book [*Baseball Prospects*], unusual since I didn't write about many rookie ball guys. . . . Not only that, I gave him a Grade B+ writing that he might develop into a George Brett-class hitter. 'Yes, I know what I'm saying,' I wrote, 'but I have a great feeling about this one.' A month after the book came out in the spring of 2000, I talked with a major league GM who told me Blalock's makeup was exceptional, and that he was the steal of the draft, although the GM thought the Brett comp was overdone."

The twenty-one-year-old had started the 2002 season with the Rangers, but hit only .211 and was sent back down to Triple A. No one expected he'd be there long, as he was considered the best everyday prospect in the game by *Baseball America*, the bible of the minor leagues.

In 2003, Blalock, who batted left and threw right, finally proved what all the fuss was about. He was the starting third baseman for the Rangers, an up-and-coming team with young stars. Alex Rodriguez was the starting shortstop, Michael Young was playing second, and a young Mark Teixeira was at first. The Rangers had little pitching, but were building what looked like a bright future.

Angels manager Mike Scioscia selected Blalock, then twenty-two and hitting .323, for the All-Star Game that was held at U.S. Cellular Field in Chicago on July 15, 2003. Angels third baseman Troy Glaus played the first seven innings for the American League, but Scioscia sent Blalock up to bat in the eighth.

It was no favor.

Blalock was going to face Eric Gagne, the fireballing right-hander of the Los Angeles Dodgers, who hadn't blown a save since August 26, 2002, and was on his way to winning the Cy Young Award. The National League was leading, 6–4.

Gagne enticed Boston's Nomar Garciaparra to ground out to short. Anaheim's Garret Anderson followed with a double. Pinch-hitter Carl Everett grounded out, moving pinch-runner Melvin Mora (for Anderson) to third. Toronto's Vernon Wells then doubled to bring Mora home and cut the lead to 6–5.

With two outs and Wells at second, Blalock received his shot on the big stage. He worked the count to 3–1. Gagne threw a fastball, of course.

Blalock boomed it to right-center field for what proved to be the game-winner. The next time Gagne coughed up a game was almost a year later, on July 5, 2004.

Gagne was dominant in 2003, going 55 for 55 in save opportunities, recording 137 strikeouts in 82⅓ innings, and pitching to a 1.20 ERA. He surrendered only three home runs that year: to Montreal's Vladimir Guerrero, Colorado's Todd Helton, and Blalock's All-Star blast.

Blalock finished his season with 29 homers, 90 RBIs, and a .309 average.

He was even better in 2004, surpassing his numbers from the previous year with 32 homers and 100 RBIs, and was selected for his second All-Star Game. Scouts raved about his improved defense, and teammates praised his work ethic. He was being talked about as the best third baseman in Rangers history.

In Texas, Blalock even had a fan club called Hank's Homies. They would arrive at The Ballpark in Arlington wearing cowboy hats, eye black, and Blalock jerseys.

In 2005, however, they had less of a reason to dress up.

Blalock hit 25 homers with 92 RBIs in 2005, but there was talk that he had begun swinging for the fences instead of trusting a stroke that was made for hitting doubles up the gap. There were also rumors the Rangers were going to put him on the market.

Blalock hit his 100th career homer in 2006. He missed much of the 2007 season after being diagnosed with thoracic outlet syndrome, a term used to describe a group of disorders that occur when there is an injury of the nerves or blood vessels in the lower neck and upper chest. Due to the syndrome, he needed to have his first rib removed.

In 2008, he was nagged by hamstring and shoulder woes. The Rangers tried him at first base before abandoning the idea and returning him to third. He did hit 25 homers in 2009, but struck out more than 100 times in fewer than 500 at-bats. "Enigmatic" was the word being used to describe Blalock. He ended his career with Tampa Bay in 2010 at age twenty-nine.

He finished with 153 home runs in nine big-league seasons, but none bigger than the one he slugged on a July night in Chicago.

97 SCOTT PODSEDNIK: A SPEEDSTER GOES DEEP

The count was 2–0. It was Game Two of the World Series.

The score was tied 6–6 in the bottom of the ninth at U.S. Cellular Field in Chicago. Rain was falling.

Never a power hitter, Scott Podsednik was nevertheless thinking about swinging away.

He looked into the Chicago White Sox dugout and spotted Ozzie Guillen, his manager.

"He shook his finger and said, 'Don't even think about it; take one,'" Podsednik recalled. "So I took a strike right down the middle."

The left-handed hitter stepped out of the box and took a practice cut.

Podsednik was thinking that Houston reliever Brad Lidge, who had a good fastball, was going to throw it again. And on October 23, 2005, Podsednik wanted to put a good swing on it.

He didn't look into the dugout again to see what his manager was signaling.

Like Podsednik, Lidge had been selected for his first All-Star Game in 2005. He was a 6-foot-5, right-handed fireballer who struck out 103 batters in 70 innings of work that season. In the process, he had recorded 44 saves in helping the Astros to their first World Series.

Lidge didn't want to walk Podsednik, who had led the National League in steals the year before with 70, and had swiped 59 in 2005. Walk him and he'd steal. That would give them a man on second with one out and two shots at bringing him home.

The White Sox thought they had it won when first baseman and new father Paul Konerko had slugged a grand slam in the seventh inning, making the score 6–4.

But the Astros had tied the game in the top of the ninth with two runs.

It was a momentous time for both teams. Established in 1962, Houston had never been in a World Series. The last time the White Sox had won one was 1917.

Podsednik and Lidge were also looking for a little redemption. Podsednik, never known for his arm, had been unable to throw out the potential winning run in the ninth, which started some grumbling in the stands and owner's box. In Lidge's previous game he had surrendered a three-run homer to Albert Pujols, which put a National League Divisional Series contest in doubt. He said he wasn't thinking about Pujols when he faced Podsednik, but the home run was on everyone else's mind.

A third-round draft pick by the Texas Rangers in 1994, Podsednik was a prototypical leadoff hitter for his time. He slapped at the ball, got on base, and always looked to steal another. Podsednik's speed, not his power, was on Lidge's mind.

In fact, Podsednik had not hit a home run for the White Sox that season. None. In 568 at-bats.

The White Sox had traded power (Carlos Lee) to Milwaukee for Podsednik's speed in December 2004. And while their roster didn't exactly gleam with All-Stars, it all worked under the guidance of Guillen. The White Sox won the American League Central Division by six games with a 99–63 record and swept the Red Sox in the Divisional Series.

The White Sox captured Game One of the 2005 World Series against the Astros, and beating them in Game Two would put them in a commanding position.

Lidge's next pitch to Podsednik: fastball. He swung, sending it over the 408-foot sign in right-center field.

"I don't think anybody in the ballpark was thinking about me hitting the ball out of the ballpark," the speedster admitted.

Tyler Kepner of the *New York Times* described the scene: "The White Sox players leaped joyously from their dugout, crashing into each other and bouncing together at the plate as Podsednik trotted into the throng."

It was the 14th walk-off home run in World Series history.

"I didn't think that he was going to walk me," Podsednik said. "Luckily, I got into a hitter's count. I was looking fastball the entire at-bat."

The blow helped the White Sox vanquish the ghosts of the 1919 team, better known as the "Black Sox" since eight players were accused, but eventually acquitted, of throwing the World Series (though they were suspended indefinitely from baseball).

Following Podsednik's blast, the White Sox went on to capture the 2005 Series in four straight games.

Lost a bit in the excitement of the shocking game winner by the speedster was the fact that while Podsednik went homerless in the regular season, he had hit another one in the playoffs.

In the Division series opener against the Red Sox, a 14–2 win, Podsednik homered off Geremi Gonzalez in the sixth inning.

It didn't mean a lot in a rout, but it still counted.

96 BERT CAMPANERIS: THE UBIQUITOUS CAMPY

Bert Campaneris is probably best known for playing all nine positions in a single game.

The Cuban native and shortstop by trade was small and wiry, and could steal a base almost at will. Six times he led the American League in swipes, and when he retired after the 1983 season, he ranked seventh in baseball history, with 649 bases stolen.[3] As part of his small-ball game, Campy also thrice led the AL in sacrifice bunts. But there was nothing small about his game in the biggest of postseason contests—Campy had three homers, four doubles, a triple, 11 RBIs, and six steals in October games.

"Ubiquitous" is the word often used to describe his game.

In response to the first pitch he saw in the big leagues, on July 23, 1964, he slugged a home run off Minnesota's Jim Kaat, who would go on to win 283 games in 25 seasons (and finally be elected to the Hall of Fame in 2022).

Later in the same game, Campy would hit another one over the fence. He's one of only five players ever to hit two homers in their big-league debut.

In 19 seasons, Campy was selected to six All-Star Games. As a leadoff hitter, he was integral to the success of the great Reggie Jackson/Sal Bando/Vida Blue/Catfish Hunter/Rollie Fingers-led green-and-gold Oakland A's of the early 1970s. But on September 8, 1965, Campy was playing for the Kansas City A's. The team was owned by the eccentric, visionary, and never boring Charlie O. Finley. The team wasn't drawing fans to the stadium, so Finley came up with the promotional idea of having Campy play all nine positions in a single game.

Before the game, Finley took out a million-dollar insurance policy on his young star.

Campy even pitched ambidextrously in the eighth inning. It was no big deal to him. He had once done that in the minors. The first batter he faced for the Los Angeles Angels was his cousin, the fine outfielder Jose Cardenal, who popped out.

---

3 As of the conclusion to the 2015 season, Campaneris was 14th all-time in stolen bases.

Campy allowed one hit and one run, walked two, and had one strikeout in his lone inning on the mound. He went 0-for-3 at the plate, but did steal his 49th base of the season. His only error occurred while playing right field. In the ninth, he was catching when Angel Ed Kirkpatrick collided with him at a play at the plate. Campy held on to the ball to preserve the 3–3 tie, but he had to leave the game for precautionary X-rays. The Angels ended up winning in 13 innings. A crowd of 21,576 showed up to see Campy play all nine positions. The following game had less of a draw, with only 1,271 fans in the seats at Kansas City's Municipal Stadium.

Campy finished the '65 season with a team-leading .270 average. He also led the league in triples (12) and stolen bases (51), which broke Hall of Famer Luis Aparicio's nine-year streak as the American League stolen base champion.

When the A's moved to Oakland in 1968, Campy became a fan favorite from day one. His best season might have been in '68, when he led the AL in hits (177) and all of baseball in steals (62). Two years later, Campy swatted 22 of his career 79 home runs. But the following year, in 1972, he gained national attention for another reason.

He'd lead off Game Two of the American League Championship Series against the Detroit Tigers with a single. He then stole second and third base, and scored the first run on a Joe Rudi single. Pure Campy baseball.

He already had three hits and two steals when he came up to bat against Detroit reliever Lerrin LaGrow in the seventh inning.

The speculation was that fiery Detroit manager Billy Martin ordered LaGrow to hit Campy, taking the bat out of his hands.

LaGrow plunked Campy on the left ankle, and he fired his bat out at LaGrow. The benches emptied. Campy and LaGrow were suspended for the rest of the series, but Campy was allowed to play in the World Series win against the Cincinnati Reds. It was Oakland's first world championship.

* * *

Campy ensured the A's would repeat in 1973. In the AL Championship Series, he led off Game Two against the Baltimore Orioles with a home run off of Dave McNally, a 17-game winner.

In Game Three, with the score tied 1–1 in the bottom of the 11th, Campy homered off Baltimore's Mike Cuellar, a fellow Cuban and an 18-game winner. It was the turning point for the A's in the five-game series.

In the '73 World Series, the A's met the New York Mets, the team with the lowest winning percentage ever to make it that deep into October. The Mets had won only 82 games in the regular season. The Cincinnati Reds, already the Big Red Machine, had won 99. But the Mets toppled the Reds in a five-game series.

The A's won Game One of the World Series, thanks to a double by starting pitcher Ken Holtzman, batting for the first time all year (because the American League had instituted the designated hitter rule). He scored when Campy hit a routine grounder that bounced between the legs of Mets second baseman Felix Millan. Campy then stole second and scored the winning run when Joe Rudi singled.

Campy had the game-winning hit in Game Three, but the Mets extended the Series to seven games. Holtzman was pitching against Jon Matlack, who had won 14 in the regular season and had been the NL Rookie of the Year the previous season.

In the third inning, Holtzman once again led off with a double. By that time in the Series, the A's, despite their powerhouse lineup, had yet to hit a home run. Campy solved that with a long drive to right that cleared the distant fence at the Oakland-Alameda County Coliseum. It would prove to be the game-winning drive. Reggie Jackson hammered a two-run homer later in the inning to seal the deal.

Campy would catch Wayne Garrett's pop-up for the last out of the game, putting the exclamation mark on the A's second of three consecutive World Series championships and a 5–1 Game Seven victory.

* * *

Campy hit .353 in the '74 World Series against the Los Angeles Dodgers, helping his team to another world championship.

Since Campy played all nine positions, only Cesar Tovar of Minnesota in 1968, Scott Sheldon of the Texas Rangers in 2000, and Shane Halter of the Detroit Tigers, also in 2000, have duplicated this feat.

Billy Martin held no grudges from his Detroit days. He told the Yankees to sign Campy when Martin was managing New York in 1983. Playing second and third base, Campy, then forty-one, hit a career-high .322 in a utility role.

Hall of Famer Rickey Henderson went on to break many of Campy's offensive records, but none of that makes his play and accomplishments any less ubiquitous.

95 HAROLD BAINES: A LATE BOMB FOR BAINES

On May 8, 2014, the thirtieth anniversary of Harold Baines's most famous home run, ESPN's Doug Padilla asked the Chicago White Sox great what he remembered about the game.

Baines paused, and then admitted, "I don't remember anything about it."

Wait.

He did.

A little.

"The only details I know is that [Tom] Seaver won both games [a day later]," he recalled. "Obviously I hit the home run in the 25th inning, but I don't know anything more than that. Oh, and I remember the error by [Milwaukee's] Randy Ready when they had a three-run lead or something like that."

Another thing Baines remembers: he was 1-for-9 before he ended the longest game in major-league baseball history with his home run in the bottom of the 25th inning.

Baines, a left-handed hitter with a small right leg kick, clubbed the 757th pitch of the game to center field off Milwaukee's Chuck Porter, the Brewers eighth pitcher.

No, he doesn't remember what the pitch was.

"I was just glad it was over," Baines told Tyler Kepner of *the New York Times* in 2014. "I think every player is excited to hit a home run for your team to win. I wish I did it in the ninth instead of the 25th."

Baines would hit 29 that season, a career high, in his remarkably consistent 22-year career.

The game was played over two days and took eight hours and six minutes to complete. It started on May 8, 1984, at Chicago's Comiskey Park and was a pitcher's duel between Milwaukee's future Hall of Famer Don Sutton and Chicago's Bob Fallon, a rookie who would never start another game in the big leagues.

The Brewers took the lead in the ninth, scoring twice, but the White Sox tied the game in the bottom of the inning. The score remained 3–3 until the start of the 18th, when the game was suspended because of the American League's 1:05 a.m. curfew. The teams had six men in scoring position during the extra innings, but couldn't push across a run.

When the game resumed the following day, Milwaukee's Ben Oglivie hit a three-run homer in the top of the 21st, but the White Sox knotted the score in the home half of the inning.

It seemed as if the game would never end.

During the 24th inning, Chicago manager Tony La Russa asked Tom Seaver to start warming up. The pitcher emerged from the clubhouse, where he was sipping coffee and working on a *New York Times* crossword puzzle. Seaver hadn't pitched in relief since 1976.

"All of these things went through my mind: 'I don't do relief. I don't do this. When I go in to pitch, I'm calm, cool, and collected, and I've done my mental preparation,'" he told the *Times*. "I was so nervous, I could barely get dressed."

Seaver, La Russa, and Sutton were just three of the six Hall of Famers who participated in the game. The others were Milwaukee's Robin Yount and Rollie Fingers and Chicago's Carlton Fisk, who caught all 25 innings.

Seaver pitched a scoreless 25th.

"I get to the dugout and I'm so hyper, I'm chirping like a baby robin: 'What a good reliever I am!'" Seaver told the *Times*. "Then I hear the crack of the bat." It was the homer by Baines. The game was over.

For the record, the White Sox stranded 24 runners.

Seaver then worked 8⅓ innings in the second game of the doubleheader for his second win of the day and the 276th of his career.

Jim Evans, the plate umpire on May 8, told the *New York Times* thirty years later that the longer the game went on, the looser the players got.

"Guys would look at the catcher and smile or hit him on the shin guards: 'You awake?' It doesn't become comical, but it's sort of lighthearted, like, What's going to happen next?"

Only one previous major-league game, between the National League's Brooklyn Robins and Boston Braves in 1920, had gone longer than 25 innings. It ended in a tie and in less than four hours.

The longest game in professional baseball took place on April 18–19, 1981, when the International League Rochester Red Wings played the Pawtucket Red Sox for 33 innings over 11 hours and 25 minutes. Future Hall of Famers Cal Ripken Jr. and Wade Boggs were on the field.

Harold Baines didn't play in either of those games. But in 1984, he was still playing right field for the White Sox. His knees weren't that bad yet.

He'd been taken by the White Sox with the first pick in the 1977 draft. He was in the big leagues by 1980, a star by 1982, and a team leader when the Pale Hose won the 1983 American League Western Division.

He wasn't so much a power hitter as a terrific all-around hitter, someone who could bullet line drives to all fields. Early in his career, he was a disciple of the hitting guru Charley Lau, who was instrumental in Hall of Famer George Brett's career.

In 1984, baseball historian Bill James wrote of Baines, "He is gorgeous, absolutely complete. I've seen him drop down bunts that would melt in your mouth, come up the next time and execute a hit and run that comes straight off the chalkboard. I've seen him hit fastballs out of the yard on a line, and I've seen him get under a high curve and loft it just over the fence."

In James's 2001 *The New Historical Baseball Abstract*, he rated Baines the 42nd-best right fielder in baseball history.

Baines, whose long face was usually adorned with a trimmed beard or a Van Dyke, hit better than .300 eight times—and .324 in 31 career postseason games. From 1980 to 1997, he reached double figures in home runs every year, and five times he stroked at least 29 doubles.

Baines was at his best in the clutch. He is tied for seventh in AL history for grand slams with 13. He is fourth in the category of three-homer games. He is tied for seventh in major-league history in walk-off dingers.

Until Seattle's Edgar Martinez and Boston's David Ortiz started piling up numbers as designated hitters in recent years, Baines held most of the DH records. The White Sox retired his number 3 in 1989—and he had 12 more seasons to go—but have unretired it three times on his return to the Pale Hose.

Baines finished his career with 384 homers, 2,866 hits, and 1,628 RBIs.

The Baltimore Orioles inducted Baines into the team's Hall of Fame but, as of 2015, he has not yet been elected to the National Baseball Hall of Fame.

Seventy-five percent of the vote is needed for induction in the National Baseball Hall of Fame. Baines has never received more than 6.1 percent.

94 JIMMY PIERSALL: THE CRAZY 100TH

Lost in the story of Jimmy Piersall is the fact that he was a very good baseball player.

Ted Williams, the Boston Red Sox great, thought Piersall was the best defensive center fielder he ever saw. And in Boston, Piersall had replaced a pretty good one in Dom DiMaggio.

Piersall was twice selected to the American League All-Star team (in 1954 and '56). He won two Gold Gloves and hit as high as .322 in 1961. In 1956, he led the American League in doubles with 40. The following year he had a career-best 19 dingers. He was also a terrific bunter.

Hall of Famer Rogers Hornsby, who didn't lead the league in handing out praise, said, "Piersall in my opinion is a throwback to the old time ball player."

Hornsby liked how Piersall would use batting practice to hone his skill at playing various depths and angles in center. Hornsby also might have recognized in the Waterbury, Connecticut, native something from his own no-holds-barred era. The bench jockeying nature, the fights he'd start, and how he engaged with fans. Overall, he had fun playing baseball.

But there was another side to that fun. Piersall was always nervous, fidgety, and edgy.

He seemed to collect stress the same way pockets accumulate lint. The only thing he did better than play center was worry. He'd also mimic opposing pitchers and rant at umpires.

What at first could seem like a prank, on second look appeared cruel or simply odd.

No one had a name for all of it (though some teammates called it "bush") until he was a member of the Boston Red Sox in 1952. Piersall started the season as the Sox's starting shortstop. That was manager Lou Boudreau's idea. He and Boston general manager Joe Cronin were former star shortstops and thought Piersall could make the switch. Instead, he worried.

During his rookie season, that anxiety manifested in different ways. He had been ejected from three games, started a brawl with New York's Billy Martin, and instigated a fight with a teammate. In one game, he mimicked Hall of

Famer Satchel Paige and DiMaggio. When the bullpen cart would putter by, he would stick out his thumb.

By June, Piersall was in right field, starting to hit, but losing his grip. By July, he was in a mental institution undergoing shock treatments. He was only twenty-two.

Piersall was diagnosed with a nervous breakdown and emotional exhaustion, then manic-depression. Later he was considered to have a bipolar disorder. (His mother had also suffered with mental illness.)

Piersall spent seven weeks in the hospital and didn't return to baseball until the following spring. In conversations with Cronin during the winter, he said he couldn't remember playing for the Red Sox in 1952.

But in 1953, Piersall won the starting right fielder's job with the Sox. He played in 151 games, finished with a .272 average, and led the league with 19 sacrifice bunts. He made a grab in right field on May 9 that Yankee Hall of Famer Phil Rizzuto called "the greatest catch I've ever seen."

In 1954, Piersall raised his average to .285 and hit eight homers. He was named to his first All-Star team and also collaborated on his life story with *SPORT* magazine's Al Hirshberg.

Piersall was even better in 1955: .283 average, 13 home runs, and 25 doubles. It was his first full season as a center fielder. His book, *Fear Strikes Out: The Jim Piersall Story*, was a national best seller, and the film rights were later sold.[4]

Reporting from the front lines of mental illness, the book was unblinkingly honest—startling for the day and age—earning Piersall great praise for its candor.

"I was aware that many others had been afflicted like I was," he said, "or were even now experiencing the same mental sickness and I felt if they learned how I had conquered mine, they would become encouraged in their own efforts at rehabilitation."

Piersall didn't like the movie. He felt it was too hard on his father, played by Karl Malden. Also, he believed Anthony Perkins didn't look like much of a baseball player. Or like him, black-haired and lantern-jawed.

But, due to the film, Piersall's fame spread. He became a popular off-season speaker. He needed the money, as he was the father of nine.

---

4 Piersall would eventually disown the film due to what he believed was its distortion of the facts.

* * *

Piersall continued to be hot with the bat and led the American League with 40 doubles in 1956 while hitting .293 and knocking in 87 RBIs. He was selected to his second All-Star team.

But after Piersall's first down season with the Sox in 1958, his nemesis, Billy Martin, had landed on Piersall's ribs. They hurt all season. Piersall was sent to the Cleveland Indians for Vic Wertz and Gary Geiger. The trade broke his heart.

This showed in his first season in Cleveland, when he hit just .246 and lost his job to Tito Francona, the father of future big-league manager Terry Francona. Piersall rebounded in 1960, with 18 homers, a .282 average, and brilliant defense. But the shadow of his mental illness was still there.

Due to his flickering belligerence, he was ejected from three games in 1959 and six in 1960. When he caught the last out of a game against the White Sox, he threw the ball into Comiskey Park's electronic scoreboard. He also once took solace—saying he was having a conversation with Babe Ruth—behind the center field monuments at the old Yankee Stadium. He tried to distract Ted Williams's at-bat by running from center field to right—and back. His teammates were embarrassed and confused. The Indians asked him to seek psychiatric help.

* * *

Piersall had a great year in 1961, hitting a career-high .322 and winning a Gold Glove. But in a game at Yankee Stadium—growing up in Waterbury, a Yankee town, he hated the Yankees—two men came running toward him. One was bellowing, "You crazy bastard, we're going to get you."

Piersall hit the first man with a right to the face, then took off after the other, barely missing kicking him in the backside.

The men were arrested. No one blamed Piersall. For a change.

Still, the Indians in the off-season shipped him to the Washington Senators. Then, in May of 1963, the Senators traded him to the New York Mets for the former Brooklyn Dodger Hall of Famer, Gil Hodges, who was named manager of the Senators.

Piersall was scuffling at the plate when he came to bat in the fifth inning on June 23, 1963, for the Mets at the Polo Grounds. Dallas Green (who would later manage the Mets) was on the mound for the Philadelphia Phillies.

Piersall was hitting only a buck-something. Even so, he still had 99 career home runs.

Piersall also knew that on June 14, Duke Snider, the legendary Dodger, had belted his 400th homer to little fanfare. Piersall decided he was going to have some fanfare when he hit his 100th.

It turned out it was a long, lazy fly ball to right. The Polo Grounds had a short right field, but Piersall's hit counted.

He started running around the bases—backward.

He concentrated so as not to trip. He even shook third-base coach Cookie Lavagetto's hand while rounding third. Some teammates laughed. Green steamed. So did baseball Commissioner Ford Frick. The Mets released him within a week.

Piersall ended up signing with the California Angels where, the following season, only two months after the arrival of the Beatles, he came up to bat wearing a Beatles wig and pretending to play guitar with his bat.

* * *

Piersall finished his career in 1967 when he realized he could no longer hit. For his career, he batted .272 and had 104 home runs.

Piersall took acting lessons in Hollywood, but usually played himself in television appearances. He worked in a variety of roles for renegade Oakland A's owner Charlie Finley. In the 1970s and '80s, he called White Sox games with legendary broadcaster Harry Caray. He always knew what he was talking about, even if the players disagreed.

He was who he was: Jimmy Piersall.

93 RICK WISE: DOUBLE TROUBLE ON MOUND

Rick Wise was still battling the effects of the flu when his turn in the rotation arrived.

Wise wasn't the kind of pitcher who skipped starts. In a long career that stretched from 1964 to 1982, Wise would win 188 games, complete 138 starts, and pitch more than 3,000 innings.

He was a gamer who would be traded twice, for Hall of Famers Steve Carlton and Dennis Eckersley. He'd also be the winning pitcher in one of the greatest games ever played: Game Six of the 1975 World Series. Besides, his Philadelphia Phillies teammates were counting on him, he would note in recalling the historic game of June 23, 1971.

When Wise woke in Cincinnati that morning, the temperature was already above 80 degrees and starting to soar. And he was still dealing with the flu.

"I came up the stairs from the coolness of the clubhouse to field level and the heat of the field sucked the breath out of me," he would say later. "These were the days of cookie-cutter stadiums with Astroturf. It was probably 120 degrees on the field at 6:30 p.m."

The ace of the Phillies, easily spotted because he was one of the few players to wear glasses, Wise slowly made his way to the bullpen, not wanting to expend more energy than needed.

"My warm-up pitches seemed to stop half way [sic] to home plate," he said. "I felt very weak and thought to myself, 'You'd better locate your pitches or you won't be around for long.'"

The Reds weren't quite yet the Big Red Machine, but they were getting there. The lineup included Pete Rose, George Foster, Johnny Bench, Tony Perez, and Dave Concepcion.

The first 12 Reds went in order.

"I felt myself getting stronger," Wise said, "possibly because I had sweated out the remnants of the flu."

The Reds were also swinging early in counts and hitting loads of groundballs, making for quick innings.

"My tempo increased, my focus increased and my command and location were excellent," he said.

Wise, who always prided himself on his hitting, came to bat in the visitor's half of the fifth against Cincinnati starter Ross Grimsley, a twenty-one-year-old southpaw who would later become a 20-game winner for the Montreal Expos.

Phillies right fielder Roger Freed had opened the inning with a double, and the Phils were holding a 1–0 lead.

With Wise at the plate, Grimsley left a pitch up in the zone, and he parked it over the left-field fence for his sixth major-league home run and a 3–0 lead.

The following inning, Wise walked Cincy shortstop Concepcion.

The perfect game was history, but the no-hitter lived on.

And now the game was still on the line.

Wise knew too well that, with the powerful Reds lineup, all they needed were a couple of bloops and a blast and, before the other team could react, the game would be tied.

Wise led off the eighth inning against Clay Carroll, who won 10 games out of the pen in 1971 and topped the National League in saves in 1972. Wise was ahead on the count, 2–0.

"I checked the third-base coach for a sign and [George Myatt] just turned his back on me," Wise said. "In other words the green light was on—swing at it! Clay threw the next pitch right down Broadway and I was ready."

He homered again, knocking in his third run of the game. The extra run wouldn't hurt, he knew, but Wise still had to retire six straight batters to preserve his no-hitter.

Wise set down five straight without much worry. The Cincinnati crowd was on its feet.

Two outs, bottom of the ninth, and up came Pete Rose, the man who would eventually break Ty Cobb's career hit record. Rose worked the count to 3–2. Wise decided on a fastball, down. Rose lashed a line drive right at Phillies third baseman Pete Vuckovich. The game was over.

Rick Wise became the first and only pitcher in baseball history to pitch a no-hitter and hit two home runs in the same game.

In 1931, Cleveland's Rick Ferrell was the first pitcher to throw a no-hitter and homer in the same contest. In 1944, Boston Braves pitcher Jim Tobin followed, and in 1962, Earl Wilson of the Boston Red Sox also accomplished the rare baseball feat. No pitcher has done so since then.

On February 25, 1972, in the midst of a contract dispute with the Phillies, Wise was dealt to the St. Louis Cardinals for Hall of Famer Steve Carlton, who was also in the middle of a contract haggle.

In the 1973 off-season, Wise was packaged with outfielder Bernie Carbo and sent to the Boston Red Sox for switch-hitting outfielder Reggie Smith.

Wise won 19 games in 1975 for the American League East champion Red Sox. He won the deciding game in the American League Championship Series against the Oakland A's and was the winner in relief in Game Six of the epic 1975 World Series, which was won on a Carlton Fisk home run in extra innings.

He missed hitting, once he was traded into the American League, which established the designated hitter in 1973, unlike the National League.

"I always figured I had an advantage over my opponent because I could swing the bat pretty well," he said of his time in the National League.

Wise finished his 18-year career in 1982. For his career, he recorded four one-hitters and whacked 15 home runs.

He was a minor-league pitching coach when his playing days were over. Sometimes he'd double as the team's hitting coach, too.

92 JOE MORGAN: "LITTLE JOE" JACKS ONE FOR THE GIANTS

Joe Morgan was in the Houston Astros organization, née Houston Colt .45s, for ten years.

Signed out of Oakland, California, in 1962, the 5-foot-7 second baseman made the big club for parts of 1963 and 1964, but was finally able to unpack his bags in 1965.

Morgan took the job of Nellie Fox, another short, left-handed swinging second baseman who, like Morgan, would end up in the Hall of Fame.

Fox was called "Little Nel." Morgan was dubbed "Little Joe." The two men immediately bonded.

It was Fox, in the twilight of his career, who is given credit for fixing a flaw in Morgan's swing. Morgan tended to keep his back elbow down low, and Fox suggested he flap his back arm like a chicken to keep his elbow up.

Unorthodox, sure. But Morgan tried it. And it worked. It also became a Morgan trademark.

"I think of Nellie Fox all the time," Morgan told Bill Jauss of the *Chicago Tribune* in 1990, on the eve of being inducted into the Hall of Fame. "I would not be the player I am without his help."

Along with instituting the arm flap, Fox was a constant instructor.

"He taught me in one year what it takes most players five years to learn," Morgan said. "He told me I had twice as much ability as he had. He taught me mental sides of baseball I'll never forget."

When Fox was dying from skin cancer in 1975, Morgan visited him at the hospital.

"He told me, 'I really hope you win the MVP,'" Morgan said. "He said, 'I'm pulling for you. You deserve it.'"

Fox died on December 1, 1975. He was forty-seven.

Joe Morgan would go on to win the National League MVP in 1975, hitting .327 with 17 homers and 94 RBIs.

His Cincinnati Reds manager Sparky Anderson said, "I have never seen anyone, I mean anyone, play better than Joe has played this year."

* * *

In an old-fashioned blockbuster of a deal, the Astros had traded Morgan to the Reds on November 29, 1971, for power-hitting first baseman Lee May (who'd broken Morgan's kneecap with a batting-practice line drive in 1966) and second baseman Tommy Helms. The Reds also received future Gold Glove center fielder Cesar Geronimo, starting pitcher Jack Billingham, and minor-league outfielder Ed Armbrister.

It wasn't a good trade for the Astros.

Morgan was an All-Star for the Reds from 1972 to 1979. Citing Morgan's walk-to-strikeout ratio, stolen base percentage, and fielding numbers, baseball historian Bill James named him the best second baseman in history, ahead of the Philadelphia A's star Eddie Collins and the St. Louis Cardinals star Rogers Hornsby.

The Sporting News listed Morgan as the 60th-best player in history when the magazine ranked the best of the best in 1999.

Morgan's run with the Reds ended in 1979. He next signed as a free agent with the Astros. His veteran attitude and winning ways helped them to a National League West pennant in 1980. Later in the same year, he was released by his old team and signed by the San Francisco Giants.

In 1982, as a Giant, he had his last good season, with 14 homers and 61 RBIs to go with a .289 average.

And while the Reds and Astros lay claim to Morgan, to some he'll always be the Little Giant.

* * *

Giants fans hate the Los Angeles Dodgers. And on October 3, 1982, the Giants, on the last day of the season at home in Candlestick Park, had a chance to exact baseball revenge by ending the Dodgers playoff chances.

The day before, the Dodgers had eliminated the Giants from the Western Division title race. It ended a great streak by San Francisco, which had been 14 games out of first on July 30, and nine games out on September 1.

Morgan was batting second for the Giants.

He came up in the seventh with two outs and two on in a 2–2 game. Morgan, then thirty-eight, had struck 21 homers in his two seasons in San Francisco.

The Dodgers, who had lifted starter Fernando Valenzuela for a pinch-hitter in the top of the seventh, called upon left-hander Terry Forster to get out of the jam. Morgan fell behind in the count, 1 and 2. Forster threw a slider, and Morgan redirected it deep to right field and over the fence. The crowd of 47,457 went crazy.

Circling the bases, Morgan thrust his right arm into the air. The Little Giant had hit a big dinger.

"I got my A-No. 1 swing at it, and when I hit them that good they usually go out," Morgan said after the game. "I've been in the big leagues 19 years and I've learned a lot of humility. It is tough to be over there [the Dodger clubhouse]. . . . But I wanted this one for the Giants and the fans."

Morgan, who was reunited with former Reds Tony Perez and Pete Rose on the 1983 Philadelphia Phillies, retired after the 1984 season and was elected into the Hall of Fame in 1990.

Of course, he mentioned Nellie Fox in his induction speech.

91 ED SPRAGUE JR.: A CANADIAN MILESTONE

By way of introduction, broadcasters and sportswriters would note that Ed Sprague Jr.'s father pitched in the big leagues. (He was on the 1972 world champion Cincinnati Reds roster but didn't pitch in that World Series.)

Or they'd mention that Ed's wife, Kristen Babb, had been a 1992 Olympic gold medalist in synchronized swimming at the summer games in Barcelona.

Sprague's bio, though, was presented almost as an afterthought. But he had a terrific one. He'd helped Stanford University to the 1987 and 1988 NCAA championships as a hard-hitting third baseman. He'd played on the 1988 U.S. Olympic team that won a gold medal when baseball was a demonstration sport.

The Toronto Blue Jays drafted Sprague in the first round of the 1988 amateur draft. He was a 6-foot-2, 215-pound right-handed hitter with power. The club was thinking he might be a catcher. Or a first baseman.

Sprague made his big-league debut in 1991 and came up to stay on July 31, 1992.

The Jays were loaded then, boasting future Hall of Famers Roberto Alomar and Dave Winfield. Their pitching staff was led by the likes of Jack Morris, David Cone, and Pat Hentgen.

Sprague's first career home run was delivered against the Minnesota Twins. Batting eighth and catching that Sunday in Toronto, he hit a three-run homer off Mike Trombley to beat the Twins, 4–2.

It stopped the rumble of boos Sprague was routinely greeted with while playing at home in Toronto; his wife had earned the gold medal ahead of Canadian swimmer Sylvie Frechette. The judging was called into question. Two years later, Frechette would be awarded the gold, though Babb-Sprague was allowed to keep her medal, too.

But early in Sprague's career, he mostly sat on the bench. The Blue Jays had Kelly Gruber at third, a two-time All-Star who knocked in 118 runs during the 1990 season. Members of the Blue Jays bench had been dubbed "The Trenches." No one quite knows where the name came from, but spare outfielder Derek Bell liked it so much that it stuck.

The Blue Jays, under the calming influence of fourth-year manager Cito Gaston, won the American League East by four games, then upset the Oakland A's in the American League Championship Series, four games to two.

Toronto went to Atlanta to start the World Series, where the Atlanta Braves easily won Game One.

The Jays were trailing in the eighth of Game Two. Toronto tried to rally. Roberto Alomar doubled to left with one out. Joe Carter and Dave Winfield followed with back-to-back singles, slicing the Braves lead to 4–3.

Atlanta starter John Smoltz was pulled from the game and left-hander Mike Stanton was summoned to face the lefty-swinging John Olerud. Stanton got his man, enticing a pop-up. Closer Jeff Reardon was called upon.

When Atlanta's closer Alejandro Pena went down for the year, the Braves acquired Reardon from the going-nowhere Red Sox. At that time, both Reardon and Smith were tied with 357 lifetime saves.

Reardon, then nearly thirty-seven, was 3–0 with three saves and a 1.15 ERA down the stretch for the Braves.

In the National League playoffs against the Pittsburgh Pirates, Reardon won Game Seven. He also saved an earlier game in the series and gave up no earned runs.

In Game Two of the World Series, Reardon struck out Gruber to end the Blue Jays uprising in the eighth.

Reardon sported a menacing black beard and was nicknamed "The Terminator." He was the closer for the Minnesota Twins when they won the World Series in 1987 and would finish his career with 367 saves, the first pitcher ever to save 40 games in both the American League and the National League. Not bad for an undrafted guy out of the University of Massachusetts.

On Sunday, October 18, 1992, Reardon entered the ninth inning protecting a one-run lead with the hopes of leaving Atlanta with a 2–0 World Series advantage.

It seemed the entire Atlanta-Fulton County Stadium shot to its feet, tomahawk chopping and chanting.

Derek Bell, the leader of the Trenches, led off the Blue Jay ninth with a walk. Sprague was sent up to pinch-hit for Toronto reliever Duane Ward, who was part of the terrific Jays bullpen that featured closer Tom Henke.

The late Blue Jays play-by-play man Tom Cheek said of Sprague, "Watch him hit a homer."

On the first pitch Sprague did just that, deep to left field.

The man with one home run all season and no pinch hits put the Blue Jays up, 5–4. Sprague hit a fastball that went down instead of up. Sprague's homer marked the first win by a foreign team in a World Series game. It was also only the second time in Series history that a pinch home run had given the trailing team the lead.

"I knew it was gone," Reardon said in his soft-spoken way after the game. "It was no cheapie. He hit it good. When I give up home runs, that's usually how they go. They get 'em pretty good."

Pat Borders, who would go on to be named Most Valuable Player in the '92 World Series, said of the Jays bench, "Then the guys in the trenches came through . . . Bell pinch-hits and draws a walk. . . . If Sprague rolls over on that pitch into a double play we come home down 2-0. We probably don't win."

Sprague appreciated the moment, but when asked which was a bigger deal, his World Series homer or his wife's gold medal, he said, "I think hers is the bigger accomplishment. It just took me one swing. She had to train fourteen years. I've been fortunate to have some nice moments."

Gaston said of Sprague, "You guys will hear from this young man for a long time. He studies the game, he works hard and he'll be around."

Sprague had his best year in 1996 for the Jays, with 36 homers and 101 RBIs. He was also an All-Star for the Pittsburgh Pirates in 1999, when he slugged 22 homers and knocked in 81 runs. But he ended up a journeyman after that, playing for Oakland, San Diego, Boston, and Seattle.

His 11 years in the majors were over in 2002. Sprague finished with 152 career homers, and as the only player ever to win championships in the College World Series, the Olympics, and the World Series.

90 SCOTT HATTEBERG: HATTY SAVES THE STREAK

The Oakland A's had won 19 games in a row, the last two in walk-off fashion, thanks to shortstop Miguel Tejada, who was having a MVP-type of season. On September 4, 2002, the hottest team in baseball was aiming for its 20th straight, an American League record.

The A's took an 11–0 lead that night at home against the Kansas City Royals. Tim Hudson, on his way to a 15–9, 2.98 season, was on the mound for the A's.

The winning streak was built with starting pitching, lead by Barry Zito, Mark Mulder, Tim Hudson, and the surprising Cory Lidle (a journeyman who was 3–0 and gave up only one run in August), dominant relief pitching (especially from closer Billy Koch), and home runs. Ten players had combined to smack 26 homers during the streak and, as a team, the A's would bop 205 during the season. In 14 of the games, the A's never trailed. They were behind by two runs only twice.

Billy Beane had assembled this team. He was a former number one draft choice of the New York Mets in 1980. He had failed as a player but succeeded in player development, buying in early and relying on statistical analysis in building financially-challenged teams with undervalued talent. Beane believed in walks the way bankers believe in money. His work drew the attention of best-selling writer Michael Lewis, who was interested in writing a book about this baseball revolution.

In the 2001 off-season, the A's lost slugging first baseman Jason Giambi to the big-moneyed New York Yankees. Beane responded by signing free agent Scott Hatteberg, a catcher with a ruptured nerve in his throwing elbow, who had never played first base. Beane liked Hatteberg's ability to draw walks and was also confident that the A's could return to their fourth consecutive postseason with Hatteberg and a payroll under $40 million.

* * *

Scott Hatteberg grew up idolizing Yankee great Don Mattingly. He was good enough to be drafted by the Boston Red Sox as a sandwich pick (between the first and second round) of the 1991 draft as compensation for the Kansas City Royals signing pitcher Mike Boddicker.

In parts of seven seasons with the Red Sox, Hatteberg slugged 34 homers and hit .267 with an on-base percentage of .358—about 40 points better than the league average—a stat few noticed. But after he hurt his elbow, the Sox traded Hatteberg to the Colorado Rockies for infielder Pokey Reese. Forty-eight hours later, the Rockies released Hatteberg, and the A's came calling, signing the injured player for less than $1 million. Oakland infield coach Ron Washington was charged with converting Hatteberg, who couldn't throw, to first base.

Hatteberg was hitting .271 with a .363 on-base percentage by September 4. With the A's comfortably in first place in the American League Western Division, he started the game on the bench.

The A's had built an 11–0 lead that night, but then almost blew it, as the Royals tied the game in the top of the ninth.

Outfielder Jermaine Dye led off the bottom of the ninth with a flyout against Kansas City reliever Jason Grimsley.

Oakland manager Art Howe decided to pinch-hit Hatteberg for outfielder Eric Byrnes.

Hatteberg, who had one career hit off of Grimsley (a two-run homer a year earlier, of course), took ball one.

The thirty-three-year-old then powered a no-question drive to deep right-center field, and the 55,528 fans at Network Associates Coliseum in Oakland rose in a can-you-believe it roar. The A's had set the new American League consecutive-game winning streak with 20 on the back of their third walk-off in a row.

As he circled the bases, Hatteberg bowed his head and raised his right arm, the elbow slightly crooked—the one that almost ended his career—in a low-key celebration.

It was a Hollywood moment in real time.

The A's 20-game winning streak was snapped two days later by the Minnesota Twins.

The team still went on to win 103 games and the American League West, but only to lose to the Twins, three games to two, in the American League Division Series. Tejada was the AL Most Valuable Player and Zito the Cy

Young Award winner. Beane accepted the job as Boston Red Sox general manager for five years and $12.5 million, then changed his mind and decided to stay in Oakland. Michael Lewis later wrote *Moneyball: The Art of Winning an Unfair Game*, and it became a *New York Times* best seller. In 2011, the book became a movie, with Brad Pitt starring as Beane and Chris Pratt as Hatteberg.

Hatteberg retired in 2008 with 106 career homers and a lifetime .361 on-base percentage, which is better than Hall of Famers Willie Stargell, Kirby Puckett, Eddie Murray, Roberto Clemente, and Hatteberg's hero, Don Mattingly. Beane hired Hatteberg as a special assistant after his playing days had ended.

89 REGGIE JACKSON: TITANIC ALL-STAR CLOUT AT TIGER STADIUM

If Minnesota's Tony Oliva hadn't dove for the liner off Oakland's Joe Rudi's bat on June 29, 1971, Reggie Jackson would never have gotten the chance to hit one of the longest dingers in baseball history.

But on June 29, 1971, Oliva, despite an already iffy right knee, gave it all he had diving for a shot to right field. Rudi ended up with a meaningless double in a 5–3 Minnesota win over Oakland, while Oliva, who was hitting .375, tore a ligament in his right knee, was sidelined for more than a month, and was never the same player again. (He was finally elected to the Hall of Fame in 2022.)

Oakland's Reggie Jackson was selected by Baltimore manager Earl Weaver to replace Minnesota's star right fielder, who would go on to win his third American League batting championship.

Reggie was already Reggie.

He was selected by the then Kansas City A's with the second pick in the 1966 amateur draft out of Arizona State, and made his big-league debut the following year, starting off with a triple.

By 1969, the A's were in Oakland and Reggie, then twenty-three, was challenging Roger Maris's single-season home run record with 37 in the first half of the season. He finished with 47, but was already a star. And in Detroit on July 13, 1971, Reggie was a star among stars. It was estimated that 60 million viewers tuned in to NBC as 23 future Hall of Famers participated in the final All-Star Game staged at Tiger Stadium.

It was also the first time two black pitchers, Vida Blue for the American League and Dock Ellis for the National League, would start against each other in the sport's showcase.

Thanks to Cincinnati catcher Johnny Bench's booming two-run homer in the second and a solo shot by Atlanta's Hank Aaron in the third, the National League owned a 3–0 lead off Vida Blue, who was 17–3 at the All-Star break, heading into the bottom of the third.

Boston Red Sox shortstop Luis Aparicio led off with a single off Ellis, who later would say he pitched the game drunk, and also would admit to pitching a no-hitter under the influence of the psychedelic drug LSD.

After Ellis's single, Reggie was sent up to pinch-hit for Blue. He was dressed in the A's uniform of the day: Kelly green and gold, white spikes. He was nursing a strained left hamstring.

The summer wind, sometimes gusting to 35 miles per hour, was blowing out to right. Reggie fell behind in the count. He choked up.

"A ball and two strikes," he would recall. "It was a hanging slider right out over the plate. I got the ball up in the air, the wind was blowing out. The neat thing for me, I was really trying to keep from striking out."[5]

Cincinnati manager Sparky Anderson, guiding the National League team, later said, "For me that's the hardest home run I've ever seen."

The ball kept rising.

"All I can say," Reggie noted later. "Is that ball had places to go."

Hall of Famer Al Kaline, who hit 399 career homers for Detroit, said, "It was one of those hits, when the bat hit the ball, it had a tremendous ringing noise. . . . I had a great view from the dugout. It was still going up with plenty of steam when it hit the tower on the roof in right. Nobody knows how far that could've gone."

In a *Detroit News* story, writer Lynn Henning described a test by Wayne State University to see how far Reggie's ball would have gone. Researchers concluded that the ball would have traveled 650 feet if it hadn't hit the transformer 100 feet above, and 100 feet from, the field. The ball landed back on the playing field, where San Francisco's Willie Mays retrieved it for Jackson. There were huge cheers and audible gasps. It was the intersection of science, power, and baseball.

Two batters later, Frank Robinson hit a two-run homer to put the American League in the lead. Robinson became the first player in history to hit home runs for both leagues in All-Star Games.

The midsummer classic would feature two more homers from Hall of Famers—Pittsburgh's Roberto Clemente and Minnesota's Harmon Killebrew. The American League broke an eight-game losing streak with the 6–4 victory. A dinger from a Hall of Famer produced every run.

Detroit's Hall of Fame broadcaster Ernie Harwell described the game as the second-best All-Star contest in history. Only 1941's was better, he said, recalling the event also held in Tiger Stadium, then known as Briggs Stadium, and ending with Boston's Ted Williams's walk-off home run.

---

5 He had good reason to worry, as he would strike out 161 times during the 1971 season.

Vida Blue would later call Reggie's home run the start of Reggie's "coming out party."

"It was his way to say to the world: 'See, I told you,'" Blue said. It was his signature on all his smack—and he wasn't afraid to talk smack. I liked that. He backed it up, and he always did it on a national stage."

And for Reggie, the stage would only get bigger, as would his homers. He ended his career with 563 homers, plus 18 in the postseason. But his 1971 moon shot was the only homer he hit in an All-Star Game.

88 JOHNNY CALLISON: MAJOR BLAST FROM A MODEST MAN

Johnny Callison remembered how Dick Radatz's fastball hummed in the seventh inning.

The Philadelphia Phillies right fielder playing in his first All-Star Game felt he was lucky to get wood on the big Boston right-hander's heater.

He wasn't alone.

The word "overpowering" didn't do Radatz justice in 1964.

He was 6-foot-6 with the body of an any-era football lineman.

New York Yankee Hall of Famer Mickey Mantle had dubbed Radatz "The Monster" with good reason. The right-hander fanned Mantle 44 times in 63 at-bats.

Before Radatz faced Callison, he had struck out Cincinnati's Johnny Edwards and New York's Ron Hunt. In the eighth, Radatz encored by fanning St. Louis's Bill White and Cincinnati's Leo Cardenas, and enticed Chicago's Billy Williams, a Hall of Famer, to weakly ground to second.

American League manager Al Lopez, who skippered the Chicago White Sox, let Radatz bat in the top of the ninth. Why not? It was an era when players took the All-Star Game seriously. The American League was leading, 4–3. The National League was sending up three right-handed hitters who had won or would win Most Valuable Player Awards: San Francisco's Willie Mays and Orlando Cepeda, and St. Louis's Ken Boyer.

The 50,000-plus at the new Shea Stadium were in a frenzy. It was hot and sunny on the July 7 afternoon. With 18 future Hall of Famers in uniform, the game felt bigger than the nearby World's Fair.

Mays fouled off five Radatz pitches before earning a walk to lead off the ninth. He then stole second. Cepeda followed with a bloop single to right. Mays held on third, but Yankees first baseman Joe Pepitone made an errant throw home and Mays scored to tie the game at four. Cepeda took second, and was pinch-run for by Curt Flood.

Radatz overpowered Boyer, retiring the third baseman on an infield pop. With first base open, Lopez called for Radatz to intentionally walk Edwards to set up a potential double play to end the game.

National League manager Walter Alston of the Los Angeles Dodgers countered with Milwaukee's Hank Aaron, the man who would best even Babe Ruth in career home runs, to pinch-hit for Hunt.

Aaron became Radatz's fifth strikeout victim of the afternoon.

Then up came Callison.

His number 6 in Philadelphia was treated like Mickey Mantle's number 7 in New York. He was an emerging star, to say the least. When Callison's manager Gene Mauch first saw him play, thought he was watching the second coming of Mel Ott, the great New York Giant who had hit 511 home runs in his 22-year career.

Bobby Wine, a Callison teammate, used the word "magnificent" to describe the young right fielder's play.

"But he was a funny guy in that his confidence never matched his ability," Wine later said. "Real humble, maybe too humble. It was like he was ashamed to be great."

At 5-foot-10, 170 pounds, Callison looked small compared to The Monster.

When he dug in to face Radatz again, Callison was using a lighter bat loaned to him by Billy Williams. Callison usually preferred a heavier stick, but felt he couldn't get around on Radatz's heat.

Callison blasted Radatz's first pitch to the loge section in Shea's right field for a three-run homer and a National League win, 7–4. He was the third player in history—Boston's Ted Williams and St. Louis's Stan Musial the others—to hit a walk-off home run in an All-Star Game.

"He reared and threw me a high hard one," Callison later said. "As soon as I swung, I thought it was a homer. You can just feel it—hear it! I was on cloud nine as I rounded the bases. By the time I rounded second, I saw Radatz throw his glove into the dugout."

He could also see a contingent of Hall of Famers–Mays, Aaron, Williams, Marichal, and Clemente—at home waiting to greet him.

Callison was sure his homer was an omen the Phillies were going to win the World Series in '64.

He was wrong.

The Phillies blew a 6½-game lead in the final dozen of the regular season. Had the Phillies won the pennant, Callison probably would have been the league MVP. Instead, Ken Boyer of the championship Cardinals won the award.

87 BILLY HATCHER: POSTSEASON PHENOM

If Bill Doran got on base, Billy Hatcher was supposed to bunt him to second.

That was the plan.

But Bill Doran struck out, swinging.

The Houston Astros were down to their last two outs in the bottom of the 14th inning on October 15, 1986, in Game Six of the National League Championship Series.

"Right beside the dugout, there was this lady with a little girl," Hatcher would later say. "I can't remember how old she was, but she said, 'It's all right, Billy's going to hit a home run.'"

Hatcher had only six all season.

The Astros had acquired him in the 1985 off-season for Jerry Mumphrey from the Chicago Cubs. Houston liked Hatcher's speed and defense but weren't counting on home runs.

Hatcher was shocked when he was traded. He thought he was going to be a Cubbie for life, as he has been drafted by the club in the sixth round of the 1980 draft, worked his way through their farm system, and made his big-league appearance for the club in 1984.

He hadn't initially been that excited about being traded to the Astros, who weren't expected to be very good in 1986. Pundits had picked them to finish fifth in the National League West. But Houston ended up having the last laugh.

An expansion team born in 1962, they were in October in '86, in their first postseason, still fighting against the mighty New York Mets, the team to beat since April (and the other expansion team to come into the league in '62). The Mets were leading the seven-game series, three games to two.

Starter Bob Knepper had shut out the Mets for eight innings, allowing just two hits. Then came the ninth.

With two strikes, New York's Lenny Dykstra tripled. Mookie Wilson followed with a two-strike single to right. After a groundout by Kevin Mitchell, Keith Hernandez poked a double to right center for a run. Knepper's day was over. The Astros were clinging to a 3–2 lead. It didn't last. A Ray Knight sacrifice fly tied the game.

In the top of the 14th, the Mets went ahead, 4–3, and were on the verge of winning the NL crown.

But the Astros believed if they could get to Game Seven, with their ace Mike Scott (who had struck out 306 batters in the regular season) back on the mound, there was no way they would lose. Scott, who had been drafted and discarded by the Mets, had already dominated New York twice in the fall of '86.

All that was hope and speculation. To force a Game Seven, the Astros had to win Game Six. And Houston hadn't scored a run in 12 innings.

Left-handed relief ace Jesse Orosco was pitching for the Mets.

Hatcher hit .258 his first year as an Astro, and was second on the team to Doran with 38 steals. He might have had only six dingers, but one in August was crucial—a grand slam in a must-win game against the Los Angeles Dodgers. In September, he'd delivered a homer in the 18th inning to beat his former team, the Cubs.

Orosco's first pitch to Hatcher in the 14th was a fastball that was drilled down the line in left. The Astrodome crowd of 45,718 stood as Hatcher missed a home run by inches, but the fans were back in the game.

Hatcher wasn't thinking home run at the time. He was just trying to get on base—and possibly steal second. He already had three stolen bases in the series and didn't believe the Mets could throw him out.

"I was trying to hit the ball hard and run," he recalled.

With the count 3-and-2, Orosco threw another fastball, a touch inside. Hatcher hit a towering fly deep to left. Running down the first-base line, he kept shouting, "Stay fair, stay fair!"

This time the ball did, hitting the foul pole.

"I remember her [the girl in the stands] saying that, and when I hit the home run, I was running around the bases saying, 'She knew this was going to happen before it happened.' It was unreal. It was an out-of-body experience . . . I don't think my feet hit the ground."

The fun, however, was short-lived.

The Mets scored three times in the 17th, and despite a rally by the Astros, one in which Hatcher stroked an RBI single, New York won the game and was headed to the World Series.

"We should have won [Game Six]," Hatcher said. "It wasn't just that one game; I think it was the whole series. That was probably one of the best series in baseball, ever. Both teams left everything they had out on the field. There was no second-guessing anything that you did. . . ."

When he hit the biggest home run of his career for Houston, one of his coaches was the great Yankee Yogi Berra, who occasionally would show off his World Series rings.

Hatcher remembers, "He would have them on, and he had one for every finger. I just said to myself, 'I want a ring.' I mean, after seeing Yogi and being around him and seeing what type of person he was and how much he loved baseball, I said, 'All I ever want is an opportunity—and I'm going to get that opportunity one day.'"

And he did.

86 LENNY DYKSTRA: NAILS HAMMERS ONE

Growing up in Orange County, California, Lenny Dykstra was a California Angels fan. His favorite player was Hall of Fame second baseman Rod Carew.

Like Carew, Dykstra batted left.

Dykstra was obsessed with baseball. His goal was to be a major leaguer.

While hockey was in his blood, baseball was in his dreams.[6] Even if so many friends, teammates, and coaches scoffed, all seeming to say a version of the same thing—you're too small.

And he was.

One high school coach said Dykstra was 5-foot-8 on his tippy-toes.

"Lenny's big saying always was 'if they only knew,' meaning that if only they knew where we would wind up, they'd treat us better," childhood friend Mark Baker told *Newsday*'s Jim Baumbach in 2012.

Baker wanted to be a professional bowler, and it was at the lanes in Garden Grove that Dykstra's nickname was born: Nails. It would also become the name of his 1987 book.

"I got it going pretty good, threw a bunch of strikes, and he was saying I was throwing 'nails,'" Baker recalled. "From then we just called everything Nails. . . . If a girl was good-looking, she became Nails. If you hit a baseball really hard, that was Nails."

It wasn't Nails when Dykstra showed up at a 1981 Southern California tryout camp and was mistaken for a batboy.

Joe McIlvaine, the Mets scouting director, recalled Dykstra's reaction. "I'm Lenny Dykstra, and I'm the best player you're going to see here today."

McIlvaine, who had pitched in the Detroit Tigers system and spent a decade as a scout, would come to think enough of Dykstra's skill

---

6 His uncle, Tony "Mighty Mouse" Leswick, had scored the winning goal for the Detroit Red Wings in overtime to win Game Seven of the 1954 Stanley Cup Finals against the Montreal Canadiens.

set—especially his speed—to consider taking him in the third round of the 1981 draft.

But his scouts told him there was no need to rush—no other team was that impressed. The Mets ended up drafting him in the 13th round.

Dykstra, all of eighteen, informed the Mets he didn't want to start in rookie ball. He wanted to begin his career in Class A.

"Some people may call it cockiness, but it was a good kind of cockiness because he 100 percent believed in his ability," McIlvaine told writer John Baumbach. "Lenny could never fail in his own mind."

* * *

Dykstra made the major leagues in 1985. By 1986, he was a Mets star on a team with a constellation that included Darryl Strawberry, Gary Carter, Keith Hernandez, Doc Gooden, and Mookie Wilson. Dykstra was installed as the team's leadoff hitter. His energy, recklessness, daring, toughness, cockiness, and all-out hustle made him a Shea Stadium favorite as the Mets won the National League Eastern Division by 21½ games while rolling up 108 wins, a massive total.

Dykstra, still a sprig, wore his number 4 with a dirty pride. The *New York Times*' George Vecsey would write, "The only place Lenny made sense was in a uniform with the number 4 on the back. (The Yankees had the aura of (Lou) Gehrig; the Mets had the aura of Lenny.) For a few fun years, Lenny was the personification of the franchise, hitting the dirt, head-first."

That was Dykstra in 1986. Add a mouthful of Red Man chewing tobacco, and there is your man who, in his first full big-league season, hit .295 with eight homers, 45 RBIs, and 31 steals.

In the 1986 National League Championship Series, the Mets split the first two games with the Houston Astros in the Astrodome.

As mighty as the Mets were, they feared having to face Houston's Mike Scott three times in a seven-game series. Scott was 18–10 with a 2.22 ERA en route to the Cy Young Award.

In Game One, Scott struck out 14 in a 1–0 win. His split-finger fastball was filthy.

Scott was Houston's scheduled Game Four starter.

In Game Three, the Astros owned a 5–4 lead on the Mets heading into the bottom of the ninth.

Houston called upon closer Dave Smith, who saved 33 games in the regular season. He was known for his forkball and changeup.

Leading off the ninth, Mets second baseman Wally Backman beat out a bunt single. The Astros argued that Backman had gone out of the baseline to avoid the tag by Houston first baseman Glenn Davis, but the call stood. Backman moved to second on a passed ball. Danny Heep, pinch-hitting for shortstop Rafael Santana, flied out.

Dykstra, who entered the game as a pinch-hitter in the seventh, strode to the plate. He had been slumping the last month, hitting only .214 in September. Not that Nails knew that.

On Smith's second pitch, Dykstra golfed a low, inside fastball high and deep to right.

"When the ball took off, all I said was 'Maybe.' What else could I say?" he told Marty Noble of *Newsday*, who ghostwrote Dykstra's 1987 book. "Maybe, maybe, maybe. And my voice got higher with each one. Most of the time I can tell if a ball I hit is going out. But I haven't hit that many home runs that I can always tell. Straw can tell on his. He can just stand there and watch it go out. Me, I've got to get going and get to first base at least. I'd look pretty weak if I watched it and it hit the wall. So I headed to first, saying 'Maybe' and hoping 'Yes.'"

He told reporters that the last time he hit a game-winning homer in the bottom of the ninth, he was playing the board game Strat-O-Matic with his brother.

It was the first time that a player in the postseason had hit a walk-off home run with his team trailing.

The Mets beat the Astros in six games. Dykstra hit a crucial home run in Game Three of the 1986 World Series against the Boston Red Sox. He would star again for the 1993 Philadelphia Phillies, who lost to the Toronto Blue Jays in the World Series.

Nails was out of the game by 1996. He was thirty-three, no longer a sprig.

85 STEVE GARVEY: "SENATOR" CONNECTS WITH PADRES

This was what the San Diego Padres had signed Steve Garvey for: Game Four, bottom of the ninth, a must-win situation in the 1984 National League Championship Series. The score was tied, 5–5.

Garvey had been a Los Angeles Dodger for so long that, even in his second year with the Padres, he still looked strange in Padre brown as opposed to Dodger blue.

But there he was, number 6 on his back, solid as an old blocking fullback, in the right-handed batter's box. Teammate Tony Gwynn, who won the National League batting championship in his breakout season, was on first. There was one out. Big Lee Smith was on the mound for the Chicago Cubs.

It was the first postseason appearance for the Cubs since 1945. It was also the initial playoff experience for the Padres, who joined the National League in 1969.

The Cubs had won the first two games by a combined score of 17–2. They were the sentimental choice of the nation because they hadn't won the World Series since 1908.

Behind the pitching of Ed Whitson, the Padres won Game Three, 7–1. But Game Four was a seesaw affair. Jack Murphy Stadium in San Diego was bedlam.

Garvey had signed a six-year, $6.6 million contract just before Christmas of 1982 after refusing the Dodgers offer of $5 million. The Padres were looking for a solid middle-of-the-order bat, leadership, and a chance to goose their attendance. Garvey turned thirty-four the day the Padres announced the deal. He promised San Diego fans that the team would be championship caliber in the "very, very near future."

The team, which had had only one winning season in its 15-year history, finished 1982 with an 81–81 record.

With his well-groomed black hair and chiseled movie-star looks, Garvey was the face of the Dodgers. Teammates called him "Senator" because they thought he had a future in politics. He was known for honoring every autograph request.

Garvey would break the National League consecutive-game streak of Cubs star Billy Williams on April 16, 1983, in his first game back at Dodger Stadium as a member of the Padres. He would go on to play in 1,207 games before the streak ended on July 29, 1983, after he injured his thumb in a collision at home.

Garvey was having a good first year in San Diego—.294 average, with 14 homers and 59 RBIs—until July 29, when he dislocated his left thumb while trying to score on a wild pitch.

San Diego manager Dick Williams would say of Garvey, "When I managed Oakland, Reggie Jackson had some great seasons for me. And when I managed Boston, Carl Yastrzemski for one year was as good as anybody I ever saw.

"I don't hesitate to put Garvey with those guys, not necessarily because of his power, but because he hits in the clutch against good pitchers. It doesn't make a difference whether Steve is ahead or behind in the count, either; you know when he's really needed he's going to drive the ball somewhere."

The Cubs Lee Smith was a good pitcher on the brink of being great when the Cubs met the Padres in the National League Championship Series of 1984.[7] He was also a 6-foot-5 and 220-pound right-hander who threw HARD.

He had saved Game Two, and 33 others in the regular season.

Smith had spun a scoreless eighth in Game Four, but Garvey was coming up, and was 3-for-4 with three RBIs on the night.

The Padres had built a 2–0 lead in the third on a sacrifice fly from Gwynn and a run-scoring double from Garvey. Chicago took the lead in the fifth on a two-run Jody Davis homer and a solo shot from Leon Durham.

The Padres tied the game in the home half of the fifth, thanks to a Garvey RBI single. They went ahead with another RBI single in the seventh, 5–3. The Cubs had knotted the score in the eighth.

In the ninth, with one out, Gwynn had singled.

Garvey then stepped up to the plate and drilled a ball to right center at the 370 sign.

"I could see Tony [Gwynn], who was on first, start to run toward second base, and as I looked toward right field all I could see was Henry Cotto [the Cubs right fielder] heading toward the wall," Garvey recalled 30 years later. "I

---

7 From 1993 to 2006, Smith owned the all-time save record with 478.

really didn't know if I had gotten all of it and I started to think, 'He [Cotto] is going to make the greatest catch in playoff history.'"

Cotto didn't.

The ball was gone.

"As I rounded first base the roar increased," Garvey recalled. "At some point it just gets so loud that you don't even hear it anymore. Then I remember my teammates jumping all over me at home plate."

The Padres beat the Cubs in Game Five.

ESPN's Steve Wulf reported, "When *The Natural* was shown on a plane from Chicago to San Diego for the start of the Series, the passengers chanted, 'Gar-vey! Gar-vey!' at the climax."

The Padres would play the Detroit Tigers in the Series but would lose in five games.

Garvey finished his postseason career with a .356 average.

He thinks people remember his 1984 home run so clearly because it was against the Cubs. "[T]heir postseason history," he would note. "Had it been any other team . . ."

As noted by ESPN's David Schoenfield, that home run got Garvey's number 6 retired by the Padres.

84 JACK CLARK: CLARK SLAYS THE BUFFALO

There were two outs in the top of the ninth, with men on second and third. The Los Angeles Dodgers were clinging to a 5–4 lead over the St. Louis Cardinals.

It was a do-or-die game for the Dodgers, who trailed the 1985 National League Championship Series three games to two.

Tom Niedenfuer was pitching for the Dodgers. The 6-foot-5, 225-pound hard-throwing right-hander had recorded 19 saves during the regular season, a career high. He was Dodger manager Tommy Lasorda's go-to man out of the bullpen. "Buff"—short for buffalo ("he has a big head," Lasorda once noted)—had pitched 106 innings during the season, a large number for a reliever.

In the 1981 World Series, during Niedenfuer's rookie year, he pitched five innings of scoreless ball against the New York Yankees. He hadn't given up a postseason run in seven October appearances, including earning a save in Game One of the 1985 NLCS, until St. Louis Hall of Fame shortstop Ozzie Smith, a switch-hitter who had never hit a homer left-handed and who had only 28 in his career, drove a fastball down the right field line, barely clearing the fence to win Game Five. Fans voted the home run the greatest moment in Busch Stadium history.

In Game Six, Niedenfuer was called upon again. This time he replaced Dodger starter Orel Hershiser, who had entered the seventh inning with a 4–1 lead.

But the St. Louis seventh started with consecutive singles by catcher Darrell Porter and left fielder Tito Landrum. Steve Braun moved runners into scoring position with a groundout. Willie McGee then singled in both runs before Lasorda signaled for Niedenfuer to face Ozzie Smith . . . again.

Smith tripled in the tying run.

Niedenfuer walked Tommy Herr, then struck out Cardinals sluggers Jack Clark and Andy Van Slyke swinging to end the inning.

Niedenfuer retired the Cardinals in order in the eighth. In the bottom of the inning, outfielder Mike Marshall hit a fly ball to right that kept drifting and drifting before landing over the fence to give the Dodgers the lead. They were three outs away from forcing a Game Seven.

The top of the ninth inning opened with pinch-hitter Cesar Cedeno striking out. Then center fielder Willie McGee came up to bat. He singled and stole second. McGee had replaced Vince Coleman, who was injured when a Busch Stadium tarp ran over his left leg before Game Four.

Facing Smith again, Niedenfuer walked him. Tommy Herr followed and grounded out to first, advancing the runners.

Jack Clark then stepped to the plate, but was pretty sure that he would be walked.[8] A rib injury had curtailed Clark's numbers during the regular season, but he still had hit 22 homers and knocked in 87 runs. He also still had the arrogance of a cleanup hitter.

Clark was called "Jack the Ripper" when he was a member of the San Francisco Giants. He'd made his major-league debut with the Giants as a nineteen-year-old in 1975 and was a star by 1978. Clark had a big bat and a big mouth, and both got him traded to the Cardinals for four players in the off-season of 1984.

"Not that he's wrong and I'm right," Cards manager Whitey Herzog later said, "but I was shocked that he didn't walk [Clark]. The winning run already was on second. With the type of club we had and the speed we had, we hit a lot of topped balls, a lot of choppers that scored runs.

"I'm not trying to second-guess here, but a walk sets up a force out. Tommy said he didn't want to load the bases with a base on balls and then have a walk force in a run. I can understand that."

Clark had changed bats in 1985, going to a lighter model, one that Hall of Famer and former Giants teammate Joe Morgan had used. While in the on-deck circle, Clark later told a reporter how he started thinking about Hank Sauer, his hitting coach in San Francisco.

"He always told me to be ready for fastballs, to anticipate strikes and to get three swings," Clark said. "If you swing hard and miss, you don't have to sit down. You get two more swings."

In the back of Clark's mind was this thought, too: "[They] were going to put their arm up [for the walk] and then sit down real quick and try to throw a quick strike."

It didn't matter what the Dodgers were going to do.

"I said to myself I was going to look for a fastball middle in," Clark recalled.

The fastball came. And it went, like a bullet from a gun. Clark thought it was going to sail out of Dodger Stadium.

---

8 The Dodgers had pitched to him carefully in the series, walking him five times.

"When I hit it, I knew it was gone," he told Gordon Edes of the *Los Angeles Times*. "I'd always dreamed of hitting a ball out of Dodger Stadium. I'd never hit one out, not even in batting practice. I think maybe I reached the back wall. [Dave] Kingman and [Willie] Stargell had done it, and I thought it was within reach."

Dodger left fielder Pedro Guerrero pulled up before the wall and dropped to his knees.

The ball landed halfway up the Pavilion in left field. Niedenfuer said he thought the ball would hit the Goodyear blimp on the way down. On-deck hitter Andy Van Slyke told Edes it was a laser shot "straight out of *Star Wars*."

Niedenfuer got the final out of the inning, but the Dodgers went meekly in the bottom of the ninth, and St. Louis traveled to the World Series, though they lost in seven games to the Kansas City Royals.

Dodgers manager Tommy Lasorda was heavily criticized for pitching to Jack Clark. He didn't care. He'd done what he thought was right. "A second-guesser is someone who doesn't know anything about the first guess," he said. "And the second-guesser is somebody who needs two guesses to get one right."[9]

When asked how he would have pitched to himself in the sunlight of Dodger Stadium on October 16, 1985, Clark said: "I would have unintentionally walked me. Don't give him anything good. If he wants to swing at those pitches, fine, but if it's 3-and-0 and he hasn't swung, I would have walked him."

Niedenfuer claimed he never considered walking Clark with the left-handed swinging Andy Van Slyke on deck. Van Slyke, in his second full season, hit .255 with 13 homers and 55 RBIs in 1985. His batting average in the playoffs to date was .091.

Clark said hitting the homer was like winning a gold medal.

He'd sign with the New York Yankees in 1988, but would end up being traded to the San Diego Padres later that year. He'd finish his career with the Boston Red Sox in 1992.

Clark was a four-time All-Star and hit 340 homers—impressive when you consider his home fields in San Francisco, St. Louis, New York, and San Diego did not help right-handed power hitters.

---

9 Yet Lasorda had used the intentional walk nine times in the series. And, in each instance, the following batter made an out.

Even with all that, a day doesn't go by that someone doesn't ask him about his home run on October 15, 1985.

"It's the way I always imagined the big leagues to be like," Clark once said.

83 TONY FERNANDEZ: A BLAST IN PLACE OF BIP

Bip Roberts was supposed to start at second base in Game Six of the 1997 American League Championship Series.

He had been acquired by the Cleveland Indians from Kansas City on August 30, 1997, for rookie pitcher Roland de la Maza, and had been a spark for the Tribe in the final days of the regular season.

The Baltimore Orioles were starting ace hurler Mike Mussina, who was having an October for the ages.[10]

The Indians were one game away from the World Series. The Orioles, the best team in the American League all season, were at home in Camden Yards. During batting practice Bip (his real name was Leon) was taking balls at second base. Tony Fernandez, the former Toronto Blue Jays great, was completing his BP hacks in the cage. He buzzed a line drive in Bip's direction.

As Bip told George Vecsey of the *New York Times*, when he put his glove up, he "Caught all thumb, no glove at all. I knew it was bad right away."

Bip retreated to the clubhouse for a painkiller to ease the throbbing in his left thumb. It didn't help. But he still took his turn in batting practice.

Roberts had been a first-round pick of the Pittsburgh Pirates, but the 5-foot-7, 165-pounder made his reputation in the 1980s as a San Diego Padre.

He was a gamer, but he couldn't grip the bat properly after he hurt his thumb. "I kept changing my grip," he said, "and once you start doing that, you're dead."

He was scratched from the lineup before the game. Cleveland manager Mike Hargrove inserted Fernandez at second and batted him second. He then moved shortstop Omar Vizquel to the leadoff slot.

For eight innings it didn't make a difference. Mussina, again, was great.

In Game Three of the series, he threw seven shutout innings of one-hit ball, striking out 15. Only Bob Gibson, with 17 in the 1968 World Series, had recorded more strikeouts in a postseason game.

Mussina had 31 strikeouts in three postseason starts. He could throw hard, but also deceived hitters with a knuckle curve. He was four strikeouts

---

10 In four October starts, Mussina was 2–2 with a 1.24 ERA.

away from tying the record for Ks in the postseason, something only Bob Gibson of the St. Louis Cardinals (1968), Tom Seaver of the New York Mets (1973), and Orel Hershiser of the Indians (1995) had accomplished.

On October 15, 1997, Mussina bettered it. He struck out 10 in eight scoreless innings against the Indians. The only hit he allowed was a double by Cleveland's David Justice.

"Christy Mathewson and Walter Johnson would have been proud of Mussina," wrote Thomas Boswell of the *Washington Post*. "No one has ever pitched better at this time of year and for these stakes." In 29 innings against the two highest-scoring teams—Cleveland and Seattle—Mussina allowed just 11 hits (a .118 batting average) and four walks (1.24 earned run average) while striking out 41 batters. In the middle of the Indians 1997 lineup were first baseman Jim Thome and right fielder Manny Ramirez. They'd combine to hit 1,167 career home runs.

"Locked in a draining scoreless duel with Charles Nagy, Mussina evoked images of Gibson's intensity and Sandy Koufax's overpowering stuff. They made huge hitters with clubs in their hand look like a pitiable breed with little future," the *Post*'s Boswell continued.

Nagy wasn't as sharp. He kept pitching in and out of trouble, but was tough and more than kept the Tribe in the game.

Mussina left the contest after throwing eight innings and 108 pitches. Into the 11th, the score was still tied.

* * *

A slick fielder in his prime, Fernandez won four straight (1986 to 1989) Gold Gloves for the Toronto Blue Jays.

For his defensive theatrics, sportswriters called Fernandez the Ozzie Smith of the American League. *Sports Illustrated*'s Ivan Maisel described Fernandez's defense as having "the range of a Texas cattleman."

Fernandez was a long and lean switch-hitter who modeled his stance after Hall of Famer Rod Carew, though he would sometimes change his stance depending on the pitcher and hitting situation.

The Jays had traded him to San Diego on December 6, 1990, in a blockbuster deal that included second baseman and future Hall of Famer Roberto Alomar for first baseman Fred McGriff and outfielder Joe Carter.

Against Mussina, Fernandez, now thirty-five years old, was 0-for-3.

Baltimore's reliever in the 11th inning was Armando Benitez, 6-foot-4, 220 pounds and all heat, who recorded the first two outs of the frame. He fell behind Fernandez, the third hitter, 2–0, on fastballs just outside.

Benitez had a history with Cleveland.

A year earlier in the playoffs, Cleveland's Albert Belle had boomed a grand slam off the hard-throwing righty. In Game Two of the '97 series, he surrendered Marquis Grissom's game-winning eighth-inning homer. In Game Four, he coughed up Roberto Alomar's game-winning hit, which built the Tribe a 3–1 series lead.

"This time, the blow was like a bolt of lightning on a night with no storm in sight," Boswell wrote in the *Washington Post.*

With the count now 2–0, Fernandez hit a Ruthian fly ball off Benitez to right in Babe's hometown, which landed in the temporary bleachers in right field. The Orioles had upset the Indians in 1996; now it was the Indians turn.

Jose Mesa silenced the O's in the bottom of the 11th and, just like that, the Indians were on their way to the World Series.

After the game, Fernandez told Jack Curry of the *New York Times*, "I don't believe in destiny. I believe that the Lord arbitrated it this way. He wanted me to play for some reason and I did."

According to Curry, Bip Roberts, who couldn't play because of a freak injury, couldn't stop smiling, even though his hand wouldn't stop hurting.

"This," Roberts said, "is the greatest feeling I've ever had."

82 STEVE YEAGER: A DODGER'S SHOT INTO THE GREAT BLUE YONDER

No, Chuck Yeager is not Steve Yeager's uncle.

The first pilot to have traveled faster than the speed of sound in 1947 and the catcher who helped the Los Angeles Dodgers to the 1981 world championship are cousins, not uncle and nephew. Steve Yeager has made the point many times through the years, but sometimes that fact gets mixed up.

What is not in question is that Steve Yeager hit one of the most important home runs in Los Angeles Dodgers history. He was also one of the great defensive catchers of his time.

St. Louis Cardinals outfielder Lou Brock, a Hall of Famer who stole 938 bases—second all-time in baseball history—called Yeager "the best-throwing catcher in the game."

That was when Johnny Bench of the Cincinnati Reds, also a Hall of Famer, was winning 10 consecutive Gold Gloves.

In one game, a Yeager throw from a catcher's crouch to second was clocked at 98 miles per hour. Second base is 254 feet from home plate.

In 1978, Yeager tossed out almost half the runners trying to steal.[11]

When Yeager would draw comparisons to Bench, he bristled and said, "When I'm the All-Star catcher and have won an MVP award and have led the league in home runs and RBIs like Johnny has, then maybe I can compare myself with him."

Yeager was the starting catcher for the Dodgers when they lost to the New York Yankees in the 1977 and 1978 World Series.

By 1981, Yeager, almost thirty-three, was a backup to a young Mike Scioscia, the future manager of the California–Los Angeles Angels. Yeager had hit only .209 with fewer than 100 at-bats, but the Dodgers were back in the Series against the New York Yankees.

Because New York was starting left-handers Ron Guidry, Tommy John, and Dave Righetti, the right-handed-hitting Yeager got a chance to play more

---

11 In an extra-inning game in 1972, Yeager tied a then–National League record for catchers with 22 putouts.

than usual. In Game One, he slugged a homer in a losing cause off of ace Ron Guidry at Yankee Stadium.

Future Dodger manager Tommy Lasorda fell in love with Yeager in 1972, when guiding LA's top farm club in Albuquerque: his arm, hustle, toughness, and his occasional power.

In the pivotal Game Five, with the Series tied at two, Guidry was again on the mound and working on a two-hit shutout and a 1–0 lead.

He struck out the dangerous Dusty Baker to open the seventh. Guidry had retired 15 of the last 16 Dodger hitters. Vin Scully, the voice of the Dodgers, said the Yankee southpaw showed no sign of wilting on this sunny Sunday afternoon.

Baker, who would later manage the San Francisco Giants, Chicago Cubs, Cincinnati Reds, and Washington Nationals, suggested to Pedro Guerrero and Yeager that they should move up in the batter's box to combat Guidry's late-breaking slider.

They listened.

Guerrero, who baseball historian Bill James once said was "the best hitter God has made in a long time," swung and missed at Guidry's first offering, but smoked the second one high and deep, far beyond the bleacher walls in left center. The score was now tied.

Yeager missed Guerrero's dinger. He was swinging a weighted bat in the on-deck circle when the weights fell off, and he had turned his head to gather them.

"I heard the crowd going wild, and when I looked up Pedro was trotting around the bases," he said.

Yeager, wearing number 7 and batting seventh, swung and missed the first two Guidry offerings with fierce swings.

"I wasn't looking for a home run," he said. "But those two swings must have looked like I was trying to air it out to the parking lot."

Guidry then threw a fastball.

Yeager stroked it almost as far as Guerrero did, to the same left-center area code. The Dodgers took the lead in the game and Series for good.

"He made me look so bad on the first two breaking balls," Yeager said, "so maybe he figured I'd be looking for another one. He's a great pitcher and it was one of those things. I just guessed right."

Yeager was 3-for-6 with a double, along with two homers against Guidry that October.

"Ask any pitcher," Yeager noted, "and there's always one particular guy on each team who gives him difficulty."

For the first time, three players shared the Series MVP: Yeager, Guerrero, and Ron Cey.

And maybe someone, somewhere, asked Chuck Yeager if he was related to Steve.

81 MIKE SCHMIDT: RECORD 48TH HR LIFTS PHILLIES

The Philadelphia Phillies had muddled in mediocrity for so much of the 1980 season.

By August 10, they were six games out, in third place with a record of 55–52, looking up at the Montreal Expos and Pittsburgh Pirates.

Then they started winning.

The team featured Hall of Fame pitcher Steve Carlton. "Lefty," as he was called, was in the midst of a 24–9 season in which he would toss 304 innings. At first was the all-time hit leader, Pete Rose. Smooth-fielding Garry Maddox patrolled center. Maddox won eight Gold Gloves, sparking New York Mets broadcaster and former Pittsburgh slugger Ralph Kiner to say, "Two thirds of the Earth is covered by water, the other third is covered by Garry Maddox." Bob Boone, son of Ray and father of Aaron and Bret, was the team's three-time All-Star catcher. Powerful four-time All-Star Greg Luzinski, "The Bull," held down left field. He had 130 RBIs in one season, 120 in another. The bullpen was anchored by two-time All-Star Tug McGraw.

But the heartbeat of the team was third baseman Mike Schmidt.

Schmidt was selected by the Phillies out of Ohio University in the second round of the 1971 draft, the pick right after Kansas City's selection of George Brett from El Segundo High School in California.

Schmidt had gone undrafted out of high school. He hadn't even made his hometown Dayton's All-City team. With his knees already hurting, Ohio University had not offered him a scholarship. He was a walk-on shortstop on the freshman team, for which he would hit one home run.

But Mike Schmidt got better. And better.

Athletic and hardworking, the college shortstop worked himself into a two-time All-American, clubbing 27 homers and 98 RBIs during his college career.

Tony Lucadello, a longtime Phillies scout who signed 52 players who would make the big leagues, was a big fan of Schmidt. In 1971 he unsuccessfully urged the team to use its first-round pick to draft him. Instead, the Phillies selected Roy Thomas, a pitcher who went 20–11 in his career with Houston, St. Louis, and Seattle.

The California Angels were also in on Schmidt. If the Phillies hadn't taken him with the 30th overall pick, the Angels would have done so seven selections later. California plucked Ron Jackson, a high school outfielder from Birmingham, Alabama, who'd eventually be the Boston Red Sox hitting coach in 2004, when the team won its first World Series in eighty-six years.

As a late-season call-up, Schmidt hit his first major-league homer on September 16, 1972. His three-run dinger beat the Montreal Expos and snapped Balor Moore's 25-inning scoreless streak.

That winter, the Phillies traded starting third baseman Don Money to the Milwaukee Brewers to clear the path for Schmidt. The Phillies knew what they had. At 6-foot-2, 195 pounds, Schmidt, intense and serious, made the team's roster for good in 1973. But he struggled.

He did hit 18 homers and drive home 52, but struck out 136 times in 443 at-bats. He finished with a horrid .196 average. He heard his first boos—and they wouldn't be his last—as a professional. Philly fans are tough, even on the new face of the franchise.

However, Schmidt rebounded. Over the next three years, he led the National League in homers with 36, 38, and 38, but also in strikeouts, with 138, 180, and 149. When Schmidt became a star, the Phillies won three straight National League East Championships, in 1976, 1977, and 1978.

He gained the nation's attention on April 17, 1976, when he hit four home runs in a game against the Chicago Cubs at Wrigley Field.

During his career, Schmidt would lead the National League in home runs eight times and finish with 548 dingers. He had 13 seasons of hitting at least 30 homers. And when you hit that many home runs, few care about how much you strike out.

Schmidt was a 12-time All-Star who was selected in 1980 as Most Valuable Player in the World Series. He won 10 Gold Gloves for his defensive work at third base (second only to Baltimore's Brooks Robinson's 16), and he led the National League in slugging percentage five times, and in RBIs in four seasons.

His number 20 was iconic, and his batting stance, in where he held his bat high and almost completely turned his back to the pitcher, was often imitated by Phillies fans. His thick auburn hair and reddish mustache were trademarks, too.

On April 18, 1987, Schmidt hit his 500th home run, a game-winning three-run shot in the top of the ninth inning off Pittsburgh's Don Robinson. "You can go down that home run list, of all the guys who hit their 500th," Schmidt told Jayson Stark of the *Philadelphia Inquirer*, later of ESPN. "And you'd be hard-pressed to find a guy who hit one with a better storybook ending."

Schmidt was the 14th player to hit 500 home runs.

But listings of Schmidt's numbers don't do him justice. He was clutch, earning National League Most Valuable Player honors three times.

The first was in 1980, as the Phillies made their come-from-behind charge. Barely over .500 on August 10, they went 36–19 down the stretch.

Schmidt hit 16 home runs in the final six weeks of the season. He had nine in the last two weeks, four in the last four games.

The Phillies pulled into Montreal on October 3, 1980, tied for the division lead with the Expos. Schmidt hit a sacrifice fly in the first, and a solo homer in the sixth, to power the Phillies past the Expos, 2–1, to take over sole possession of first place.

The next day, the game was delayed three hours by rain. With two outs in the top of the ninth, the Phillies trailed, 4–3, before Bob Boone tied the game with an RBI single.

Tug McGraw, the Philadelphia reliever, was masterful, throwing three innings of one-hit ball to keep the Expos in check. In the 11th, Pete Rose singled and, with one out, Schmidt faced Stan Bahnsen, who in 1968 was the American League Rookie of the Year for the New York Yankees.

On a one-ball count, Schmidt drove Bahnsen's offering deep to left at Olympic Stadium. As Phillie broadcaster Andy Musser described it, "Long drive to left field. . . . He buried it! He buried it!"

It was Schmidt's 48th homer, a team record, until Ryan Howard powered 58 of them in 2006. No third baseman in history had hit that many. The record would last 27 years, until Alex Rodriguez hit 54 for the Yankees.

In 1980, Schmidt finished with 121 RBIs. He was unanimously selected as the National League Most Valuable Player. (He'd win two others, in 1981 and 1986.)

The Phillies beat the Houston Astros in the National League Championship Series and went on to win the World Series in six games over the Kansas City Royals, the first World Series championship in franchise history. Schmidt did his part, hitting two homers and knocking in seven runs.

Schmidt retired in 1989 after 18 seasons. He was elected into the baseball Hall of Fame in 1995, at the time boasting the fourth-highest percentage of votes, 96.5. He was named to Major League Baseball's All-Century Team in

1999 as the best third baseman. In 2004, the Phillies unveiled a bronze statue of Schmidt outside the third-base gate at Citizens Bank Park.

"That 1980 season he was big," Dallas Green, the Phillies manager that season, told Matt Baron of the *Philadelphia Inquirer*. "Every time we needed a jump-start or every time we needed a special home run or an at-bat, Michael usually was there for us."

80 ROBIN YOUNT: KID SHORTSTOP DELIVERS HARVEY'S WALLBANGERS

It was a crazy season.

The Milwaukee Brewers were scuffling at 23–24 on June 1, 1982, stalled in sixth place in a seven-team division.

Team general manager Harry Dalton fired skipper Buck Rodgers and replaced him with hitting coach Harvey Kuenn. In his playing days, Kuenn was a terrific hitter, winning the 1959 American League batting championship with a .353 average for the Detroit Tigers. The Brewers responded to the relaxed and let's-have-fun style of Kuenn, and immediately won 20 of their next 28 games.

Behind Robin Yount, Gorman Thomas, Paul Molitor, Ben Oglivie, Ted Simmons, and Cecil Cooper, the Brewers powered their way back into contention. As a team, the Brewers ended up slugging 216 home runs. Their ninth hitter, second baseman Jim Gantner, chipped in with a .295 average, giving you an idea of their powerful lineup.

The team started to be widely known as "Harvey's Wallbangers." It was ironic in a way, since Kuenn was really a singles hitter, once traded for a home run champion, the often overlooked Rocky Colavito.

But all that winning wasn't all that easy.

Though their ace, Pete Vuckovich, did win the AL Cy Young Award in 1982, the Brewers weren't blessed with great starting-pitching depth. The fact that Hall of Fame relief pitcher Rollie Fingers, the AL's MVP and Cy Young Award winner in 1981, started to suffer elbow woes didn't help the cause, either.

So Dalton made a late-season deal for thirty-seven-year-old starting pitcher Don Sutton to help solidify the staff. The longtime Los Angeles Dodger, who had been pitching for the Houston Astros, was just what the Brewers needed. Sutton went 4–1 down the stretch.

Sutton, then in his 17th season, would say of Yount, "[He is the best all-around player I've ever played with. As a shortstop, Dave Concepcion of the Reds has been the standard in the National League, and on a scale of 10 he's 9.5, but Robin Yount is 9.6."

Kuenn, who made his big-league debut in 1952, agreed, and expanded on what Sutton said. The Brewers manager told Dave Anderson of the *New York Times* in 1982 that Yount, who batted second, was a "picture ballplayer—just the way he runs, his defensive grace . . . He comes in on a ball, plays the short hop and makes the throw better than anyone I've ever seen. He's the best shortstop I've ever seen play."

Gorman Thomas, who led the American League in homers with 39 in the summer of 1982, added that Yount, was "the best ballplayer I ever saw. Other people have their own opinions and they talk about different players. That's because they didn't see this guy. I saw this guy every day for 10 years. Home to second, first to third, nobody was better. Had the greatest range to his left of anybody I've ever seen. Hit for average. Hit for power. He was the perfect package."

By early September 1982, the Boston Red Sox and Detroit Tigers had become pretenders rather than contenders for the American League East Division title, but the Baltimore Orioles, managed by Hall of Famer Earl Weaver, were still alive on the last weekend of the regular season. They were also playing at home, hosting Harvey's Wallbangers. Yount had just turned twenty-seven.

The Brewers had to only win one of four games at Memorial Stadium to clinch the division crown, but they made things difficult for themselves by dropping the first three games to the Birds by a combined score of 26–7. The season had come down to one game, a winner-take-all, for the first time since the Red Sox and the New York Yankees in 1949.

Two future Hall of Famers, Sutton and Baltimore's Jim Palmer, started the pivotal contest. But then Robin Yount became the story.

In the first inning, he homered to right. In the third, he homered to center. The Brewers could exhale.

In the eighth, he tripled and scored. The Brewers won the game, 10–2, and the division.

Yount finished the season with 29 home runs and 114 RBIs. He also hit .331. The stat was .001 shy of glory—if he'd gotten a hit in the ninth instead of being struck by a pitch, he would have won the batting crown, too. His defense at shortstop was stellar, earning him a Gold Glove.

The Brewers rebounded from an 0–2 deficit in the American League Championship Series with the California Angels to win the AL pennant and play the St. Louis Cardinals in the World Series. The Cardinals won the "Suds Series" (as it was called because of the famous breweries in both cities), four games to three. Yount hit .414 with a homer and six RBIs in the Fall Classic, but it wasn't enough.

He was a nearly unanimous choice for the AL MVP, though, his first of two. Yount became the first shortstop since Minnesota's Zoilo Versalles in 1965 to be awarded the honor, and just the fifth in AL history, joining Washington's Roger Peckinpaugh in 1925, Cleveland's Lou Boudreau in 1948, and New York's Phil Rizzuto in 1950.

Born in Danville, Illinois, in 1955, but growing up in Woodland Hills, California, Yount was the third pick in the June 1973 draft, one pick ahead of another future Hall of Famer, Dave Winfield. Both would have more than 3,000 hits in their careers. Winfield ended up well traveled on his starry path, wearing the jerseys of San Diego, the New York Yankees, California, Toronto, Minnesota, and Cleveland.

Yount played his entire 20-year career in Milwaukee.

He was just eighteen when he made his big-league debut in 1974. After going hitless in his first four games, he slugged a game-winner in his sixth off Baltimore's Ross Grimsley. He was the last eighteen-year-old to hit a big-league home run, and played more games at that age than anyone in history. Yount was elected to the Hall of Fame in 1999, his first year of eligibility.

Long and lean, with a head of shaggy, sandy hair and a distinctive bushy mustache, it's not surprised that Yount's favorite player as a kid had been Oakland outfielder Joe Rudi.

"Growing up, I didn't admire any particular shortstop," Yount once said. "I liked the way Joe Rudi hit, and when I was a rookie I used to talk to him about hitting. I was an A's fan then. They were winning the World Series then."

Yount was such a good athlete that he once considered playing on the pro golf tour, and also had mused about a career as a professional motorcycle racer. By 1985, shoulder woes forced him to switch from shortstop to the outfield.

He was a star there, too.

Two years after the move, he made a game-ending catch to save a no-hitter by southpaw Juan Nieves.

In 1989, he won his second MVP, putting up .318/21/103 numbers, making him the third player in history to win an MVP at two positions. (Detroit's Hank Greenberg had been the first, St. Louis's Stan Musial the second; New York's Alex Rodriguez would also earn an MVP at third base in 2009, after starting his career at shortstop.)

Yount, always on the quiet side, considered offers from other teams in 1989, when his contract with Milwaukee expired, but returned to the Brewers with a new three-year, $9.6 million agreement. He would average 143 games played a season.

Yount collected his 3,000th hit—an infield single off Cleveland's Jose Mesa—on September 9, 1992, at Milwaukee's County Stadium. He was the 17th player to reach that plateau, and the third-youngest. He retired after the 1993 campaign with 3,142 hits. The Brewers retired his number 19 the following year.

"What can you say that hasn't been said?" former teammate Charlie Moore once noted of the man fans still refer to as "The Kid." "If he had played in New York or Los Angeles, he could have been a god."

79 FRANK ROBINSON: ROBBY'S GREATEST THRILL

Frank Robinson batted himself second when he made history the freezing afternoon of April 8, 1975.

It was Opening Day and the Cleveland Indians were hosting the New York Yankees. Twenty-eight years after Jackie Robinson broke the color line as a player, Frank Robinson did it as a big-league manager—a player-manager.

When he was hired as the Tribe's skipper, Robinson, then thirty-nine and entering his 20th season as a player, already had stroked 574 career home runs. He didn't think he was done as a player yet. Always a fierce competitor, he hungered to manage in the big leagues. He'd started talking about this desire when he was in his early thirties. Earl Weaver, his manager in Baltimore, had helped get "Robby" a job managing in the Puerto Rican Winter League.

Cleveland owner Ted Bonda thought "it was the right thing to do," in offering Robinson the position for the American League club. Robinson received a standing ovation from the 56,204 at Municipal Stadium when he brought out the lineup card on Opening Day.

The ovation was louder in the bottom of the first, when he came to bat.

Doc Medich was pitching for the New York Yankees. The count was two balls and two strikes. On a fastball low and away, Robinson pulled it into the bleachers in left, his 575th home run and hit number 2,901 of his career.

The crowd got louder still.

At the time, only Hank Aaron, Babe Ruth, and Willie Mays had more career dingers.

"Of all the pennants, World Series, awards and All-Star games I've been in, this is the greatest thrill," Robinson told the *Cleveland Plain Dealer* after the 5–3 win.

One of those cheering was Rachel Robinson, the widow of Jackie Robinson, who died in 1972. "I was very proud that [Rachel Robinson] would make the trip," Frank Robinson said. "I hoped and wished that Jackie could have been there. The next best thing was having her there . . . because it kept me focused."

On October 15, 1972, nine days before his death from complications of diabetes, Jackie Robinson told a World Series crowd in Cincinnati that he hoped to see a black manager in the near future. Frank Robinson—no relation—was the obvious first choice. He was as smart as he was tough. "Leader" was a word regularly used to describe him.

"Fearless" was another.

He was also a man of immense accomplishments:

- Rookie of the Year.
- Only person to win Most Valuable Player Awards in both leagues.
- Most Valuable Player of the World Series.
- Most Valuable Player of the All-Star Game.
- Triple Crown winner.
- Gold Glove winner.
- Manager of the Year.

Frank Robinson was elected to the Hall of Fame in 1982.

Hall of Famer Roberto Clemente once told *The Sporting News* that St. Louis Cardinals great Stan Musial and Robinson were the best hitters he ever saw.

In his best-selling book *Ball Four* Jim Bouton wrote, "I was warming up in the bullpen when a fan leaned out and said, 'Hey Jim, how do you pitch to Frank Robinson?' I told him the truth. 'Reluctantly.'"

Jim Palmer, Hall of Fame pitcher and Robinson's teammate on the Orioles, described him simply as "The best player I ever saw."

He was also Ty Cobb–like on the basepaths, ruthlessly aggressive, especially when a shortstop or second baseman was trying to turn a double play.

"I never relaxed on a ball field," he said. "I have always believed in going all out all the time. The baseline belongs to the runner, and whenever I was running the bases, I always slid hard. If the second baseman or shortstop was in the way, coming across the base trying to turn a double play, I hit him hard."

He also wasn't afraid of getting hit by a pitch. Robinson, a wiry right-handed hitter, almost hovered over the plate

The year after he led the Baltimore Orioles to the 1966 World Series championship with his Triple Crown season, Robinson said, "I don't want people to say Mickey Mantle, Willie Mays, and Hank Aaron in one breath and in the next, Frank Robinson. I want them to say Mantle, Mays, Aaron, and Robinson in the same breath."

Frank Robinson was born in Texas on August 31, 1935, the youngest of ten children. He grew up in West Oakland, California, where his neighbors included future major leaguers Curt Flood and Vada Pinson, and where he was a high school basketball teammate of Hall of Famer Bill Russell, who in 1966 was the first African American to be named a head coach of a major sports franchise.

Robinson signed with the Cincinnati Reds shortly after graduating from high school in 1953. Three years later, at age twenty, he was the team's starting left fielder, hitting 38 home runs and batting .290. He was selected to the All-Star Game and was named the National League Rookie of the Year. Previously, the Reds had 11 straight losing seasons. In 1956, with Robinson leading the way, they won 91 games.

Robinson continued to improve. In 1959 he had a monster season, slugging 36 homers and knocking in 125 runs with his .311 average. By 1961, he had moved to right field, helping the Reds to the National League pennant. He hit .323 with 37 homers and 124 RBIs and was the National League MVP.

Robinson was even better in 1962 with 39 homers, 136 RBIs, 51 doubles and a career-high .342 average. In 1965 Robinson collected 33 homers and 113 RBIs, but the Reds started thinking of him as "a fading talent increasingly hobbled by leg injuries."

Reds owner Bill DeWitt said Robinson was an "old thirty."

On December 9 of that year, in one of the most lopsided deals in baseball history, the Reds traded Robinson for pitchers Milt Pappas and Jack Baldschun, and outfielder Dick Simpson.

In Baltimore, Robinson led the Birds to four World Series in six seasons.

In '66, his first season in Baltimore, Robinson rolled up 49 homers, 122 RBIs and a .316 average, and became the first Triple Crown winner since New York's Mickey Mantle in 1956.

Oriole pitching great Dave McNally would say, "As good as Frank was, it was how hard he played that really made an impact. . . . The intensity the man had was just incredible."

After six seasons with the Orioles, Robinson played for the Los Angeles Dodgers and California Angels before being picked up by the Indians in a late-season trade in 1974.

He was named manager of the Tribe on October 4, 1974. He lasted until the summer of 1977, when he was fired due to the team's lack of success. He got his next shot managing in 1981, when he was picked to lead the San

Francisco Giants, becoming the first black manager in National League history. Robinson skippered the Giants until 1984.

Four years later, the Orioles hired him to run the team. In 1989, he piloted them to second place and was the unanimous choice for American League Manager of the Year. He was fired in 1991 when the Birds were slumping.

When Major League Baseball took over the Montreal Expos in 2002, Frank Robinson, then sixty-six, was hired by Commissioner Bud Selig to manage them. Selig was looking for stability. Robinson managed the team—which three years later became the Nationals when it moved to Washington, D.C.—until 2006, one year after the extremely accomplished man was asked by a never-identified member of his team if he had ever played in the big leagues.

He won his 1,000th game as manager on April 20, 2006, the 53rd man to reach that figure.

Robinson had a reputation for eschewing statistics and managing from his gut. Pitchers, as it turned out, were afraid of him.

In recalling his first game as a big-league manager and hitting a home run in the first inning, Robinson said, "At first there was nothing running through my mind. But, by the time I got to third base, I thought to myself, 'Wow, will miracles never cease to happen?'"

78 JOHNNY LINDELL: A PITCHER WITH POP

In the bottom of the eighth, with the score 4–4, in an October game the New York Yankees had to win, manager Casey Stengel sent up left-handed hitter Bobby Brown to bat for Billy Johnson.

Then Cliff Mapes, another portsider, came up to hit for Hank Bauer.

Brown drove a deep fly to center. Mapes tapped back to Boston pitcher Joe Dobson.

Dobson, who threw right-handed, had 14 wins for the Red Sox in 1949, and more than 100 in his 10-year Boston career. He would be posthumously inducted into the Red Sox Hall of Fame.

He had entered the game in the fifth inning of the next-to-the-last game of the 1949 season and had thrown 3⅔ scoreless innings in relief of Sox southpaw starter Mel Parnell, who had won 25 games and pitched to a 2.77 ERA, but failed to hold a 4–0 lead.

The Red Sox had trailed the Yankees in the standings all season, but, in the midst of an 11-game winning streak in September, swept New York in a three-game series at Fenway to take over first place. The Sox needed to win one of the last two games to face the Brooklyn Dodgers in the World Series.

It was October 1, 1949. In China, Chairman Mao announced the establishment of the People's Republic of China.

At Yankee Stadium, Johnny Lindell stepped to the plate. It was a bit of a surprise.

He batted right-handed. He hadn't hit a homer since July. But he had two hits in the game and in his last at-bat poked a pitch far enough to force Ted Williams to the warning track in left field.

Lindell, a former pitcher who had converted to the outfield, had hit .317 in 1948. But this was 1949, and his average languished in the .230s.

The Yankees had Charlie "King Kong" Keller on the bench. Keller, while past his prime, had a left-handed power swing built for the short porch in Yankee Stadium. But he had ruptured a disc in his back in 1947 and hadn't been the same since. By 1949, he felt Stengel was avoiding him.

Yet Stengel was a big believer in the platoon system, which pitted left-handed hitters against right-handed pitchers and vice versa. He made great use of platooning with the injury-riddled Yankees in '49, mixing and matching in almost every game.

Joe DiMaggio was the team's big loss. He hadn't begun playing until late June because of a bad right heel, then had come down with pneumonia in September. Shortstop Phil Rizzuto was the only Yankee regular who played the entire season.

Relief pitcher Joe Page had kept the Yankees in the game, throwing nothing but zeroes for 6⅔ innings of one-hit relief.

In his great book *Summer of '49*, David Halberstam described Lindell as "the team rogue. He was exuberant, generous, and crude, and his humor seemed to dominate the locker room."

He was also a low-ball hitter, so Dobson decided he was going to throw only high fastballs.

The first pitch was up: ball one. The second pitch was high, too, but Lindell drove it deep into the left field bleachers, giving the Yankees a 5–4 lead.

After the game, Lindell jokingly blamed Red Sox manager Joe McCarthy for the home run. Seven years earlier, it was McCarthy, then the Yankee manager, who had converted Lindell, a 6-foot-4, 217-pounder, from a hurler—one who was 23–4 for the Newark Bears and was also the 1941 Minor League Player of the Year—to an everyday player.

After watching Lindell pitch for the Yankees in 1942, McCarthy didn't think the right-hander had enough zip on his fastball to be a success, but he loved his bat. McCarthy wasn't wrong. Lindell, who would go on to hit four consecutive doubles in a game, led the league in triples. He was selected to the 1943 All-Star Game and was the instigator of a Yankee rally in Game Three of the 1943 World Series.

The following year, Lindell had his best season, blasting 18 homers and knocking in 103 runs. In 1947, Lindell started six of the seven World Series games and hit .500 in the Series.

But what he is remembered for is the home run in the eighth inning against the Red Sox on October 1, 1949.

It would be prominent in the first line of Johnny Lindell's obituary.

Other than the Sox, seemingly the only person in the Bronx not thrilled by the home run was Lindell's son, Johnny III. He was ten. He liked the family's off-season home in Arcadia, California, better than the Bronx. When

Lindell Sr. hit the home run, Halberstam wrote, "[E]veryone in their Bronx neighborhood was happy and excited but little John Lindell. Hearing the news, he burst into tears because he was sure it meant staying in New York for an additional two weeks."

He was correct.

John's dad started a key rally the following day, when Vic Raschi pitched the Yankees into the 1949 World Series. The Yankees went on to beat the Brooklyn Dodgers in the Series.

The following year was less eventful. Lindell, not hitting, was released by the Yankees. The St. Louis Cardinals claimed him, but he didn't hit for them, either. He was sold to the Pacific Coast League's Hollywood Stars.

That's when Lindell decided to pitch again.

Back in 1948 as a Yankee, he had started working on a knuckleball just for fun. By '49, he could control it enough that Stengel gave serious thought to using him as a pitcher. But Lindell had not taken the mound in nine years, until Fred Haney, his manager with the Hollywood Stars, suggested pitching again.

And pitch Lindell did. In the 1951–52 seasons for Hollywood, Lindell went a collective 36–18. His ERA was 2.73.

The Pittsburgh Pirates brought him back to the majors in 1953. He was thirty-six when he twirled 175⅔ innings, led the team in strikeouts and complete games, but finished 5–16 on a Pirates team that lost 104 games. In Lindell's 16 losses, the team had scored a total of 36 runs.

He was sold to the Phillies in late August and went 1–1 for them.

In his time as a pitcher for the Pirates and Phillies, Lindell also hit .303. Sometimes the Pirates would bat him fifth on the days he pitched.

His last home run came in 1953 against Brooklyn. It was a 9th-inning, three-run, pinch-hit homer that tied the game.

Johnny Lindell finished his big-league career with 72 homers and eight wins.

77 AL WEIS: A MOST MIRACULOUS MET

It was the end of 1967, and Al Weis was disappointed.

He had played six years for the Chicago White Sox. Since his arrival, they were always in contention, sometimes even down to the last game of the season. Weis even had an off-season job with the Pale Hose—back when most players needed an off-season job—in public relations.

He was also a middle infielder recovering from a broken leg suffered trying to turn two in a game against the Baltimore Orioles in June.

Then, in the middle of December, he received a call saying he had been traded.

To the New York Mets.

Weis grew up in Bethpage on Long Island, about 30 minutes from Shea Stadium, the future home of the Mets. But it was the White Sox who had signed him out of the navy in 1959, three years before the Mets even played a game.

He warmed the bench at first, watching the baseball gymnastics of two future Hall of Famers, shortstop Luis Aparicio and second baseman Nellie Fox. Weis was going to be the successor to one of them. At least that was the plan.

The Mets, which he joined in 1968, were a different story. In five of the six seasons they were in existence, they had finished last in the National League.

Al Weis was twenty-nine. The clock was ticking on his career.

"My reaction was, 'Oh, no.' The stumbling, fumbling Mets," he said to a reporter looking back on his career. "After all these years with a contending team, I was going to a last-place club. It's the ambition of every player to play in a World Series; now I figured that was the end of that dream."

It was Gil Hodges, the manager of the Mets, who insisted Weis be included in the trade that brought the National League club Tommie Agee, a former Rookie of the Year for the White Sox, to play center field.

Hodges, the Hall of Fame Brooklyn Dodgers first baseman, had managed the Washington Senators from 1963 until 1967. He had seen enough of Weis's play. (In 1965, Weis, never known for his bat, did hit .296.) He also understood intangibles. Al Weis was all about intangibles.

He was a skinny switch-hitter who could play second and short. He could also run a little, twice leading the White Sox in stolen bases.

It cost the Mets outfielder Tommy Davis, a two-time National League batting champion, and Jack Fisher, the pitcher who gave up Ted Williams's last home run and Roger Maris's 60th in 1961, for the White Sox to surrender Agee and Weis.

Hodges told Weis more than once that the deal would not have been made if he weren't included.

"Things like that give you confidence," Weis said. "All through the season he let me hit in a lot of situations where other managers would have taken me out."

He played second base, mostly. But he would substitute at shortstop when the starter, Bud Harrelson, had National Guard obligations on weekends.

Early in 1968, a season in which the Mets would finish ninth in the National League, Hodges batted Weis leadoff in a game against the Houston Astros at the Astrodome. The contest went 24 innings. Weis went 1-for-9 with a walk. Worse—he let a routine groundball go through his legs to give the Astros a 1–0 win.

At his Shea Stadium debut two days later, with family and friends in attendance, Weis went 2-for-4 with an RBI in a Mets win.

Weis would end up hitting just .172 in 1968, the Year of the Pitcher.

While the Mets finished 73–89, ninth in the National League, there was a murmur of promise. They had young pitching.

How good? Only 1969 would reveal.

Weis shared second base with a kid, Ken Boswell. Tom Seaver, Jerry Koosman, and Gary Gentry were the top starters in the Mets rotation. Not that it was a big deal at the time, but Weis had stopped switch-hitting. He would bat right-handed only.

The Mets were 45–34 in early July when they had a home-and-home series against the Chicago Cubs, managed by Leo Durocher and considered the team to beat in the National League.

In the home half of the showdown, Tom Seaver almost pitched an almost-perfect game. He was this close. Jimmy Qualls, a rookie, broke it up with a single.

In the away half of the home-and-home, it was Weis who was the hero.

In the fourth inning of the second game at Wrigley Field, the contest tied at one, he was down 1–2 in the count with Art Shamsky on third and Ed Kranepool on first. He choked up a little more than usual. Weis swung and hit the ball onto Waveland Avenue. He was so shocked, he said, he had to remember to "be sure and touch every base."

It was his fifth homer in eight years.

The Mets won.

"Once, when I hit a homer for the White Sox, I came into the dugout and all the guys were lying on the floor or passed out from shock," he told reporters.

Asked if he was as surprised as everyone else in the park, he said, "I'm always surprised . . . Let's face it. I'm no home-run hitter. I'm not even a hitter. I know my place on this club. I'm a fill-in. I'm a substitute."

The next day, he was penciled in the lineup against the Cubs.

He hit another homer. The Mets won.

After the game, Seaver mentioned Al Weis and Babe Ruth in the same sentence. And Seaver is a serious man.

The Mets were behind the Cubbies by 10 games on August 13. They won 14 of their next 16, and were on their way to a divisional championship.

They had won 73 games in 1968, 100 in 1969.

They easily handled Hank Aaron and the Atlanta Braves in the League Championship Series.

Then the Mets met the mighty Baltimore Orioles in the World Series. The Birds had won 109 games in the regular season and easily dispatched the Minnesota Twins in the playoffs. The Orioles also won Game One of the World Series in Baltimore, beating Seaver, a 25-game winner in the regular season, 4–1. Weis knocked in the Mets only run with a sacrifice fly.

But this was 1969. Vietnam. The first moon walk. Woodstock.

Game Two was a pitcher's duel between New York's Jerry Koosman and Baltimore's Dave McNally. Koosman had a no-hitter for six innings. But the score was tied at one in the top of the ninth when Ed Charles, Jerry Grote, and . . . Weis, starting at second and batting eighth, strung together consecutive two-out singles. The Mets won, 2–1.

In Game Five, at Shea Stadium, with the Mets leading the Series three games to one, the Orioles built a 3–0 lead behind McNally, who won more than 20 games each season from 1968 to 1971.

New York's Donn Clendenon smoked a two-run homer in the sixth to pull the Mets to within a run. Weis, who would hit seven homers in his major-league regular season career, hit one long and deep to left in the seventh to tie the score.

It was the first homer he had ever hit at Shea.

Weis, the .219 lifetime hitter, batted .455 in the World Series.

The Mets would go ahead in the eighth and seal the World Series win, cementing a place in baseball history as the "Miracle Mets."

"I started four of the five World Series games, and I got called into the fifth game as a defensive replacement," Weis said years later to a reporter. "I would have considered myself lucky to have played in even one game. Think of all the really great players who never got into a World Series, guys like Ernie Banks and Billy Williams. I was lucky just to get the chance, and then I was fortunate enough to perform well."

76 WILLIE MAYS: CLASSIC CLOUT OFF OF SPAHN

In 22 seasons, Willie Mays played in 24 All-Star Games, hit 660 home runs, and collected a total of 3,283 hits. For eight consecutive seasons, from 1959 to 1966, he knocked in 100 runs. In 1954 and 1965 he was named the National League Most Valuable Player. He made a catch in the 1954 World Series that will be remembered as long as there is baseball. He also won 12 Gold Gloves—and the award didn't exist until his sixth season, 1957—in the big leagues for his fielding prowess. He should have been unanimously elected to the Hall of Fame. (He wasn't, securing 409 votes out of the potential 432 baseball writer ballots.) He was the 10th black player to make the big leagues.

When he was brought to the New York Giants in 1951, Mays was hitting .477 for Minneapolis in Triple A.

He struck out in his first at-bat, and went 0-for-his-first-12 against the Philadelphia Phillies at Shibe Park in the City of Brotherly Love, but the Giants—17–19 when he was called to the majors—won three in a row with him in the lineup.

The next day, May 28, in New York, at the Polo Grounds, before 23,101 fans, Mays batted third.

In the first inning, Eddie Stanky walked before Whitey Lockman hit into a double play against future Hall of Famer Warren Spahn, pitching for the Boston Braves. Up came Mays. He was twenty.

Giants scout Montague told Tim Cohane, the sports editor of *Look* magazine, that he been scouting Alonzo Perry, a teammate of Mays with the Negro League's Birmingham Black Barons in 1948, but he couldn't take his eyes off the center fielder, Mays.

"This was the greatest young player I had ever seen in my life or my scouting career," he wrote, upon seeing Mays.

Durocher, in his book *Nice Guys Finish Last*, described Mays this way: "If somebody came up and hit .450, stole 100 bases, and performed a miracle in the field every day, I'd still look you right in the eye and tell you that Willie was better. He could do the five things you have to do to be a superstar: hit,

hit with power, run, throw, and field. And he had the other magic ingredient that turns a superstar into a super Superstar. Charisma. He lit up a room when he came in. He was a joy to be around."

But on May 28, 1951, Mays was still a prospect, all promise.

Spahn, who won 363 games, more than any left-handed pitcher in the history of baseball, remembers facing Mays for the first time.

"I'll never forgive myself. We might have gotten rid of Willie forever if I'd only struck him out," he told a reporter in jest. He noted that the pitcher's mound is 60 feet, 6 inches from home plate, and his pitch to the rookie looked like "a helluva pitch" for 60 feet.

Mays launched the ball over the roof in left.

He then went hitless in his next 13 at-bats, making Mays 1-for-26. According to legend, after the game he was caught crying in front of his locker, telling Durocher he couldn't hit major-league pitching.

Durocher said, "As long as I'm the manager of the Giants you are my center fielder. . . . You are the best center fielder I've ever looked at."

Mays went 14 for his next 33. He slugged 20 homers as a rookie in 1951, the year the Giants made their remarkable comeback to win the National League pennant on Bobby Thomson's home run. Mays was on deck when that ball soared into history.

Mays missed the next year and a half because of military obligations, but returned in 1954 to hit .345 with 41 home runs, leading the Giants to the world championship.

Mays would hit 18 career homers off of Spahn, the most he would hit off any pitcher. (He also slugged 13 off another Hall of Fame pitcher, the Dodgers Don Drysdale.)

His most famous home run off Spahn came in 1963. The Giants were based in San Francisco, at homer-unfriendly Candlestick Park, where the damp wind tended to blow in.

On July 2, a Tuesday night, Spahn, forty-two, took the hill for the Milwaukee Braves. He had spun a three-hit shutout four days earlier against the Dodgers. Two years before that, in 1961, he had no-hit the Giants, his second career no-no.

Juan Marichal, twenty-five, was pitching for the Giants. Seventeen days earlier, Marichal had thrown a no-hitter against Houston.

Spahn, who had won his 300th game in 1961, was on his way to a 23–7 record with 22 complete games, his last great season.

Bud Selig, the future commissioner of baseball, making his first trip to San Francisco, was in attendance, rooting for his hometown Braves. He couldn't believe how cold San Francisco could be in July.

On that chilly evening, Marichal and Spahn both threw zeroes, inning after inning after inning after inning, in one of the greatest pitching duels in baseball history.

Mays threw a runner out at the plate in the fourth. The Giants Willie McCovey nearly hit a home run in the ninth, but the ball went foul.

Both pitchers worked out of mild jams.

Giants manager Alvin Dark wanted to take Marichal out in the ninth, 12th, and 15th innings, but the young pitcher—the midst of his breakout season—kept talking him out of it.

Spahn kept grabbing a bat when it was his turn to hit. His manager, Bobby Bragan, decided it was Spahn's game to win or lose.

After 16 innings, Marichal had allowed eight hits and four walks. He struck out 10. He allowed no runs. The only extra-base hit was a double by Spahn in the seventh. Along with being a great pitcher, Spahn was also a good hitter. He would hit 35 career home runs and once hit .333 in a season.

Entering the bottom of the 16th, Spahn's pitching line was eight hits allowed and one walk.

The game featured McCovey and Milwaukee's Hank Aaron, twenty-nine, who would lead the National League in home runs with 44 each; the Giants Harvey Kuenn, a former American League batting champion; and future Hall of Famers Eddie Mathews of the Braves and Orlando Cepeda of the Giants.

And, of course, Willie Mays, who had gone 0-for-5 with a walk when he stepped to the plate with one out in the bottom of the 16th.

Mays had this habit of always stepping on first base at home after an inning. He followed his usual script on July 2 after the top of the 16th. Marichal was waiting for him.

"When he got there, I put my arm on his shoulder and I told him, 'Alvin Dark is mad at me. He's not going to let me pitch any longer,'" Marichal recounted to the *San Jose Mercury News* on the 50th anniversary of the game.

"So [Mays] touched my back and said, 'Don't worry. I'm going to win this game for you.'"

And he did. A long drive that cleared the fence in left. The Giants won, 1–0.

Marichal fired an incredible 227 pitches, mostly fastballs, in the game. Spahn mixed it up, but threw 201 pitches.

The next day, the *San Francisco Chronicle* quoted Spahn as saying he threw Mays a screwball that "didn't break worth a damn."

In his next start, Spahn tossed a shutout to beat Houston.

Marichal would finish the season with 25 wins. He threw 321⅓ innings that year, a massive total.

Mays added 38 homers to his lifetime totals.

In 1968, he would hit a 15th-inning home run off of Cincinnati's Ted Abernathy, which set another baseball record: most innings in which a player hit a home run. Mays, who retired in 1973 at forty-two, still holds the mark: 16.

75 HANK GREENBERG: RETURN OF THE FIRST HAMMERIN' HANK

He didn't know if he could still hit.

How could he?

The last time Hank Greenberg had played in a major-league game was more than four years earlier. That was a whole different world. Before everything changed.

The two-time American League Most Valuable Player was the first major-league player drafted into the U.S. Army in 1941. At first he was classified 4-F because of his flat feet, but the decision was reversed while he was in spring training with the Tigers. He was now 1-A. He went from being the Detroit Tigers cleanup hitter to basic training.

But on December 5, 1941, Greenberg, after serving seven months, was released from his military obligation. He was past twenty-eight—and thus ineligible to be drafted. With 249 career home runs, he started thinking about getting in shape for the 1942 season.

Two days later, the Japanese attacked Pearl Harbor. The United States was at war.

Greenberg became the first active major leaguer to enlist. He joined the U.S. Army Air Corps and was sent to Officer Candidate School, where he was commissioned a First Lieutenant.

He requested a transfer to a war zone and was sent to the China-Burma-India Theater, where he became part of the first B-29 teams.

By the time Germany surrendered on May 7, 1945, Greenberg was an Air Force captain with four battle stars. He had hardly swung a bat in four-plus years. He was also thirty-four.

On July 1, 1945, Greenberg started in left field in a game against Hall of Fame manager Connie Mack's Philadelphia A's. He was, of course, batting cleanup.

The Briggs Stadium crowd of more than 47,000 stood when he first came to bat.

Greenberg thought he was in pretty good shape, but was unsure about his legs. Ballplayers always worry about their legs, especially sluggers.

But in the previous month, Ted Williams of the Boston Red Sox, another World War II hero, told a reporter, "Greenberg will hit, and you can count on it. At the end of the season, he'll be the most dangerous hitter on the Detroit team."

The Tigers were in contention. With the Yankees, of course. Greenberg had helped lead Detroit to three American League pennants and a 1935 World Series championship before entering the army. Long before Hank Aaron, Greenberg was the first "Hammerin' Hank."

He was also the first Jewish baseball superstar, once hitting 58 homers in a season and knocking in 183 in another.

He gained national attention in 1934—the year in which he hit 26 homers and drove in 139 runs—when he decided not to play on Yom Kippur, the holiest of Jewish holidays.

Still, he had to face the slurs.

"How the hell could you get up to home plate every day and have some son of a bitch call you a Jew bastard and a kike and a sheenie and get on your ass without feeling the pressure?" he once asked. "If the players weren't doing it, the fans were. I used to get frustrated as hell. Sometimes I wanted to go into the stands and beat the shit out of them."

He didn't. Instead, he hit.

Greenberg, born to Jewish immigrants on January 1, 1911, had grown up in the Bronx. The Yankees had tried to sign him, but he opted for the Tigers in 1929 because Lou Gehrig was playing first base for the Bronx Bombers.

He was tall and strong (6-foot-4, 215 pounds) and smart, but a bit awkward physically. He worked very hard at playing baseball. Very, very hard, initially getting a handle for first base and later learning left field. He could always hit. He made his major-league debut in 1930, when he was nineteen.

Hank Greenberg was discharged from the Air Corps on June 14, 1945.

In the eighth inning of the first game of a Sunday doubleheader on July 1, 1945, Greenberg launched an eighth-inning home run off of Philadelphia's Charlie Gassaway, a left-hander, to the deepest part of left field.

The Tigers swept Philadelphia that day to extend their lead over the Yankees to 3½ games.

Four days later, with two outs in the bottom of the ninth, Greenberg slashed a single to center, knocking in two runs to beat the Red Sox, 8–7.

More than four years after he'd last played in the major leagues, Greenberg would finish the 1945 season with 13 homers, 60 RBIs, and a .311 average in just 78 games.

Ted Williams was right.

So was Associated Press sportswriter Whitney Martin, who wrote in 1945, "He will be watched as a symbol of hope to all other baseball players in the service who fear their absence from the game might impair their effectiveness and money-earning capacity."

But as inspiring as that home run was off of Gassaway, Greenberg was even more clutch down the stretch. The Washington Senators, instead of the Yankees, were the team to beat in the American League in 1945, and the pennant race went down to the wire.

The Tigers had to wait out three days of rain in St. Louis to play the Browns (the future Baltimore Orioles), needing a split of a doubleheader to go to the World Series.

The Tigers were trailing by a run in the top of the ninth. Browns starter Nels Potter had put two runners in scoring position when he intentionally walked forty-year-old Doc Cramer, a pretty good player for the A's and the Boston Red Sox.

Up came Greenberg. It was raining hard. Potter, a righty, was hoping to induce a game-ending double-play grounder.

Greenberg stroked the second pitch he saw. The ball flew just inside the left field foul pole for a grand slam and a 6–3 Tiger win to capture the American League pennant.

"I took the first pitch from Nelson Potter for a ball. As he wound up on the next pitch I could read the grip on the ball and I could tell he was going to throw a screwball," he told Ira Berkow, his biographer and *New York Times* columnist. "I swung and hit a line drive toward the corner of the left-field bleachers. I stood at the plate and watched the ball for fear the umpire would call it foul. It landed a few feet inside the foul pole for a grand slam. We won the game, and the pennant and all the players charged the field when I reached home plate and they pounded me on the back and carried on like I was a hero."

The second game was canceled due to rain.

It was Greenberg's first trip to the Series since 1935. The opponent was again the Chicago Cubs, as it had been ten years earlier.

In '35, Greenberg hit 36 homers and knocked in 168 runs while being named the American League MVP.

But in the second game of the 1945 Series, Greenberg's left wrist was broken by a pitch. He stayed in the game, actually trying to score from second on a hit in the same inning. But his wrist swelled, and his season was over. Greenberg hit two homers and three doubles, and knocked in seven runs before getting hurt.

The Tigers went on to win the World Series. It was the last time the Cubs made the Fall Classic.

The following year, Greenberg smacked 44 homers and knocked in 127, leading the Tigers to a second-place finish. Following the season, Greenberg was listening to the radio when he learned he had been waived by the Tigers.

He was stunned.

"I don't understand it," he told reporters, "and I never will."

The Pittsburgh Pirates offered him a $100,000 contract, the first one in baseball history, and owner John Galbreath sweetened the deal with a racehorse. The Pirates also shortened the distance to the left-field fence by 30 feet.

But he was thirty-six, and it showed. Injuries didn't help—especially bone chips in his elbow.

Greenberg closed his career with a career-low .249 batting average, but still slugged 25 homers. In his last season he reached out to Brooklyn rookie Jackie Robinson, the first black player in the big leagues. Not everybody did.

He also mentored Ralph Kiner, the future Hall of Famer slugger and broadcaster.

Greenberg was elected to the Hall of Fame in 1956. He had 331 home runs in his career and a .313 lifetime average.

Bill Veeck, who owned the Cleveland Indians, St. Louis Browns, and Chicago White Sox at various times, was known for his imaginative thinking. He was sure Hank Greenberg would have made a fine baseball commissioner.

74 BABE RUTH: BABE'S FIRST IN THE HOUSE BUILT FOR HIM

Yankee Stadium was a big deal.

A very big deal.

When the New York Yankees purchased Babe Ruth in 1920 from the Boston Red Sox, they had been playing in the Polo Grounds, the home of perennial National League powerhouse New York Giants. It was an uneasy landlord-tenant relationship, more so after Ruth arrived.

The Yankees attracted 1.3 million fans to the park in 1920, Ruth's first year in New York, outdrawing the Giants, who drew 929,609.

Giants owner Charles Stoneham was not pleased. He spoke more often and more loudly about how the Yankees should find a real home. Stoneham was said to have remarked that the Yanks should move "to Queens, or some other out-of-the-way place."

After looking at various Manhattan sites and the Long Island City area of Queens, Yankee owners Jacob Ruppert and Cap Huston decided to build on a 10-acre former lumberyard in the Bronx.

They spent $2.3 million of their own money to construct a three-tiered stadium that could hold more than 70,000 people in an era of 30,000-seat baseball parks. And it was to be called a stadium, not a park. Some also called it a huge gamble.

Before the "Roaring '20s" roared, sportswriters, politicians, and fans asked if the city could continue to support three baseball teams—the Yankees, Giants, and Dodgers. It didn't help when details of the 1919 World Series betting scandal, in which games were thrown, became public. The Chicago White Sox lost the Series to the Cincinnati Reds, and eight players were accused of intentionally losing games for money. The Sox players were acquitted in court in 1921, but banned from baseball. The game's reputation hung in the balance.

Construction of Yankee Stadium commenced on May 5, 1922, and Opening Day was April 18, 1923. Dubbed by generations "The House That Ruth Built," it would host papal masses and Billy Graham revivals, fights by Joe Louis and Muhammad Ali. U2, Billy Joel, and Pink Floyd staged concerts there. Notre Dame Football Coach Knute Rockne gave his famous "Win one for the Gipper" speech in one of its dressing rooms. Soon after being freed from a South African prison, Nelson Mandela spoke there.

Babe Ruth's wake was also held at the Stadium in 1948.

But a quarter of a century earlier, on April 18, 1923, Babe, twenty-eight, was alive and in his prime. In a deal announced on January 5, 1920, the Boston Red Sox famously sold him to the Yankees for $125,000. Red Sox owner Harry Frazee, who'd purchase the Carmine Hose in 1916 for $500,000, was selling Ruth for reasons more complicated than the myth that he wanted to fund the Broadway play *No, No, Nanette*.

"Ruth is our big ace," he once said. "He's the most talked of, most sought for, most colorful ballplayer in the game."

And Ruth then was only just starting. His first year with the Yankees, he shattered baseball's single-season home run record by swatting 54. St. Louis Browns slugger George Sisler was second in home runs with 19.

Ruth encored in 1921 with a new record, 59. In 1922, Ruth bopped 35 dingers.

Prior to the Stadium's opening, Ruth told reporters, "I'd give a year off my life if I can hit a home run in the first game in this new park."

Legendary composer and conductor John Philip Sousa led the Seventh Regiment Band in pregame ceremonies. New York Governor Al Smith threw out the first pitch to Yankee catcher Wally Schang.

At 3:35 p.m., home plate umpire Tommy Connolly bellowed, "Play ball!"

The day was bright, but windy and chilly, topcoat-and-sweater weather. Ruth was playing right field and batting third. Hitting in front of him was third baseman Jumping Joe Dugan and, behind him, first baseman Wally Pipp, who would gain fame two years later when he sat out a game with a headache, giving Lou Gehrig the opportunity to play, which he would not relinquish until he was too sick to stay in the lineup.

Pitching for the Red Sox was right-hander Howard Ehmke, who had a funky sidearm delivery and terrific control, and was known to throw a slow ball and a slower ball. He would pitch a no-hitter for the Red Sox later that season and finish the campaign with 20 wins, his career best. When he retired, Ehmke started a company that made the first tarpaulins to cover baseball diamonds when it rained.

But on April 18, 1923, with two on in the third inning, Ehmke's job was to get Babe Ruth out.

With two outs and a run in, he walked Yankee center fielder Whitey Witt. After an RBI single by Dugan, Ruth stepped to the plate. His jersey was lacking that iconic number 3—the Yankees didn't start wearing numbers until 1929, when they became the first team to do so. Number or not, everyone in the Stadium knew who Ruth was.

Ehmke threw a slow ball, Ruth hit it fast and hard, deep to right field. No one there measured it, but Ruth and the 70,000 in the stands knew it was a home run—

Yankee Stadium's very first.

"It was an amazing day," Witt, a great friend of Ruth's, said. "The new ballpark, the crowd, all the excitement. It was an experience that you could never repeat in a hundred years. We were in awe when we first saw the park. It seemed so big. At the time, there was nothing like it in baseball. Looking around, it was enough to make your eyes pop out."

It was just the first of 6,581 regular-season games played at Yankee Stadium, the House that Ruth Built.

Babe Ruth died of cancer on August 16, 1948. He was fifty-three. His wake at Yankee Stadium was held over two days. The lines never seemed to stop.

73 KEN GRIFFEY JR.: A FATHER'S DAY GIFT FROM JUNIOR

The Seattle Mariners had the first pick in the 1987 draft.

Team owner George Argyros wanted to select Mike Harkey, a 6-foot-5 right-handed pitcher out of California State University, Fullerton. Scouting director Roger Jongewaard and head scout Bob Harrison were adamant about taking Ken Griffey Jr., a high school outfielder, with the top pick.

Argyros bowed to the wishes of Jongewaard and Harrison, but warned them that if Griffey was a bust, they might need to look for new jobs.

Harrison, to whom Argyros once had offered the general manager's job, wasn't worried about that threat. His scouting report on Griffey included this: "He's the best player I've ever seen . . . he has all the tools to be a superstar."

(Harkey ended up being drafted with the fourth pick by the Chicago Cubs. Injuries curtailed his career. He retired with a 36–36 record and became a pitching coach.)

Griffey was seventeen when the Mariners grabbed him, the first son of a major-league player ever selected with the top choice in the draft. He was the kid with the big talent and the smile.

In the 1970s and '80s, Ken Griffey Sr. was a three-time All-Star, and had been a cog for the Cincinnati Reds when they were known as the Big Red Machine. At the time his oldest son was drafted, Griffey Sr. was thirty-seven and playing for the Atlanta Braves. He'd finish the 1987 season with 14 homers, 64 RBIs, and a .286 average.

His first year as a pro, Junior Griffey tore it up with Bellingham in the Class A Northwest League, hitting .313 with 14 homers and 40 RBIs in 54 games. He made his major-league debut for Seattle in 1989, and the Mariners signed Griffey Sr. late in the following season.

They played a total of 51 games together before Senior retired in 1991, the first time in major-league history a father and son took to the field at the same time. Senior played left, with Junior in center. "A lot of times I'd look over [to center field] and, this is no lie, I still see the hat too big for his head, a baggy uniform and he's got number 30 across his chest and back," Griffey Sr. told Sherwin. "That's a father-son game I was remembering when he was just a little kid and I was with the Reds. Then reality comes back when I have to get ready for the pitch."

On September 14, 1990, facing California's Kirk McCaskill, Griffey Sr. banged a two-run homer in the first inning. The encore was Junior rifling a dinger to nearly the same spot at Anaheim Stadium in California, making them the first father and son to hit homers in the same game.

Ken Jr., of course, became one of the greatest players ever, hitting 630 home runs, winning 10 Gold Gloves (only Hall of Famers Willie Mays and Roberto Clemente had more among outfielders) and electrifying fans in ways no statistics could properly illustrate.

During his 22-year career, he played for Seattle, his hometown Cincinnati Reds, and the Chicago White Sox.

Injuries, including a torn hamstring and labrum, dislocated patella, fractured wrist, and broken hand, started piling up as he got older. He would have hit more than 700 home runs if not for all the injuries.

When Junior Griffey hit his 500th home run, his father was in attendance.

After he made his familiar path around the bases, he ran to his father, seated in the first row next to the Reds dugout. It was Father's Day, June 20, 2004.

Junior had spent almost a week trying to reach number 500. He hugged his dad and said, "Happy Father's Day. I love you."

Griffey Sr. said later, "He's always done that on Father's Day. It was a nice gift but he does that so he doesn't have to buy me anything."

Junior Griffey said his father gave him this advice en route to number 500: "Pick out a pitch you can hit, still get your base hits, and one is going to fly out."

Another bit of advice from his dad helped Junior through the rough patches of his career.

"It all comes down to patience. He sometimes expects it all to come easy. Even Junior has to work. He was talking 'I . . . me . . . me.' I told him to stop that and think of the team. Do the little things to help them and you'll see changes all around you. He did and saw what happened."

Father knows best.

72 KEN GRIFFEY SR.: DAD SHOWS JUNIOR HOW IT'S DONE

In 1988, after a seven-season absence, Ken Griffey Sr. returned to the Cincinnati Reds.

It felt good. Right.

In the 1970s, Griffey Sr. had been a fleet young member of the Big Red Machine, winners of back-to-back World Series in 1975 and '76.

A left-handed hitter, Griffey Sr. hit .300 or better five times for the Reds as a top-of-the-order stick. He was one of manager Sparky Anderson's "Great Eight," the starting lineup that powered through the National League.

In '76, Griffey lost the batting crown by one point to Chicago's Bill Madlock.

Griffey Sr. was from Donora, Pennsylvania, the same hometown as St. Louis Cardinals Hall of Famer Stan "The Man" Musial.

Now he was back in Cincinnati after forays with the New York Yankees and Atlanta Braves, and playing a different role, that of elder statesman and spare part. In 1990, Griffey Sr.'s Reds were in first place every day of the season.

But the team felt Senior—at forty called "Gramps" by teammates—was at the end of his career. He was released on August 24. His teammates were angry. When the Reds went on to win the World Series that fall, the club's first since 1976, Griffey Sr.'s former team voted him a full share of the Series earnings and a ring, his third.

He is only the third player in the Reds storied history to own three rings.

As disappointed as Griffey Sr. was by the release, it worked out well for him.

The Seattle Mariners signed him on August 29 to play with his son, their star center fielder Ken Griffey Jr.

Two days later, they stood in the same outfield, Senior in left and Junior in center, the first father and son to play on the same team in major-league history. To mark the occasion, they delivered back-to-back singles against the Kansas City Royals.

Junior Griffey was in his second big-league season. He had already made his first All-Star Game. Like his father, he batted left-handed, but he was taller and sleeker, with more power.

Junior was in his early teens when he used to take batting practice with the Reds at the old Riverfront Stadium. Hall of Fame first baseman Tony Perez watched "The Kid," as he soon would be called, take a few hacks. Perez then turned to Griffey Sr. and said, "Don't let anybody ever change that swing. That's a big-league swing right now."

Indeed. It was a swing that launched 630 career home runs.

More of a gap hitter, Griffey Sr. popped 152 homers and finished his career with a .296 lifetime average.

"My dad hit 152 home runs and that's the person I wanted to be like," Junior Griffey once said. "My hero growing up. That's the person who taught me how to play and is still telling me how to play."

Junior had been touted since he was young. Seattle selected him with the number 1 overall pick in the 1987 draft. He was in the big leagues two years later.

Senior was never considered a big prospect. He was a 29th-round draft choice in 1969. It took him four years to make the big leagues.

Two weeks after their first game together, the Griffeys wrote another piece of baseball history, hitting back-to-back home runs.

Kirk McCaskill was pitching at home for the California Angels that night, September 14, 1990. He walked Seattle second baseman and leadoff hitter Harold Reynolds.

McCaskill got back to throwing strikes when Griffey Sr. came to the plate. He had him down 0-and-2 when Junior's dad lashed a long drive to deep left-center field for a home run.

His son greeted him at home plate.

McCaskill then fell behind Junior, 3-and-0. The next pitch was too good to take, and Junior, then still only twenty, launched it in the same direction as his father's shot.

All of baseball applauded.

Six times in Junior's career he would hit home runs on Father's Day.

As Griffey Sr., who was elected to the Reds Hall of Fame in 2004 put it, they were gifts far more appreciated than the Old Spice and ties Junior once gave him.

Ties and aftershave go out of style; home runs never do.

Especially when they are hit by your son.

71 SHAWN GREEN: SENSATIONAL SLUMP BUSTER

The slump was over.

Finally.

Shawn Green, who had powered 49 homers to set a Los Angeles Dodgers team record in 2001, had gone 24 games and 110 at-bats without a dinger. It was May 21, 2002, and Green had only three long balls.

The week before, he had endured an 0-for-18 drought in which he failed to hit the ball out of the infield. He was booed and benched. His batting average was the definition of anemic: .231.

But the first two games in Milwaukee seemed to be a kind of elixir. Milwaukee, after all, was where Green hit his first major-league homer, on May 14, 1995, at the former County Stadium, when he was a member of the Toronto Blue Jays, and the Brewers were still in the American League.

Green had homered twice to help build a 5–0 Dodger lead that Tuesday night in May. But the Dodgers would blow the game and lose, 8–6. The next day, Green tripled home the only run in a 1–0 Dodger win.

On May 23, a Thursday, the Brewers opened the roof at Miller Park for sunshine at the afternoon game. Green, a smooth left-handed hitter, knocked in a run with a double off of Milwaukee southpaw starter Glendon Rusch in the first.

In the second inning, with two on, Green hit a three-run homer to give the Dodgers a 6–1 lead.

But Shawn Green's afternoon was only starting.

In the fourth and fifth innings, Green, who was still batting third despite his slump, slugged homers off of Milwaukee reliever Brian Mallette. The Dodgers now owned a 10–1 lead.

Green batted again in the eighth. He singled to center, making it a 5-for-5 afternoon. But to get a chance to hit a fourth home run in the game, he needed at least three Dodgers to reach base.

Hiram Bocachica, who had earlier pinch-hit for left fielder Brian Jordan and stayed in the game, homered off Jose Cabrera to score Green. Catcher Chad Kreuter opened the ninth with a double. Cabrera managed to retire two straight batters. Third baseman Adrian Beltre, then a twenty-three-year-old kid making a name for himself, was the batter. He powered a two-run homer.

Up came Green.

On a 1–1 pitch, he hit his bomb to write his name into the baseball record book as the 14th major leaguer to hit four homers in a game.

Green said he had been looking for a pitch to hit out. "I felt that if I got something to hit, I was going to hit it hard and in the air. Fortunately, I got that last pitch and didn't miss it."

The ball sailed more than 425 feet over the fence in right-center field.

"As the day went on, all of a sudden [the ball] kept getting bigger and bigger," Green said after the game. "After getting the double and a home run, things just took off from there."

Along with the four homers, he scored six runs and knocked in seven. His box score line was a ridiculous 6–6-6–7.

Green also established a record for total bases in a game with 19, breaking the mark of 18 set by Joe Adcock of the Milwaukee Braves on July 31, 1954.

Green also joined Gil Hodges as the only other Dodger to hit four homers in a game. Hodges had hit four on August 31, 1950, at Ebbets Field in Brooklyn.

In the three games, Green raised his average from .231 to .265.

But he wasn't through. Green hit a homer in the next game against Arizona, then two more on Saturday, finishing the week with nine home runs, a National League record.

Three weeks earlier, Seattle's Mike Cameron had hit four homers in a game against the Chicago White Sox. Two players had never before hit four home runs in a game in the same season.

Green ended up being voted to the All-Star team. He finished 2002 with 42 homers, third in the National League, and 114 RBIs, good for fourth place.

Green, then twenty-nine, had been acquired by the Dodgers from the Blue Jays in a deal for outfielder Raul Mondesi in the 1999 off-season.

Green had told the Jays that, when his contract expired in 2000, he would be thinking about returning home to California. Soon after the trade, Green signed a six-year, $84 million contract with the Dodgers.

When he hit 49 homers for the Dodgers in 2001, he became the fifth player in history to record 40 homers in both leagues. He finished with a .283 career batting average, but was even better in the clutch, hitting .337 with men in scoring position.

Almost 15 months before he hit four dingers in one game, he hit three in one.

On August 15, 2001, Green had three homers in a 13–1 win over the Montreal Expos.

He is only the fourth player in history to have both a three-homer game and a four-homer game. The others are Cleveland Indians and Chicago White Sox outfielder Pat Seerey, and two Hall of Famers, Lou Gehrig of the New York Yankees and Mike Schmidt of the Philadelphia Phillies.

Green, who retired in 2008, finished with 328 career home runs.

70 ALFONSO SORIANO: THE ONE THAT SHOULD HAVE BEEN A WINNER

Alfonso Soriano thought he had won the World Series.

And why shouldn't he have?

The seventh game of the 2001 World Series was tied in the top of the eighth. Arizona's Curt Schilling, pitching on three days' rest, had dominated all night long. But on a 0–2 pitch, Soriano, only twenty-five, all coiled and sinewy power, rifled a low-and-away split-fingered fastball into the left field seats to put the New York Yankees ahead, 2–1.

"Unless I buried it, I couldn't have thrown it any lower," Schilling said.

It was less than two months after 9/11.

The whole country was rooting for New York. Even Red Sox fans. Or so it seemed.

"Oh, man," Soriano said years later. "I felt like, 'We got this.' When I hit that ball, I said, 'It's gone, that's all we need.' I was happy for the team, the city, for me."

Soriano was a rookie second baseman. He had finished the regular season with 18 homers, 73 RBIs, a .268 batting average and 43 steals, with flashes of a whole lot more promise.

In 2002, he was almost a 40–40 man, with 39 homers and 41 steals, hitting an even .300. Soriano was the second Yankee in history to hit more than 30 homers and steal more than 30 bases in a season. In 2003, Soriano piled up the same kind of numbers. Bobby Bonds, father of Barry, is the only other 30–30 man in the Yankees storied history.

Soriano would finish his career in 2014, with 412 homers, more than Hall of Famers Duke Snider, Al Kaline, Johnny Bench, Jim Rice, Orlando Cepeda, and Tony Perez.

But on a November night at Bank One Ballpark in Phoenix, Arizona, he was drawing comparisons to the then-home run king, Hank Aaron.

Soriano, 6-foot-1, 195 pounds, swung the heaviest bat in the bigs (34½ ounces) and looked so much like a young Aaron that the man who hit 755 career home runs thought so, too. Aaron couldn't help but notice Soriano's forearms and wrists. Broadcaster Jim Kaat, who won 283 games in the big leagues, noted at the time, "I can't believe how much they resemble each other. It's the speed in their wrists, how they swing, even how they stand at the plate. When I look at Alfonso, it's like looking at a young Hank."

Soriano hailed from the Dominican Republic. He played pro ball in Japan for two years before the Yankees signed him in 1998.

As he was coming through the Yankee farm system, the organization wasn't sure what position he would play. He was tried at second, third, and the outfield. But the Yankees knew "Sorrie," as he was called, had a place in the batting order.

The Yankees had long been interested in acquiring Schilling from the Diamondbacks.

Yankee owner George Steinbrenner admired Schilling's bulldog attitude. He also liked the fact that Schilling had named his son Gehrig, after Yankee great Lou.

In the winter of 2003, Arizona asked for Soriano and first baseman prospect Nick Johnson in exchange for Schilling. The Yankees said no; the price was too steep. As much as they liked Schilling, he was going on thirty-four.

But in 2001, it looked like Schilling was going to be a Diamondback for life.

The big righty, at 6-foot-5 and 220 pounds, dominated the Yankees in Game One of the World Series, throwing seven innings of three-hit, one-run ball. He struck out eight. On Halloween night at Yankee Stadium, he was just as great. Maybe even better: seven innings, one run allowed, nine strikeouts.

The Diamondbacks, leading 3–1, handed the ball to their star relief pitcher, Byung-Hyun Kim. He'd struck out 113 batters in 98 innings during the regular season, and struck out the side in the eighth before surrendering a game-tying two-run, two-out homer to Tino Martinez in the ninth. He then gave up a Derek Jeter home run in the 10th to complete the Yankee comeback.

The following night, the Yankees made another audacious comeback behind Scott Brosius's ninth-inning dinger, again off Kim.

Before the World Series started, Schilling had said he wouldn't be intimidated by pitching against the Yankees at the old Yankee Stadium. "When you use the words mystique and aura, those are dancers in a nightclub. Those are not things we concern ourselves with on the ball field."

After watching the two Yankee comebacks, Schilling, when asked again about mystique and aura, replied, "I didn't know they'd make an appearance at Yankee Stadium."

In Game Seven, back in Arizona, Schilling was leery of Soriano, the kind of hitter who could look really bad on one pitch, then send the next one on a searing ride somewhere deep.

Soriano had hit a walk-off homer off Seattle closer Kazuhiro Sasaki to win Game Four of the American League Championship Series at Yankee Stadium, and had singled in the winning run in the bottom of the 12th in Game Five of the World Series.

In the eighth inning of Game Seven, Soriano was only trying to get on base. If he did, he was hoping for the steal sign. He had a career-high 43 swipes that season, and in his 16 years in the majors he recorded a total of 289 steals.

"The third pitch, he [Schilling] threw me a fastball up and I hit a foul ball," Soriano recalled. "I was concentrating hard and thought, 'If he throws me something in the [strike] zone, I just want to make contact.' He threw me a nasty split in the dirt and I threw my bat out there and I had good contact."

It soared high to left. It was a no-brainer.

The great reliever Mariano Rivera struck out the side in the bottom of the eighth. In the ninth, the Diamondbacks came back against Rivera to win the game and World Series.

Schilling and Randy Johnson were brilliant in the Series for the Diamondbacks. They combined to go 4–0 with a 1.40 ERA, and were named the Series co-MVPs and *Sports Illustrated* Sportsmen of the Year.

Soriano never lived up to the Aaron hype, but was selected to seven straight All-Star games and was the All-Star Game MVP in 2004. While never a great defender, he did twice lead National League outfielders in assists. The Chicago Cubs signed him to a $136 million contract after the 2006 season.

Soriano was also once good enough to be traded by the Yankees for Alex Rodriguez.

69 STAN MUSIAL: STAN THE MAN'S ALL-STAR GAME-WINNER

"How good was Stan Musial? He was good enough to take your breath away."
—Vin Scully, Hall of Fame broadcaster

In 1955, Cincinnati's slugging first baseman, Ted Kluszewski, received 150,000 more All-Star Game votes than Stan Musial.

"Big Klu," as he was called, would finish the season with a career-high 47 home runs.

Musial, the St. Louis first baseman and outfielder, was selected as a reserve for the National League. It was Musial's 12th All-Star Game. (He would finish his career having played double that number.)

Musial was in the midst of a typical number 6 season—.319 average, 33 home runs and 108 RBIs. Musial won seven NL batting titles in his 22 seasons as a Cardinal. Three times he was named the league's Most Valuable Player, a league record. He missed winning the Triple Crown in 1948 by one home run. Brooklyn's Preacher Roe said he had the best strategy to stop Musial: "I throw him four wide ones and try to pick him off first base."

When he retired in 1963, Stan the Man, as he was called first by Bob Broeg of the *St. Louis Post-Dispatch*, had accumulated 3,630 hits, the most in NL history, second all-time to Ty Cobb. Musial had 1,815 of those hits at home and 1,815 hits on the road. Add to that resume 475 career homers and a .331 lifetime average.

In 1962, when he was forty-one, he hit .330. In 22 seasons, he struck out only 696 times. Stan the Man was inducted into the Hall of Fame in 1969, only the fourth person at the time to be voted in during his first year of eligibility.

He never said no to an autograph request and probably didn't go a day without playing "Take Me Out to the Ball Game" on the harmonica he always carried.

Before the 1952 season, Cobb, the gnarliest of the old-time players, penned a piece on modern baseball players for *Life* magazine. He wrote that Musial and New York Yankees shortstop Phil Rizzuto were the only players "who can be mentioned in the same breath with the oldtime greats."

Cobb didn't stop there.

He said Musial was "a better player than Joe DiMaggio in his prime."

Modest as usual, Musial responded, "Cobb is baseball's greatest. I don't want to contradict him, but I can't say that I was ever as good as Joe DiMaggio."

Modestly, Musial accepted his place on the National League bench at Milwaukee's County Stadium for the 22nd All-Star Game on July 12, 1955. If it was any consolation, he shared room in the dugout with a couple of future Hall of Famers—Milwaukee's Hank Aaron and the Giants Willie Mays—who also hadn't been elected to the starting team.

The American League jumped to a 4–0 lead in the first, thanks in big part to Mickey Mantle's three-run homer. The AL added another run in the sixth.

This was at a time when the All-Star Game wasn't just an exhibition, but a grudge match. Pride was on the line. Reputations could be made or lost. Other than in the World Series, it was the only time that the game's greats from both leagues could play against each other. Interleague play wasn't introduced until 1997.

Ninety miles away from the All-Star Game in Milwaukee, Arch Ward's funeral was concluding in Chicago. Ward was the *Chicago Tribune* sports editor who'd come up with the idea of a baseball All-Star Game, and had helped launch the first one in 1933. He also founded the Golden Gloves boxing tournament and was twice offered the job as commissioner of the National Football League. He'd died of a heart attack at age fifty-eight. Heavyweight champion Rocky Marciano and former Notre Dame football coach Frank Leahy attended his funeral.

By the fourth inning of the game Ward conceived, National League skipper Leo Durocher pinch-hit Stan Musial for Philadelphia's Del Ennis.

Stan the Man struck out.

In the sixth, he hit into a double play.

But in the seventh inning, the NL started mounting a comeback.

Mays opened the inning with a single off New York Yankee left-hander Whitey Ford. With two outs, Aaron walked, and his Milwaukee teammate Johnny Logan singled to break the shutout. Philadelphia Phillies catcher Stan Lopata reached on an error, scoring Aaron.

After Musial made the second out of the eighth, Mays, Kluszewski, and Chicago Cubs third baseman Randy Jackson hit consecutive singles for another run. Boston Red Sox hurler Frank Sullivan replaced Ford on the hill.

Hank Aaron singled to plate one run, and a second run scored on an error, making the score 5–5.

The game went into extra innings.

Sullivan was a 6-foot-6 right-hander who was making his first All-Star Game appearance. He threw 3⅓ shutout innings with four strikeouts.

Musial led off the 12th. He'd hit .317 in All-Star Games. He made his first appearance in 1943, at twenty-two, and hit his first All-Star home run in 1948. He finished his career with a record six All-Star Game home runs. (He also has the most pinch hits: three.)

He supposedly told New York Yankees catcher Yogi Berra before he dug in, "Yogi, let's end this thing."

Berra did admit to being tired.

Uncoiling from his distinctive peekaboo stance—Hall of Famer Ted Lyons, who made his reputation as a Chicago White Sox pitcher, once described Musial's stance as that of "a kid looking around the corner to see if the cops are coming"—Musial rocketed a drive to right field that wasn't going to land in the field of play.

"I never even looked back," Sullivan admitted after the game. "As soon as he hit it, I knew that was that."

George Vecsey, a *New York Times* columnist and Musial biographer, wrote in 2013, "It needs to be said, over and over again, that Stan the Man was voted by *The Sporting News* as the best baseball player of the postwar decade. . . . These were the late years of DiMaggio and Feller, the time of Williams and Robinson, the years of Mays and Aaron. Stan the Man was considered the best, a potent mix of power and consistency."

68 TONY CONIGLIARO: THE COMEBACK KID

Boston Red Sox shortstop Rico Petrocelli was kneeling on deck that sweltering Friday night in the summer of 1967.

Fenway Park was almost full, 31,027 in attendance. New England was starting to believe in its team (on Opening Day only 8,324 had attended).

While Carl Yastrzemski was in the midst of a season that would be historic, the fan favorite was right fielder Tony Conigliaro, a local guy.

He'd gone to St. Mary's High in Lynn, a city a few miles up the road from Boston. He had black hair and dark eyes. Long and lanky, he moved with a movie star's swagger. The Red Sox had needed some of that. The team hadn't won a pennant since 1946 and really hadn't been in contention since 1949.

The first pitch Tony C saw at Fenway Park on Opening Day of 1964 was from Chicago White Sox right-hander Joel Horlen, which he powered high and far over the Green Monster in left field. Tony C was three months past his nineteenth birthday. He finished his rookie season with 24 home runs, the most by a teenager in baseball history.

In 1965, Tony C led the American League, with 32 dingers.

On July 23, 1967, two weeks after he made his first All-Star Game, he became the youngest player in American League history to record his 100th home run. Tony C was twenty-two years and six months old.

The only person to reach that plateau faster was New York Giants Hall of Famer Mel Ott, who hit his 100th in 1931 at twenty-two years and four months. Ott finished with 511 career homers.

Conigliaro seemed on the same path to baseball immortality.

Cleveland Indians manager and former big-league catcher Birdie Tebbetts was convinced Tony C, with his power and the friendly confines of Fenway, was going to break the single-season home run mark of 61 set by New York Yankee outfielder Roger Maris.

Boston Hall of Famer Ted Williams, who hit 521 homers in his lengthy career, once told Conigliaro, "Don't change that solid stance of yours, no matter what you're told."

Tony C crowded the plate. Pitchers used to say that only Frank Robinson, a Hall of Famer with 586 home runs, stood closer.

It was a form of intimidation. Back then, inching closer to the plate was all about the battle of who controlled the inside part of the plate. Standing close also helped hitters with their plate coverage.

Johnny Pesky, Tony C's first big-league manager, told Tony's biographer David Cataneo, "He was fearless of the ball. He would just move his head, like Williams did. He thought the ball would never hit him."

But it always seemed to find him.

A pitch broke his wrist in his second month in the big leagues. His arm was broken by a pitch in July of 1964. He was out a month, which probably cost him Rookie of the Year honors. Within fourteen months of his debut, he had suffered two broken wrists and a broken left arm.

He still crowded the plate.

According to sabermetrics, the study of baseball statistics, the players Tony C most resembled at the same age were New York's Mickey Mantle and Cincinnati Reds product Frank Robinson, both first-ballot Hall of Famers.

On August 18, 1967, Conigliaro was batting sixth for the Sox. He had 20 homers, 67 RBIs, and a .287 average. He was also in a bit of a slump. The previous day, Ed Penney, Tony C's partner in the music business—Tony C had a regional hit in 1965—had been at the Ted Williams Baseball Camp in Lakeville, Massachusetts, watching his two sons play. Williams gave him a message for the Red Sox right fielder. "Tell Tony that he's crowding the plate. Tell him to back off," Williams said. "It's getting too serious now with the Red Sox."

Tony C told his brother Billy, a Red Sox prospect, that if he backed off the plate, pitchers wouldn't take him seriously.

That Friday night in his first at-bat, as usual, Tony C crowded the plate and then singled.

In the fourth, George Scott tried to stretch a single into a double and was thrown out. The game was delayed for 10 minutes after a fan threw a smoke bomb into left field.

When it resumed, center fielder Reggie Smith flied out to center.

Tony C dug in.

Years later, Petrocelli would say of his buddy, with whom he practiced doo-wop singing on the road, "I always believed there was a spot where Tony couldn't see the inside pitch. If you threw it to the right spot, he'd hit that ball nine miles. But then there was this blind spot, a little more inside. Sometimes he moved too late to get out of the way, and sometimes he never moved at all."

Petrocelli later told the *Boston Globe* sportswriter Bob Ryan that when California Angels pitcher Jack Hamilton's fastball hit Tony C's head, "It was a 'squish,' like a tomato or melon hitting the ground."

Ryan, then a Boston College student, was in the stands. He would write on the 47th anniversary of Tony C being hit in the head, "I remember the hush. The sound of silence from 31,027 is an eerie sensation. There was no hubbub, no low buzzing, as Tony lay at the plate. He wasn't popping up and running to first base. That was obvious. It was also obvious something very bad had just taken place."

California catcher Bob Rodgers and home plate umpire Bill Valentine were first on the scene. Petrocelli was next, arriving in a sprint.

"I didn't like what I saw," he recalled. "Tony's face was swelling up like there was somebody inside his skull blowing up a balloon. The first thing I thought was he was going to lose his left eye. Blood was pouring out of his nose."

Tony C regained consciousness in the Red Sox clubhouse. "It hurts like hell," he told a doctor. "I heard a hissing sound, and that was all."

He thought he was dying. A doctor would later say that if the ball had hit Conigliaro an inch higher and to the right, he indeed would have died in the batter's box.

The official diagnosis was a linear fracture of the left cheekbone, a dislocated jaw, and a cracked orbital bone encasing his left eye. There was also severe damage to the retina of his left eye.

The Red Sox said he'd be back in three weeks. He wasn't.

Tony C missed the rest of the season.

The Red Sox went on to win their first pennant since 1946, but lost to the St. Louis Cardinals in the World Series in seven games.

"The Impossible Dream" season was scarred.

Tony C would miss all of 1968, too. His eyesight in his left eye was 20/300.

But he stayed in baseball shape. He tried pitching, something he'd done in high school. In one Instructional League game, he gave up 15 runs in an inning. He also kept taking batting practice and would shag fly balls when he wasn't pitching. His eyesight improved, slowly but surely.

Tony C not only made the Red Sox in 1969, he was in the Opening Day lineup against the Orioles in Baltimore, batting fifth, playing right field. He received a long ovation from the crowd in Baltimore. He struck out in his first at-bat.

In the 10th inning, Tony C drove a ball over everything in left for a two-run homer off left-hander Pete Richert. When he returned to the bench, manager and notorious toughie Dick Williams kissed him. The Comeback Kid had come back all the way. But the story continued.

In the 12th, Tony C scored the winning run.

He finished the year with 20 homers and 82 RBIs. He also played in 141 games and was named the American League Comeback Player of the Year.

In 1970, he stroked 36 dingers and drove in a career-high 116 RBIs.

Then the Red Sox traded him to the California Angels. Red Sox fans were shocked.

In California, Conigliaro's eyesight deteriorated. He admitted he couldn't pick up the spin of the ball.

He retired in 1971, at age twenty-six.

Tony C made a comeback with the Red Sox in 1975. When he singled on Opening Day, he received a three-minute standing ovation from the Fenway faithful. He hit two home runs in that pennant-winning season, both off former Cy Young Award winners, Baltimore's Mike Cuellar and Oakland's Vida Blue.

He retired for good after a stint at Pawtucket in the Triple-A International League. He was thirty, with a total of 166 major-league home runs.

He suffered a massive stroke in 1982 and lived in a vegetative state for eight more years.

Tony C was forty-five when he died on February 24, 1990.

67 JACKIE ROBINSON: THE SHOT THAT PRECEDED "THE SHOT HEARD 'ROUND THE WORLD"

The mere mention of Jackie Robinson embraces so much history. So much that bears his imprint.

If he's not the most important person in baseball history, he's second only to Babe Ruth, who also changed everything.

Brooklyn Dodgers president and general manager Branch Rickey decided in 1945 that Robinson would be the man to break the color line. He'd been looking for someone to be that pioneer, and in the summer of 1945 sent his chief scout and right-hand man, Clyde Sukeforth, to scout the Negro Leagues. He saw Robinson playing shortstop for the Kansas City Monarchs.

Robinson wasn't that young for a baseball player in 1945. Sukeworth told the twenty-six-year-old that the Dodgers were thinking about placing a Negro League team in Brooklyn. He didn't say anything about the actual Dodgers.

Robinson wasn't the best player in the Negro Leagues at the time—a long line actually stretched in front of him, including Larry Doby and Monte Irvin. But Rickey wanted more than just a ballplayer.

He was impressed by Robinson's education (UCLA, where he lettered in baseball, basketball, football, and track), and by someone who had grown up and competed in a racially mixed atmosphere. Rickey also liked the fact Robinson was a lieutenant in the U.S. Army and that he wasn't a smoker, drinker, or womanizer. Robinson, like Rickey, was also a Methodist, and Rickey took his religion seriously.

Andy McCue wrote about Rickey's playing career for the Society of American Baseball Research. His piece included this line: "He spent parts of the next three seasons in the majors, earning a reputation as a marginal catcher, a poor hitter, and an odd duck for refusing to play baseball on Sundays."

Rickey signed Robinson on October 23, 1945. After a year playing for the Triple A Montreal Royals in 1946, Robinson became a Brooklyn Dodger in 1947 and changed baseball with every at-bat.

Signed as a shortstop, Robinson was converted to first base, and then second base.

He was the National League Most Valuable Player in 1949, winning the batting championship (.342) and stealing more bases (37) than anyone in the NL had in 19 years. He finished second in runs batted in, with 124, and in hits with 203. He finished third in doubles (38) and triples (12).

The Dodgers won the National League pennant on the final day of the 1949 season.

Robinson was just as good in 1950 and 1951, but the Dodgers lost the pennant both years on the last day of the season.

On August 11, 1951, the Dodgers were 70–35 and owned a 13½-game lead over the New York Giants. The Dodgers played just above .500 ball the rest of the way, going 26–23, but were caught by the Giants.

Behind pitchers Sal Maglie (23–6) and Larry Jansen (23–11), third baseman Bobby Thomson (32 homers, 101 RBIs, and a .293 average), future Hall of Fame outfielder Monte Irvin (24 homers, 121 RBIs, and .312) and Willie Mays, a rookie center fielder, the Giants streaked to a 37–7 record down the stretch.

At one point in their hot streak, the Giants won 16 straight games.

Leo Durocher, the former skipper of the Dodgers, was managing the Giants. Rumors that the Giants had a system for stealing signs in 1951 became public fifty years later when an article in the *Wall Street Journal* revealed that coach Herman Franks used a telescope to eye pitch signs from the catcher. The coming pitch was relayed to the Giants dugout via buzzer.

But that wasn't known outside the Giants organization in 1951.

On the last day of the regular season, the Giants beat the Braves in Boston to take over first place for the first time that season. Meanwhile, in Philadelphia, the Dodgers trailed the Phillies, 8–5, before knotting the score in the eighth. In the 12th, Brooklyn ace Don Newcombe was trying to work out of a bases-loaded, two-out jam. It was getting dark.

Philadelphia's Eddie Waitkus sliced a low liner that was destined to land in right field.

"The ball is a blur passing second base, difficult to follow in the half-light, impossible to catch," Red Smith wrote in the *New York Herald Tribune*. "Jackie Robinson catches it. He flings himself headlong at right angles to the flight of the ball, for an instant his body is suspended in midair, then somehow the outstretched glove intercepts the ball inches off the ground."

The fall, according to Arnold Rampersad's 1997 book *Jackie Robinson: A Biography*, jammed Robinson's left elbow into his solar plexus so hard that he was knocked out.

"In the stands, word spread that a heart attack had felled him," wrote Rampersad.

In the next day's *New York Times*, Roscoe McGowen reported that Robinson's catch was "one of the greatest, if not the greatest, clutch play I have seen in almost a life time of watching major league games."

In his column, Red Smith wrote that Robinson "stretched at full length in the insubstantial twilight, the unconquerable doing the impossible."

Robinson had saved the season; the Dodgers were still breathing.

In the 14th, against future Hall of Famer Robin Roberts, Robinson, batting cleanup in a lineup that included Duke Snider, Roy Campanella, and Gil Hodges, walloped a towering home run into the fading light at Shibe Park.

The Dodgers won, 9–8.

"There's no stopping us now," Robinson said after the game. "The breaks haven't been going our way during the past month, but now that we've gotten this far we aren't going to look back."

The Dodgers and Giants were scheduled to play a three-game series to determine the National League champions.

The Giants won Game One at Ebbets Field in Brooklyn behind homers from Bobby Thomson and Monte Irvin off Brooklyn starter Ralph Branca.

The Dodgers overpowered the Giants at the Polo Grounds in Game Two. Robinson contributed a homer and knocked in three runs.

In Game Three, Bobby Thomson hit his famous home run, "The Shot Heard 'Round the World," in the bottom of the ninth, and the Giants won the pennant, the Giants won the pennant, the Giants won the pennant for the first time since 1937.

While the Giants celebrated, the Dodgers mourned, and the baseball world marveled at the comeback in the first nationally televised game. Robinson made sure Thomson touched every base.

Robinson was one of the few Dodgers to duck into the Giants clubhouse afterward and offer congratulations. Ralph Branca, the losing pitcher, said Robinson was the only teammate who went out of his way to console him. As always, Jackie Robinson was one of a kind.

66 CARL YASTRZEMSKI: THE NEW TED WILLIAMS

In the 1966 off-season, Carl Yastrzemski met Gene Berde.

A Hungarian refugee who once was a trainer for his country's national boxing team, Berde was working as a fitness director at a Wakefield, Massachusetts, health club.

Yaz was twenty-seven, the star left fielder for the Boston Red Sox, and already an American League batting champion. Twice he had hit better than .300 in a season. Three times he had led the league in doubles. He already owned two Gold Gloves for his defensive excellence in left field.

Yaz was six feet tall and 180 pounds. He wore uniform number 8, a coveted single-digit designation usually saved for someone with Hall of Fame potential.

Berde's assessment of his new client: "You think you're in shape? You, the big baseball player, you, the big champion. You can't even run a hundred yards. You no athlete . . . I make you an athlete."

And he did.

The previous season had been a rough one for Yaz. His average dropped to .278, and he swatted only 16 home runs.

Boston manager Billy Herman, the former great Chicago Cubs second baseman voted into the Hall of Fame in 1975, said that Yaz, the team captain, didn't hustle. Herman wanted him traded, but Herman was the one who was shown his way out of town when he was fired in the closing days of the 1966 season.

The Sox hired Dick Williams, who had played as a spare part for the Red Sox in 1964, to manage in 1967. He was brash, and it was said that Yaz found him abrasive. The new manager stripped Yaz of his captaincy, but that in itself didn't bother Yaz much—he wasn't into that sort of thing.

On Opening Day of 1967, only 8,324 Red Sox fans took their seats. Three-quarters of the park was empty, illustrating New England's lack of faith in the team. (Boston drew only 811,172 in 1966, eighth out of 10 teams in the American League in attendance.) The club had finished ninth in 1966, a half-game above the last-place Yankees, but they flickered with potential.

The last team to integrate, twelve years after Brooklyn's Jackie Robinson broke the color line in 1947, the Sox finally had started developing black players. George Scott, at first, and Joe Foy, at third, stood out in 1966. And outfielder Reggie Smith was on his way to area code 617.

Local hero Tony Conigliaro, the home run-hitting outfielder, was already a star and was only getting better. Pitcher Jim Lonborg, at twenty-four, was 10–10 with a bad team, but flashed the kind of potential that suggested a future 20-game winner.

The Red Sox muddled along the first couple of months of the 1967 season. Williams had predicted the Sox would win more than they lost, and they were doing that. Barely.

Thanks to an off-season of workouts designed by his Hungarian trainer, the newly ripped Yaz was hitting .300 early on, but he wanted more.

In mid-May, he sat down with Sox hitting coach Bobby Doerr. Yaz wanted to hit more home runs. It wasn't his ego talking. He thought it would be good for the team.

Doerr wasn't a home run hitter. He'd been a second baseman for the strong Red Sox teams of the 1940s, a quiet man who'd done it all in the shadow of Ted Williams and who would finally be elected to the Hall of Fame in 1986.

But in Boston, on May 13, 1967, the future Hall of Famer talked hitting with Yaz a day before a doubleheader with the Detroit Tigers.

Hitting is arithmetic, geometry, and chemistry combined. Yaz said that, as strong as he felt and as hard as he was stinging the ball, he still didn't feel as if he had home run power. He and Doerr decided he should hold his bat higher.

The decision gave birth to an iconic batting stance. Well-cocked over his left ear, Yaz's bat became as lethal as anything could be in the Summer of Love. During a doubleheader sweep on May 14, he hit homers off of Detroit's best: Denny McLain, who would win 31 games the following year, and Mickey Lolich, who would become the hero of the 1968 World Series. They were the third and fourth dingers of the season for Yaz, who was only getting started.

In June, Chicago White Sox manager Eddie Stanky said Yaz was an All-Star from the neck down. In a doubleheader against the Pale Hose, Yaz answered Stanky with a 6-for-9 performance. He hit a homer in his next-to-last at-bat and tipped his hat to Stanky when he rounded third.

But the Yaz story of 1967 didn't really explode until September, when the temperatures got cooler, and four American League teams within a whisper of first place got hot.

Then hotter.

The Red Sox would win the American League by one game, outlasting the Detroit Tigers, Minnesota Twins, and Chicago White Sox in what might have been the greatest pennant race in the history of the game. With a week to go in the season, they were all within a game of first place.

"The Impossible Dream" would become shorthand for the Sox as they captured one dramatic win after another.

And while Jim Lonborg won 22 games, and Jose Tartabull made a throw for the ages from right field, nailing a runner at the plate to secure a key late-August Sox victory over Stanky's White Sox, the Red Sox kept winning even after slugger Tony Conigliaro was hit in the head by a pitch that ended his season. And they had Yaz to thank.

In September, Yaz played like he was Babe Ruth. Or what those born too late could only imagine Babe Ruth to be. Yaz hit .417 in the final month of the season, belting nine home runs in 96 at-bats.

He hit .396 with two outs and runners in scoring position that year. With two or more men on base, his average was .437. With the bases loaded, he was 4-for-5.

In the final 10 games, Yaz was 20-for-37 (a .541 average), with four home runs and 14 RBIs. In the last six games, he was 13-for-21, a .619 average.

In Game 161, the Red Sox were hosting the Twins, who had a one game lead over Boston with one to play.

Yaz knocked in the go-ahead run in the fifth inning with a single. In the seventh, he put the game out of reach with a three-run dinger to give the Sox a 6–2 win.

In the last game of the season—Game 162—he went 4-for-4, but his biggest play was throwing out Minnesota's Bob Allison, who had singled to cut Boston's lead to 5–3 in the eighth while trying to stretch the hit into a double.

Yaz would become the only player in baseball history to win the Triple Crown and a Gold Glove in the same season.

Yaz finished with 44 home runs (tied with Minnesota's Harmon Killebrew) and 121 RBIs, and won his second of three batting championships with a .326 average, carrying the Red Sox to their first pennant since 1946.

"Yaz hit 44 home runs that year, and 43 of them meant something big for the team," teammate George Scott said. "It seemed like every time we needed a big play, the man stepped up and got it done."

The Sox lost the World Series to the St. Louis Cardinals in seven games. In those games Yaz was 10-for-25, with three homers.

He was the AL MVP and the *Sports Illustrated* Sportsman of the Year.

He would be the first player to record more than 3,000 hits and belt more than 400 home runs in a career.

But when you want to start the conversation on Yaz, start with a year.

1967.

65 TINO MARTINEZ: SERIES HEROICS

The first seventeen times Tino Martinez batted for the New York Yankees with men in scoring position, he went 0-for-17.

It was April of 1996, and he was replacing the beloved Don Mattingly at both first base and in the batting order.

In the winter of 1995, the Yankees had traded a choice left-handed pitching prospect, Sterling Hitchcock, and a major-league-ready third baseman, Russ Davis, to the Seattle Mariners in the deal for Martinez, who had just completed his best season with 31 homers, 111 RBIs, and a .293 average.

His Mariners had come from behind to beat the Yankees in the '95 American League Division Series. Yankee owner George Steinbrenner, who wanted to prove how committed he was to the left-handed-hitting Martinez, awarded the twenty-eight-year-old a five-year, $20.25 million contract.

Mattingly, who had battled back problems in the previous five seasons but had had a terrific postseason in '95, wasn't even officially retired.

So Yankee Stadium boos fell on Martinez like April rain in 1996, as he started out 3-for-34.

Martinez was not Donnie Baseball and was reminded of that every time he batted. He kept gripping his bat tighter. Yankees manager Joe Torre kept telling him to relax, that the hits would fall. Soon they did, and fans began to appreciate his everyday hustle, humility, and toughness.

His 117 RBIs in the middle of the lineup in 1996 were a giant help to the Yankees winning their first American League Championship since 1981 and their first World Series since 1978.

He had a big year in 1997, with 44 homers, 141 RBIs, and a .296 average. He also won the Home Run Derby at the All-Star Game in Cleveland, beating the likes of Mark McGwire, Ken Griffey Jr., Jim Thome, and Chipper Jones.

The following season, the Yankees won a spectacular 114 games in the regular season. Martinez contributed 28 homers, 123 RBIs, and a .281 average. He slumped in the American League Championship Series against the Cleveland Indians, going 2-for-19. But his teammates played well enough to get them to the World Series, where they would face the San Diego Padres.

In Game One, the Padres built a 5–2 lead into the seventh. Yankee second baseman Chuck Knoblauch tied the game with a three-run homer.

In the same inning, on a 2–2 pitch with the bases loaded, Martinez took what looked like strike three from San Diego southpaw Mark Langston. It was called a ball, low.

Martinez had entered the game with a .188 average, with one homer and five RBIs in 29 postseason games as a Yankee. Before Game One, teammate Paul O'Neill predicted the bat of Martinez would be a key to the Series.

Martinez rocketed a Langston fastball into the upper deck in right field, capping a seven-run inning.

The Yankees never looked back, in the game or the Series.

The hit was thought to be the signature moment for Martinez as a Yankee, his most important dinger.

Three years later, in 2001, Martinez was still a Yankee stalwart. He clubbed 34 homers and knocked in 113 runs with a .280 batting average. He was also in the last year of his contract. In his six years as a Yankee, Martinez swatted 175 homers.

Heading into Game Four of the 2001 World Series against the Arizona Diamondbacks, the Yankees were trailing two games to one.

It was October 31, less than two months after the attacks of 9/11.

The whole country seemed to be rooting for the Yankees.

By the bottom of the ninth at Yankee Stadium, the Diamondbacks were leading, 3–1, with one out to go. Byung-Hyun Kim was on the mound for Arizona. He had stepped up when the Diamondbacks closer Matt Mantei went down with elbow woes.

Kim recorded 19 saves and averaged over a strikeout an inning. The first South Korean to appear in a World Series, Kim had a funky sidearm delivery. The twenty-two-year-old thought of himself as a starter.

Kim relieved Arizona starter Curt Schilling in the eighth inning and struck out the side—Shane Spencer looking, Scott Brosius and Alfonso Soriano swinging.

With one out in the bottom of the ninth, Yankee right fielder O'Neill lofted a broken-bat single to left. Center fielder Bernie Williams struck out. Up came Martinez, who was batting cleanup. It was still Halloween, but inching toward November.

In the on-deck circle, Martinez had studied Kim's pitches and delivery.

"I just saw a fastball/slider, so I went up there in that situation and was looking for a fastball, something over the plate to try to drive out," he said.

Martinez powered Kim's first pitch, a fastball, deep to center field. Arizona outfielder Steve Finley tried to climb the wall, but it was so far gone he didn't have a chance.

Yankee Stadium was louder than after the ball dropped in Times Square on New Year's Eve.

In the 10th, Yankee shortstop Derek Jeter hit a two-out homer inside the right field foul pole for the game-winner.

In the clubhouse, the subject was Tino's home run.

"It seemed kind of surreal at first, like it didn't really happen," Arizona catcher Damian Miller said. "I couldn't believe it happened, really. It was probably the loudest place I have heard as a player, after Tino hit that home run."

Referring to Kim, Miller said, "He threw the ball right down the middle to the wrong guy. It's as simple as that."

The next night, Brosius boomed another dramatic two-out home run off Kim.

The Yankees would lose the Series in Game Seven, the winning hit smacked by Arizona's Luis Gonzalez, Martinez's best friend since childhood.

When Gonzalez arrived home after the Series, he played his messages. The first one was from Tino Martinez.

Martinez became a free agent after the season and signed with the St. Louis Cardinals, replacing McGwire at first base. He returned to Yankee Stadium in 2003 with his new team.

Martinez was greeted with prolonged standing ovations. He also hit a two-run homer off former teammate Andy Pettitte. He then homered in the ninth off Jason Anderson.

After the second one, Martinez was given that gift rarely granted an opponent: a curtain call.

64 MICKEY MANTLE: THE MICK'S FAVORITE BLAST

Mickey Mantle was a lot of things, but there was one thing he wasn't: a braggart.

Standing in the on-deck circle with Elston Howard, watching right-handed knuckleball specialist Barney Schultz finish his warmup pitches on October 10, 1964 (a Saturday afternoon World Series game at Yankee Stadium), Mantle turned to his teammate and said, "You can go back to the clubhouse, Elston. This game is over."

In the dugout, getting a drink of water after pitching nine terrific innings, Yankee starter Jim Bouton saw Mantle holding his bat.

"He was standing there with his bat on his shoulder, watching Barney Schultz. His warm-up pitches were coming in about thigh high and breaking down to the shin, to the ankles—two or three in a row. Mickey said, 'I'm gonna hit one outta here.' It wasn't a big announcement. He wasn't like that. He wasn't a grandstander. He might have been saying it to himself. He understood that Barney Schultz was the wrong guy for them to bring in."

The New York Yankees and St. Louis Cardinals had split the first two games of the World Series and were tied, 1–1, in the bottom of the ninth of Game Three. A Mantle error in right field led to the only Cardinal run. It really bothered him.

"By that time I couldn't run too much anymore," he told author Jane Leavy, biographer of Sandy Koufax and Mantle, in 1983. "They put me in right field and [Roger] Maris in center. Somebody hit me a groundball. I nonchalanted it. It went through my legs, and the guy scored."

St. Louis hurler Curt Simmons matched Bouton pitch for pitch.

In his eight innings, Simmons, a crafty veteran left-hander who had missed pitching in the World Series for the 1950 Philadelphia Phillies "Whiz Kids" because of military obligations, had the Yankees hitting the ball into the ground, forcing 17 ground-ball outs. Bouton, a fireballing right-hander who would became more famous six years later for writing the candid book *Ball Four*, stranded the go-ahead runner four times. He held the top five hitters

(Curt Flood, Lou Brock, Bill White, Ken Boyer, and Dick Groat) in the Cardinals lineup to two hits.

Barney Schultz was a big reason why the Cardinals won the National League pennant. The thirty-eight-year-old journeyman saved 14 games down the stretch, pitching in 30 of the final 60 regular-season games, helping the Cardinals overtake the collapsing Philadelphia Phillies, who let a 6½-game lead with 12 to play wither away.

Schultz, who owned a 1.64 ERA, had given up one homer all season. He was pitching in his first World Series. He earned the save in Game One.

The Yankees had been in third place in the American League on August 22—and looking old.

Rookie pitcher Mel Stottlemyre, who won nine games in only 12 starts that season, was a huge help. So was the September 5 acquisition from Cleveland of reliever Pedro Ramos, who saved eight games down the stretch.

Catcher Elston Howard hit nearly .400 in the final weeks of the season. Maris was a key late-stage force at the plate and in the field. Twenty-three-year-old first baseman Joe Pepitone came alive offensively, hitting 12 homers and knocking in 30 runs in the heat of a pennant race.

Mantle slugged seven homers in September, as the Yankees won 27 of their final 35 games, capturing the American League title by one game, their 14th pennant in 16 years.

Mantle, about to turn thirty-three, had his last great season in 1964: 33 homers, 111 RBIs, .303 batting average, and an OPS of 1.015.

In the ninth inning of Game Three of the World Series, the score tied 1–1, the game's greatest switch-hitter stepped into the left-handed batter's box, number 7 on his back. The crowd of 67,000 at Yankee Stadium stood with expectation.

While Mantle had hit .300 in '64 for the 10th time and had homered more than 30 times for the ninth season of a career that began in 1951, his batting average from the left side was only .241 that season. The Cardinals knew this.

Tim McCarver, the Cardinals twenty-two-year-old catcher, later told author Jane Leavy that he also knew Mantle, with knee and shoulder woes, was struggling, "a shell of the player that he once was. I could even hear him groaning on some swings. A swing and a miss were real bad."

The first pitch from Schultz, McCarver said, was a knuckler that "dangled like bait to a big fish. Plus it lingered in that area that was down, and Mickey was a lethal low-ball hitter left-handed. The pitch was so slow that it allowed him to turn on it and pull it."

Mantle hit it so high and so far that Bouton thought it was going to be the first home run slugged out of Yankee Stadium.

It wasn't, although it landed deep in the third deck.

With his 16th World Series home run, Mantle surpassed Babe Ruth as the all-time leader.

At the time, Mantle was only the fifth to hit a walk-off home run—the others were Tommy Henrich of the 1949 Yankees, Dusty Rhodes of the 1954 New York Giants, Eddie Mathews of the 1957 Milwaukee Braves and Bill Mazeroski of the 1960 Pittsburgh Pirates—in World Series history.

As usual, Mantle circled the bases with his head down. After he had crossed home plate and was drenched by champagne in the clubhouse, he was asked by reporters how many other homers he had called in his career.

"I called them about 500 times," Mantle said with a laugh. "That was the only time I did it. Usually, I struck out."

His first walk-off home run came against the Red Sox in 1953. He would hit 13 in his career (12 in the regular season), his last coming off Detroit's Fred Gladding on June 24, 1967, at Yankee Stadium.

Mantle would later say the homer off Schultz was the highlight of his career, one that would include 536 home runs.

Mantle would hit his 17th homer in Game Six off Simmons, a Yankee win, and give the Yanks a chance with his 18th in Game Seven, off Bob Gibson, but the Cardinals, his favorite team as a kid growing up in Commerce, Oklahoma, won the World Series.

It was the first time the Yankees had lost back-to-back World Series since 1921–22, when they bowed to the New York Giants.

In his final World Series, Mantle hit .333. Only Yogi Berra would play in more Fall Classics.

Mantle played in 12 World Series and hit more homers and drove in more runs (40) than anyone in baseball history.

63 EDGAR MARTINEZ: "GAR" THE YANKEE-KILLER

When Pedro Martinez was elected to the Hall of Fame in January of 2015, he was asked an obvious question at that day's press conference:

Who was the toughest hitter you faced?

Martinez, who took the mound for the Los Angeles Dodgers, Montreal Expos, Boston Red Sox, New York Mets, and Philadelphia Phillies, and finished his career with three Cy Young Awards, didn't hesitate.

"Edgar Martinez," was his quick answer.

Randy Johnson, elected in the same class, chimed in.

"The first person that comes to my mind was a teammate of mine for nine and a half years and the greatest hitter I ever played with," said Johnson, who also played with Ken Griffey Jr. and Alex Rodriguez. "I've faced a lot of Hall of Fame hitters and, my gosh, Edgar is the best hitter I ever saw."

Johnson, who won five Cy Young Awards and 303 games and was never known for being loquacious, added, "I support him because he was my teammate, and I loved him, and he did so much for Seattle and made me look good during my career there. The first person on my ballot, who would get my vote, is Edgar. Yes, I'm campaigning for him."

When Edgar Martinez reached the major leagues in September 1987, Seattle manager and future Hall of Famer Dick Williams inserted him in the lineup for an ailing Jim Presley. Martinez hit two doubles and a triple and reached base six times in three games.

Williams said he would reserve judgment and would take a look at the new guy in spring training.

Martinez, with his chin tucked, bat held high, leg kick and pigeon-toed stance, didn't become a regular until 1990. He hit .302. He was already twenty-seven.

He encored in 1991 with a .307 average. He had a breakout season in 1992, winning the American League batting championship with a .343 average, and was named an All-Star.

In an exhibition game the following spring, Martinez tore his hamstring badly enough to ruin two seasons. When he returned to the lineup full-time in 1995, Seattle manager Lou Piniella installed him as the team's designated hitter.

Screaming liners from baseline to baseline and deep into gaps, Martinez won his second batting championship with a .356 average, becoming the first DH to win the crown. His average was the highest by an American League right-handed hitter since New York's Joe DiMaggio's .381 in 1939.

If his regular season, which helped Seattle to its first American League West title, didn't imprint his name on the public consciousness, his hitting against the Yankees in the five-game '95 American League Division Series did.

The American League wild card winner, and in the postseason for the first time since 1981, the Yankees won the first two games at home. The series then shifted to Seattle and the Kingdome. The Mariners won Game Three, but the Yankees built an early 5–0 lead in Game Four.

In the bottom of the third inning, with Seattle's hopes barely flickering, Martinez, who tended to have Griffey's bat in front of him (and depending on whether the opposing starter was righty or lefty), Tino Martinez or Jay Buhner behind him, powered a three-run blast to put the Mariners back in the game.

In the eighth inning, Martinez launched a grand slam off New York closer John Wetteland to break a 6–6 tie. The Mariners won, 11–8.

And just when you'd think Martinez couldn't do any more, he did. On October 8, he whistled a double to left on a Jack McDowell split-finger fastball—the same pitch on which he'd struck out in the ninth—and Griffey raced home, notching the series-winning run in Game Five.

In Seattle it became known as "The Double." That hit is believed to have saved baseball in Seattle.

There were always rumors that the Mariners would be sold or relocated. They owned only three winning seasons in their nineteen-year existence and the Kingdome was considered a baseball dungeon. But that hit—with Joey Cora on third and Griffey on first—rallied support for a new stadium, which opened in 1999 as Safeco Field. Griffey Jr. and A-Rod would leave Seattle. Edgar Martinez didn't. He stayed and became more beloved.

He would hit better than .300 six more times in his career. Teammates alternated in calling him "Papi" and "Gar."

In 2000, at age thirty-seven, he knocked in 145 runs and had 37 home runs, both career highs. He also hit .324.

At age thirty-eight, he drove home 116 runs with a .306 average.

Former teammate Mike Cameron, who once hit four homers in a game, said of Martinez: "Edgar is that tree stump in the middle of our lineup. He's just there all the time. He's going to beat you. . . . He's always patient, he never gets 'chasey.' He's just Edgar."

After 18 seasons, Martinez retired when 2004 was over. He finished with 2,247 hits, 1,283 walks, 514 doubles, 309 homers, and a .418-on-base percentage. Only Babe Ruth, Stan Musial, Rogers Hornsby, Ted Williams, and Lou Gehrig exceeded all those numbers.

Martinez finished with a career .312 average and hit .500 against 243 different pitchers, including batting .579 with two homers and six RBIs against New York's great reliever, Mariano Rivera.

Rivera told Charlie Rose, the PBS talk show host, "The only guy that I didn't want to face, when a tough situation comes, was Edgar Martinez . . . It didn't matter how I threw the ball. I couldn't get him out. Oh my God, he had more than my number. He had my breakfast, lunch, and dinner."

The Mariners haven't issued the number 11 to anyone since Martinez retired.

"He was just a great hitter," Randy Johnson said. "You know how you love something and you carry it around with you? When I got to Seattle, Edgar was walking around with a bat all the time . . . I learned all kinds of little tidbits and secrets from him.

"I know you don't get into the Hall of Fame by being a nice guy. You get in for merit—and Edgar's merit stands by itself with all he's done. But he's also one of the nicest and most humble guys I've ever met."

62 JOE ADCOCK: THE HOMER THAT WASN'T

It actually was a dark and stormy night in Milwaukee on May 26, 1959.

The darkness was interrupted only by lightning skipping across the menacing sky. The wind was blowing in. Rain started to fall in the seventh inning. Future baseball commissioner Bud Selig, then a car dealer, was in attendance. Pittsburgh's Harvey Haddix, thirty-three, threw twelve innings of perfect baseball: thirty-six men up, thirty-six men down. No one in baseball history had ever been that perfect for so long.

Haddix was just 5-foot-9, 155 pounds. His nickname was "Kitten" because when he was a St. Louis Cardinal, teammates thought he looked like Harry "The Cat" Brecheen. Three times Haddix was elected to the All-Star team, and three times he was awarded the Gold Glove for his fielding. He would also win two games in the 1960 World Series for the Pittsburgh Pirates. He once won 20 games in a season and was 136–113 in his career.

In his historic outing, Haddix pitched to a three-ball count just once. The most pitches he threw in an inning was fourteen, and that was in the twelfth.

Pittsburgh shortstop Dick Schofield would later say, "It seemed like every time I'd glance up at the scoreboard, there were two strikes on the batter and there were two outs."

The lineup was loaded for the two-time defending National League champion Braves, including power hitters Eddie Mathews, Hank Aaron, and Joe Adcock. The trio would club over 1,600 career home runs.

Milwaukee right-hander Lew Burdette had allowed twelve singles, but no runs, either. Opposing batters and teammates thought his spitter was working especially well.

The score was 0–0 going into the bottom of the 13th.

Felix Mantilla, Milwaukee's second baseman, led off the inning with a routine groundball, but Pittsburgh third baseman Don Hoak threw the ball in the dirt for an error. The perfect game was history.

Mathews sacrificed Mantilla to second. Haddix intentionally walked Aaron.

There was still the chance for a no-hitter, but even more importantly to Haddix, the game was still winnable.

He had almost twirled a no-no while a member of the Cardinals in 1954 against the Philadelphia Phillies, only to have Richie Ashburn break it up with a single in the eighth.

Up stepped Adcock.

He was a strapping 6-foot-4, 225-pounder. Along with being a power hitter, he was also a terrific defender at first. When he retired in 1963, at thirty-six, he owned the third-highest fielding percentage for first basemen in baseball history.

He also retired with 336 home runs. In his era, his right-handed bat was overlooked because of teammates Aaron and Mathews, along with other first basemen like Cincinnati's Ted Kluszewski and Brooklyn's Gil Hodges. Adcock finished second in the National League in homers and RBIs in 1956 and was named an All-Star for the only time four years later.

The Cincinnati Reds signed Adcock out of Louisiana State University in 1947. But the club also had the slugging Kluszewski at first. Adcock was uncomfortable in left field and asked to be traded. His wish was granted in 1952.

On April 29, 1953, Adcock, settling in at first base for the Milwaukee Braves, became the first major-league player to hit a home run into the center field bleachers of the Polo Grounds, more than 475 feet away. (Later Hall of Famers Hank Aaron and Lou Brock would accomplish the same feat.)

On July 31, 1954, Adcock hit four home runs in a game against the Brooklyn Dodgers at Ebbets Field. He also hit a double off the top of the left field wall. He was the seventh player in history to hit four homers in one game, and he set a record for most total bases in a game—18—that lasted forty-eight years, until Toronto's Shawn Green broke it.

On this night in Milwaukee, Adcock, who had struck out twice swinging and grounded out twice, took ball one from Burdette.

No one knows how many of the 19,194 fans were still in the stands.

"The wind had been blowing in all night," Adcock recalled later, "and maybe it was a freak because when I came to bat, the flag in center field was still. I was thinking he'd been keeping the ball away from me all night and maybe he'd do it again, and he did and I hit it."

It was a slider. Adcock pounced.

"When he hit it, it looked like a lot of trouble," Schofield said.

Pirate center fielder Bill Virdon raced to the wall in right center.

"I started going back, but there was no chance. None," he told Bob Dvorchak of the *Pittsburgh Post-Gazette* on the 50th anniversary of the game. "Adcock was pretty strong. He could hit to any field in the park."

The ball flew into the stormy night over the 392-foot sign and over the bullpens.

But what looked like a three-run homer wasn't. At least not officially.

Mantilla scored from second, but Aaron, on first, didn't know the ball had gone over the fence. Aaron thought it was rolling around right-center field; he stopped at second and headed off the field. Adcock had his head down while running the bases. He was ruled to have passed Aaron on the basepaths and was credited with a double, the game-winning RBI, and ruining the greatest pitching performance in baseball history.

But he was not credited with a home run.

Winning pitcher Lew Burdette would quip years later, "I have to be the greatest pitcher who ever pitched, because I beat the guy who pitched the greatest game ever pitched."

Ironically, Haddix's first big-league win came in 1952 against the then-Boston Braves. The losing pitcher was Burdette.

Haddix would win his next start, a complete game, giving up his first hit on the third pitch.

Two days later, Adcock was being intentionally walked, but reached out on Philadelphia's Gene Conley's attempt to throw ball one. He grounded up the middle. Sparky Anderson—*that* Sparky Anderson of managerial fame—fielded it behind second, but his throw home was late. Aaron scored, and Joe Adcock had another different kind of game-winning hit.

61 WILLIE MAYS: WILLIE'S MOST IMPORTANT HOMER

Willie Mays was sitting on the bench, bat in hand, at the top of the third inning on September 12, 1962, at Cincinnati's Crosley Field, when he toppled over.

The star San Francisco Giant center fielder had been complaining of dizziness and fatigue. Teammates, and the two team doctors who treated him, said he was out cold for five minutes.

Mays, thirty-one, was placed on a stretcher and whisked by ambulance to a nearby hospital, where he remained under observation for two nights and three days.

The diagnosis: exhaustion.

Still, the headline in the *San Francisco Chronicle* was big enough to announce a declaration of war. And it held a question:

"What's Wrong with Willie?"

The heavy rumor at the time was that Mays suffered from epilepsy. A private, sensitive man, he was no longer the joyful "Say Hey Kid," the nickname *New York Journal-American* sportswriter Barney Kremenko gave him as a rookie in 1951. That kid was now going through a very public divorce that weighed on him. He was also trying to carry the Giants to the pennant. He would also admit in interviews that he tended to think and worry too much. While there was always the talk of his natural ability and how he made playing baseball look easy, Mays worked hard at his craft. While he was out of the lineup, the Giants lost four straight. When Mays returned, the Giants lost two more, though on his first game back he did launch a three-run homer in Pittsburgh off Elroy Face.

Mays felt as if he had more work to do.

From May 10, 1962, on, either the Los Angeles Dodgers or the Giants held first place in the National League.

By September 17, the Dodgers had built a four-game lead. They were 98–53, the Giants 94–57.

The Dodgers were sparked by shortstop Maury Wills, who was on his way to breaking Hall of Famer Ty Cobb's record of 96 steals in a season. Wills, who had 35 in 1961, would finish the season with 104 to go with his .299 batting average.

Outfielder and occasional third baseman Tommy Davis powered the team. He hit .346, with 27 homers and 153 RBIs.

The Dodgers probably would have had a bigger lead if Hall of Fame pitcher Sandy Koufax hadn't gotten hurt. The ace southpaw was 14–4 with 208 strikeouts by July 17 but lost circulation in his left index finger after an old injury flared. Right-hander Don Drysdale picked up some of the slack with a 25-win season.

Mays, who'd had two 50-homer campaigns in his 23-year career, was in the midst of another one of his great seasons. He would finish with 49 homers and drive home 141 runs. He'd also swipe 18 bases and hit .304.

First baseman-outfielder Willie McCovey hit behind him, as did first baseman-outfielder Orlando Cepeda. Both would be voted into the Hall of Fame. Brothers Felipe and Matty Alou often batted in front of Mays, along with Harvey Kuenn, who three years earlier had won the American League batting title with the Detroit Tigers.

The last two weeks of September, Mays was haunted by his missed games and convinced he had cost the Giants the pennant. The Dodgers stopped hitting and started losing, dropping 10 of their last 13 games, being shut out in the last two games of the season at their beautiful new park, Dodger Stadium.

On the last day of the season, the Giants were hosting the expansion Houston Colt .45s. Candlestick Park, which had opened in 1960, was filled to the brim.

When the Giants moved west from New York in 1958, San Francisco did not embrace Mays at first. Instead, fans fell for the rookie, Cepeda, believing Mays had left his heart in New York.

Frank Conniff, a reporter for Hearst newspapers, once wrote, "[San Francisco] is the damnedest city I ever saw in my life. They cheer [Soviet leader Nikita, who visited the city in 1959] Khrushchev and boo Willie Mays."

By 1962, however, Mays was embraced because of the consistency of his greatness. When Alvin Dark was named Giants manager in 1961, he appointed his old teammate Mays captain.

Mays, one of the great defensive outfielders of all time, also became adept at playing the fickle winds of Candlestick Park. He led NL outfielders in putouts with 429. Six years after Mays made the big leagues, the

Gold Glove Award was introduced for defensive excellence. Mays still won a dozen of them.

Jim Murray, the legendary *Los Angeles Times* sports columnist, once wrote that "Mays doesn't drink or smoke and no scandal has touched his life. He is a credit not to his race but to the human race."

Boston superstar hitter Ted Williams said of Mays and his skills, "They invented the All-Star Game for Willie Mays."

As dazzling as he was, on this, the last day of the regular season in 1962, Mays needed the Giants to win their game if they were going to have a chance at postseason play.

Houston was starting Dick "Turk" Farrell, a hard-throwing right-hander. He had come up through the Philadelphia Phillies system, was traded to the Dodgers, and then claimed by Houston in the expansion draft.

The last time Mays faced Farrell, on July 24, he had rocketed two long home runs.

But entering the final game of the regular season, Mays was 1 for his last 14 and 0 for his last 8.

Number 24 walked in his first at-bat, struck out in his second, and popped up in his third. He led off the eighth with the score tied, 1–1.

The first pitch Farrell offered was a curve, and Mays drove it deep to left, but it went foul.

The drive got the crowd of 41,327 to their feet.

Farrell tried to sneak a fastball by Mays.

He couldn't.

Mays rifled a shot to left.

Bob Stevens of the *San Francisco Chronicle* described the then-most important hit in San Francisco Giants history: "the ball became a blur of white, smashed through the noise of roaring throats, sailing high into the blue . . ."

James S. Hirsch, author of the 2010 Mays biography, *Willie Mays: The Life and Legend*, called that September 30, 1962, homer the most important of the 660 Mays hit in his sparkling career.

The Giants won the game and forced a three-game playoff with the Dodgers. Both teams had records of 101–61.

It was like 1951 all over again.

Koufax came back to pitch late in September, and Dodgers manager Walter Alston started him in the first game of the series. Mays greeted him with a two-run homer to set the pace for an 8–0 Giants win. Mays also homered in the sixth.

Los Angeles won Game Two at Dodger Stadium in a stirring comeback, 8–7.

In Game Three, also at Dodger Stadium, Mays delivered a crucial single to knock in a run and inch the Giants closer to their comeback win. (The winning pitcher? Don Larsen, six years after his World Series perfect game for the New York Yankees.)

The Giants would lose to the Yankees in seven games in the World Series.

Mays, remarkably, finished second to LA's Wills for the Most Valuable Player Award in the National League.

He would be awarded his second MVP (his first was in 1954) in 1965 and played through the 1973 season.

In 1999, when *The Sporting News* ranked the best players of the century, it tabbed Babe Ruth as Number 1

Willie Mays was Number 2.

Felipe Alou, who played with Mays and against Hank Aaron and Roberto Clemente, and managed Barry Bonds, said, "[Mays] is number one, without a doubt. . . . Anyone who played with him, or against him would agree he is the best."

60 KENT HRBEK: LOCAL HERO'S DREAM COMES TRUE

It was the concession manager at the old Metropolitan Stadium in Bloomington who told Minnesota Twins scout Angelo Giuliani about Kent Hrbek.

His kid was playing against Hrbek that spring and couldn't stop raving about him. The scout thought it would be worth an afternoon of his time to go to nearby Kennedy High School to see this first baseman-pitcher.

Hrbek had grown up in Bloomington, just twenty blocks away from where Harmon Killebrew and Tony Oliva made their names as Twins. He could see the lights of the ballpark from his bedroom window.

But one scout's interest was all it took. Giuliani was impressed by the powerful 6-foot-4, seventeen-year-old left-handed-hitting first baseman who also was nimble in the field. The veteran scout called Hrbek "the best prospect I've seen from Minnesota in thirty years of scouting."

Because no other team had eyeballed him, Hrbek wasn't taken until the 17th round of the 1978 draft.

"I think we were just happy that we got scouted," Hrbek told Joel Rippel of the Society of American Baseball Research. "It's a given in Florida, Texas, and California. There are probably ten scouts at a game. But it was a big deal that Angie Giuliani was at our game."

"He was a 17th-round pick who would have been a first rounder if people would have known about him," Giuliani insisted.

Hrbek made his major-league debut on August 24, 1981, blasting a game-winning 12th-inning home run at Yankee Stadium. He was twenty-one, and it was his first time in New York City.

"I didn't know whether to laugh or cry," he told *People* magazine in 1983.

Three weeks earlier, Hrbek was dominating the California League when he received a phone call from home. His father, Ed, fifty-one, a gas company supervisor, had been diagnosed with amyotrophic lateral sclerosis, better known as Lou Gehrig's disease.

"I wanted to return home," Hrbek said. "But I talked to my dad and he said, 'You stay right there and play hard. Don't let me spoil what you are doing.' I thought about my dad a lot, especially at Yankee Stadium. Lou

Gehrig was a first baseman like me, and this was his home field. It's such a strange coincidence."

In 1982, his first full season, Hrbek helped open the Hubert H. Humphrey Metrodome, the new roofed indoor home of the Twins, by stroking 23 homers, knocking in 92 runs, and hitting .301. He made his only All-Star Game appearance, and he finished second to Cal Ripken Jr. in Rookie of the Year voting.

The Twins were only 60–102 in 1982, but the foundation of a world championship club was being poured—solid cornerstones that included third baseman Gary Gaetti, right fielder Tom Brunansky, and pitcher Frank Viola. But Hrbek was the hometown favorite, gregarious and fun-loving. His father died that year, but got to see his son string together a 23-game hitting streak and to be in the stands when Texas manager Don Zimmer, with his team leading 3–2, walked Hrbek intentionally in the bottom of the ninth with two outs and nobody on.

"I've seen that before," Twins manager Billy Gardner said, "with Mantle, Williams, and Aaron."

Hrbek was a star by 1984, powering the Twins into surprise contention for the American League Western Division title and finishing second to Detroit's lights-out reliever Willie Hernandez in the MVP voting. Hrbek's final numbers were 27 dingers, 107 RBIs—his career high—and a .311 average.

The Twins slumped down the stretch and finished three games behind the division-winning Kansas City Royals, but the future was bright: the team had added future Hall of Famer Kirby Puckett to the lineup.

By this time, Jim Kaat, the Hall of Fame Twins pitcher turned broadcaster, was calling Hrbek the best defensive first baseman he'd ever seen.

Even though the Twins continued to stockpile young talent, they regressed in 1985 and 1986. In '86, they finished next to last, with a 71–91 record.

They hired Tom Kelly as manager, and, just before spring training, traded Neal Heaton, their top pitching prospect, for Montreal closer Jeff Reardon.

Minnesota won the AL West, but it wasn't pretty. The Twins were 29–52 on the road. They really made the Metrodome, and its rising decibels, their home, with a 56–25 record beneath its roof. Attendance topped more than two million. It was the Twins first division championship since 1970.

They beat the Detroit Tigers in the American League Championship Series, no small accomplishment. The Tigers had won 98 games—the most of any team that year—and overcome a 3½-game deficit with a week to go to capture the AL East.

The Twins faced the St. Louis Cardinals in the World Series. They were trailing three games to two by the day of Game Six in Minnesota.

Hrbek, who had a career-high 34 home runs in the regular season and who had popped a homer off Jack Morris in the ALCS, was struggling offensively in the postseason. The Twins were clinging to a 6–5 lead in the sixth. Hrbek was 7-for-40 in October, and wasn't doing so well on the basepaths, either.

In the second inning, he hit a drive to center that was dropped by Cardinal Willie McGee. If Hrbek had been running hard, he would have reached third. He wasn't, and stopped at second. Then he was picked off second by St. Louis starter John Tudor.

"We got two hits after that and I sat there the whole game thinking that if we lost by a run it would be my fault," Hrbek said.

Getting ready in the on-deck circle while the Twins loaded the bases in the bottom of the sixth, Hrbek thought of his father.

"I don't know if I've ever done that before," he said after the game.

The Cardinals walked Don Baylor to load the bases and take their chances with Hrbek, who was 1-for-14 against southpaws. Cardinal Manager Whitey Herzog called on Ken Dayley, his lefty reliever.

To that point, Hrbek had been 0-for-3 against Dayley in the Series.

Dayley hadn't given up a homer to a lefty in more than two years. Hrbek had only six homers off of southpaws in 1987.

Hrbek remembered that Dayley always started him off with fastballs. Dayley indeed threw another. Hrbek was waiting, and launched the pitch 439 feet to center field.

"I wish I could have run around the bases twice instead of once," said the hometown hero, who did sprint around the bases with arms outstretched like a plane that wasn't going to land. "But I don't know if they let you do that."

The Twins won, 11–5.

They took Game Seven, too, the first championship in franchise history since 1924, when they were the Washington Senators.

The Twins would win the World Series again in 1991, with Hrbek in the lineup. He retired in 1994, with 293 home runs and a .282 average. The Twins retired his number 14.

"Playing in the backyard with a plastic ball, a tennis ball, I used to imagine doing that all the time in Game Seven of the World Series," he'd say after his most memorable home run. "I guess I was just a game too early."

As he gleefully rounded the bases in Game Six, Hrbek looked into the stands to find his mother and wife.

"It would have been great if he had been there," he said of his father. "Sure, people ask me about him all the time. But he's probably got the best seat in the house, although he might be having a hard time seeing through that roof."

59 ROBIN VENTURA: THE GRAND SLAM SINGLE

It was pouring rain, the remnants of Hurricane Irene. Robin Ventura of the New York Mets couldn't really dig into the left-handed batter's box. It was more a puddle than anything else.

The bases were loaded. The Mets had just tied the score at 3–3 in the bottom of the 15th in Game Five of the 1999 National League Championship Series.

Ventura had hit three grand slams that year. He would club 18 in his career, tying him with San Francisco's Willie McCovey.

Only Alex Rodriguez, Lou Gehrig, Manny Ramirez, and Eddie Murray hit more.

Ventura remains the only player in history to hit a grand slam in both games of a doubleheader.

But he wasn't thinking about hitting a grand slam in the wind and the rain at Shea Stadium on October 17, 1999.

Honest.

In those conditions, it would have been asking a lot. He simply was hoping for a bloop, not a blast. He just didn't want to hit into a double play to end the inning and the threat. He had done that in the eighth inning, when it was already raining. But that was almost a whole game ago.

The Braves, in their dominant era when they finished first 14 out of 15 years in the National League East, were leading the series three games to one.

Ventura was mired in a slump. He was 1-for-18 (.056) in the NLCS.

He had enjoyed a fabulous first season in New York, with 32 homers, 120 RBIs, and a .301 average. He would also win his sixth Gold Glove for defensive excellence at third base. For a good chunk of the 1999 season, every time he came to bat at Shea Stadium fans chanted, "M-V-P! M-V-P!"

He had been a star for the Chicago White Sox, who had selected him in the first round of the 1988 amateur draft. He had a 58-game hitting streak while at Oklahoma State University. Joe DiMaggio, who owns the major-league record with a 56-game streak, sent his regards.

In spring training of 1997, Ventura suffered a compound fracture of his right ankle trying to score from second base against the Boston Red Sox. His injury was thought to be so bad he might miss the season.

"Robin means more to this team than anybody will ever know," White Sox manager Terry Bevington said. "It's kind of like somebody trying to cut out your heart and take your soul."

Ventura returned on July 24, four months after his injury, with a game-winning hit. The next day, he homered in his first at-bat. But the White Sox were already trying to trade him.

Owner Jerry Reinsdorf thought his third baseman was "deteriorating."

After the 1998 season, Ventura signed with the Mets, becoming a team leader.

On May 20, 1999, he hit two grand slams, one in each end of a double-header against the Milwaukee Brewers.

By September, he and the rest of the Mets infield—Rey Ordonez, Edgardo Alfonzo, and John Olerud—were on the cover of *Sports Illustrated*. The headline: "Best Infield Ever."

During the heat of the summer, Ventura, then thirty-two, made a team anthem of the phrase "Mojo Risin'" from the Doors hit song "L.A. Woman." The team wore shirts bearing the words. The song was played after every Mets win.

And there were plenty of them. The Mets went on a run, taking 40 of the next 55 games. Ventura ended up meeting Patricia Kennealy, who claims she's the widow of the Doors lead singer Jim Morrison. She became a Mets fan.

In late September, Ventura's right ankle was still hurting. So was his left knee, which was worse. And his shoulders were barking. Still, he had the game-winning, bases-loaded single in the final weekend of the season to beat the Pittsburgh Pirates and help get the Mets back into the wild-card hunt.

His postseason slump had Mets manager Bobby Valentine dropping him to sixth in the order. He also had sent up a pinch-hitter for Ventura in Game Three.

New York Daily News writer Bill Madden complained that the move was an insult, "a slight to the player who has carried the team much of the season and is playing on guts and a torn-up knee."

Ventura didn't say anything. He had struck out in big at-bats in the first two games against the Braves, both close losses.

But baseball often gives second and third chances.

In the bottom of the 15th, New York's Shawon Dunston, who rarely saw a pitch he didn't swing at, worked through twelve pitches before singling off Atlanta hurler Kevin McGlinchy.

Dunston stole second. Pinch-hitter Matt Franco walked. Edgardo Alfonzo bunted them to second and third. Olerud was walked intentionally.

Mike Piazza, the Met slugging catcher, had left the game after 14 innings. Up stepped Todd Pratt, his backup. He walked in five pitches, knotting the score.

It was Ventura's turn.

He took ball one, fouled off the next, and took ball two outside. Ventura then drilled a fastball into the storm, high and deep.

Braves right fielder Brian Jordan didn't even wait for the ball to come down. He knew it was over his head and the game was in the record books after five hours and 46 minutes. He didn't need to see it fly over the 371-foot sign. Roger Cedeno, in the game as a pinch-runner for Franco, scored. Olerud kept running home, too.

NBC's Bob Costas called it a grand slam. So did the Mets play-by-play man Gary Cohen.

But Todd Pratt, the runner on first, decided to stop at second to hug Ventura. Then he started lifting the 6-foot-1, 190-pound Ventura and carrying him around. The Mets dugout emptied in celebration. Ventura never got near second base, never mind touching home.

Ten minutes after the game, official scorer Red Foley, a longtime sportswriter for the New York *Daily News*, who had scored more than 3,000 games, ruled that Ventura would be credited with a single and driving in the winning run.

Foley noted that, while the drive cleared the fence, Ventura had gone no farther than first base.

The hit would be forever known as the "Grand Slam Single."

It didn't matter to Ventura.

He hadn't been thinking about a grand slam.

"As long as we won it's fine with me," Ventura said after the game. "I knew it went over. But it didn't matter. I didn't want to run that far anyway. Maybe when the guys go home, I'll do it. But then I was just happy to stop. I was tired."

58 MARK WHITEN: ALL IN A NIGHT'S WORK

The first game of the doubleheader was wild and sloppy, the Cincinnati Reds beating the St. Louis Cardinals, 14–13, on an RBI triple by Reggie Sanders in the bottom of the ninth.

That's a triple with an asterisk.

St. Louis center fielder Mark Whiten misplayed the line-drive single into a two-run triple, capping a five-run Reds comeback.

St. Louis and Cincinnati used a then-major-league-record fifteen pitchers in the game. Ninety-eight batters saw a total of 350 pitches. Five leads were blown.

The nightcap, with both bullpens exhausted, didn't start until just after 10 p.m. It was September 7, 1993, the season winding down for teams not in contention.

In the opener, Whiten went 0-for-4, with a bases-loaded walk.

At twenty-six years of age and in his fourth season in the big leagues, he was still a work in progress, a switch-hitter with the kind of arm that made scouts gasp. He was also a lean and strong 6-foot-3, 210 pounds.

Whiten hadn't taken baseball seriously until his senior year of high school in Pensacola, Florida. Two years later, the Toronto Blue Jays selected him in the fifth round of the 1986 draft, projecting a player who could produce double figures in homers and stolen bases. Then, of course, there was Whiten's arm, often compared to that of the all-time greats. Still, the Jays traded Whiten to the Cleveland Indians in 1991.

Whiten was acquired by the Cardinals in March of 1993, seven days before the season began, for pitcher Mark Clark. The trade was made because the Tribe needed pitching. Cleveland's Tim Crews, Steve Olin, and Bobby Ojeda had been involved in a horrible spring-training boating accident. Crews and Olin died. Ojeda was badly injured.

Even with his late arrival to the Cardinals camp, Whiten beat out Jose Canseco's brother, Ozzie, for a spot on the team. Ozzie had a terrific spring training—four homers and 14 RBIs—but manager Joe Torre liked Whiten's defense and speed better.

By September, Whiten was the Cardinals starting center fielder. Yet Torre and hitting coach Chris Chambliss still recommended that Whiten go to the fall Instructional League to work on his pitch selection.

In the second game of the doubleheader, Whiten was batting sixth.

Cincinnati was starting Larry Luebbers, a 6-foot-6 right-hander who made his major-league debut two months earlier.

Luebbers walked two and allowed a Gerald Perry ground-ball single, but there were also two outs when Whiten dug in from the left side. He was hitting .248, with 18 homers and 75 RBIs. In five minor-league seasons, Whiten never hit more than 15 dingers or drove in more than 64 runs.

Whiten hadn't hit a homer in almost three weeks; his last one was on August 11. He drove a pitch 464 feet into the upper deck at Three Rivers Stadium in Pittsburgh, becoming the first visiting player ever to do so. (Pittsburgh's Hall of Fame slugger Willie Stargell accomplished the feat four times.)

John Mayberry, the former Kansas City slugger, had given Whiten the nickname "Hard-Hittin' Mark Whiten" when the former was his batting coach in the Toronto system during the late 1980s.

Sometimes the nickname applied, but not often enough.

But on the first strike he saw from Luebbers, Whiten reminded fans why the nickname was still relevant. He drilled a line drive over the left-center-field fence at Riverfront, his second career grand slam.

He fouled out in the fourth.

In the sixth inning, facing Mike Anderson in the pitcher's first major-league appearance, Whiten greeted him with a three-run homer 397 feet to right.

In the following inning, he struck again—another three-run homer off of Anderson to right.

He was back at bat in the ninth, once again batting left-handed.

The Reds had Rob Dibble, one of the original Nasty Boys—the bullpen that helped Cincinnati to the world championship three years earlier—on the mound. Dibble fell behind, 2–0.

"I threw him the best stuff I've got," Dibble would say after the game.

Whiten then belted a fastball 441 feet for a two-run home run, his fourth homer and 12th RBI of the game, tying Cardinals Hall of Famer Sunny Jim Bottomley, who knocked in a dozen runs in a game in 1924. The Cardinals went on to win, 15–2.

Counting his RBI in the first game, Whiten also tied the major-league mark of 13 in a doubleheader, set by San Diego's Nate Colbert in 1972.

Whiten became the twelfth player in major-league history to hit four homers in a game, joining icons such as Hall of Famers Lou Gehrig, Willie Mays, and Mike Schmidt.

Whiten said all four homers came on fastballs.

"But even though they were fastballs down the middle, you still have to know what to do with them," Whiten's teammate Todd Zeile said after the game. "You can't even do what he did in batting practice."

Whiten finished the season with 25 homers and 99 RBIs, his career bests. He also swiped 15 bases.

The following spring, he pulled rib muscles and was never the same player again.

He ended up wearing the uniform of six teams, including the Boston Red Sox and New York Yankees, during the next six years, finishing his major-league career in 2000 with a total of 105 home runs.

But all people remember were four of those homers, and that one night in Cincinnati.

57 CASEY STENGEL: CASEY CHRISTENS STADIUM WITH SERIES SHOT

Casey Stengel, born Charles Dillon Stengel, was a pretty good baseball player.

As he would say, "You can look it up."

He hit .284 in 14 National League seasons. He stroked 60 career home runs, pretty respectable for the Deadball Era, which is when baseball relied on bunts and hit-and-runs. He also swiped 131 bases. Defensively, he was one of the best right fielders of his time.

In one of his baseball studies, statistician, writer, historian, and Boston Red Sox analyst Bill James listed Stengel as the 115th-best right fielder in the game's history.

But on July 8, 1958, Stengel, then managing the New York Yankees, a team he would guide to seven World Series titles and ten pennants in twelve years, testified before a Senate subcommittee hearing on baseball's antitrust exemption. Asked to state his baseball background, he responded, "I had many years that I was not so successful as a ballplayer, as it is a game of skill."

Maybe he was just being modest, or Casey just being Casey with his double-talk that would be dubbed Stengelese, or maybe his career seemed so long ago.

But he was better than he said.

He even hit one of the most famous home runs in World Series history.

Stengel, 5-foot-11, 175 pounds, who batted and threw left-handed, made his major-league debut at age twenty-two, on September 17, 1912, for the Brooklyn Dodgers. He collected four singles, walked once, drove in two runs, and stole three bases.

The following day, during a rain delay, he was playing cards with teammates. He won a hand. A teammate bellowed, "About time you took a pot, Kansas City," referring to Stengel's hometown.

As Bill Bishop for the Society for American Baseball Research wrote, "The other players caught on, calling the rookie 'K.C.' After one week in the big leagues, Stengel had a nickname, a .478 batting average, nine RBIs and a tremendous home run to right field that was said to be the longest hit in Brooklyn all season."

Stengel attended dental school during a few minor-league off-seasons, but discovered he was more a student of the game.

In 1913, he hit the first homer at the new Ebbets Field.

In 1914, he led the National League in on-base percentage.

Two years later, Stengel cracked a crucial September home run to lead the Brooklyn Dodgers to the National League pennant. He also hit .364 in the World Series, one the Dodgers lost to the Boston Red Sox and the pitching of Babe Ruth.

Stengel had an even better season in 1917, leading the Dodgers in homers, RBIs, doubles, and triples.

Despite his success on the field, Stengel was traded to Pittsburgh in the off-season.

He had sent back his contract—unsigned—to Brooklyn owner Charles Ebbets. Stengel included a note that the team must have confused his contract with that of the clubhouse man. Ebbets didn't find that funny.

The Dodgers received back future Hall of Fame pitcher Burleigh Grimes, the last hurler legally allowed to throw a spitball, in the multi-player deal.

Stengel didn't last long in Pittsburgh—contract demands again—before he was traded to the Philadelphia Phillies. He hit .292 and had a career-high nine home runs in 1920, but by the following summer he was hampered by nagging leg injuries. When the trainer from the Phillies handed him papers, Stengel thought he was being sent to the minors. Instead, he was heading back to New York, this time to manager John McGraw's Giants.

Historians argue to this day who was the better manager—McGraw or Stengel.

McGraw was the game's first dominant manager, and Stengel learned a lot, mostly to think outside the box.

But in 1922 Stengel was still a player and, as it turned out, an important cog in the Giants heading to the World Series. He hit .368 in 84 games. A pulled leg muscle limited him to only five at-bats in the World Series.

Come 1923, Giants manager John McGraw viewed Stengel, then thirty-three, as a spare part, no longer an everyday ballplayer. He also started helping mold Stengel as a future manager, allowing him to work with young players, coach first base, and going over at length about the marrow of the game.

But Stengel wasn't done as a player. He started the season sizzling. He was hitting .379 in early May. At one point in the summer, he had hits in 20 out of 22 games. The Giants won the National League flag again.

For the third straight year, the Giants would play the Yankees in the World Series. The Yankees had never beaten the Giants.

The Series opened at the new Yankee Stadium on October 10. With the score tied, 4–4, and two outs in the ninth, Stengel hit a line drive to left-center field. The ball kept rolling all the way to the wall. Stengel ran the bases as if he had a broken leg, but he kept running. Yankee players said later they could hear Casey saying to himself, "Go, Casey, go! Go, Casey, go!"

Around second.

Around third, heading for home.

Writing for the *New York American*, Damon Runyon described the first World Series home run hit in Yankee Stadium:

> This is the way old "Casey" Stengel ran yesterday afternoon, running his home run in a Giant victory by a score of 5–4 in the first game of the World Series of 1923 . . .
>
> This is the way—
>
> His mouth wide open.
>
> His warped old legs bending beneath him at every strike.
>
> His arms flying back and forth like those of a man swimming with a crawl stroke.
>
> His flanks heaving, his breath whistling, his head far back . . .
>
> The warped old legs, twisted and bent by many a year of baseball campaigns, just barely held out under "Casey" Stengel until he reached the plate, running his home run home.
>
> Then they collapsed.

Because Stengel was known as an eccentric—he had once popped out of a manhole to catch a fly ball and had a habit of lifting his cap only to have a sparrow fly from inside it—sportswriters thought he was having a laugh in a serious situation.

Not so.

According to Stengel's biographer Robert W. Creamer, a rubber pad placed in one of Stengel's cleats to ease a bruised heel had shifted, making him think his shoe was coming off.

In Game Three, Stengel hit the game-winning home run. He made it easier on himself. This one went over the fence in right field.

Running around the bases, Stengel started blowing kisses to the fans at Yankee Stadium and thumbing his nose at the Yankee bench.

Baseball Commissioner Kenesaw Mountain Landis fined Stengel, but also said, "Casey Stengel just can't help being Casey Stengel." His heroics were not enough as the Yankees went on to win their first World Series. Babe Ruth hit three homers to pace the Yankees.

A month later, Stengel was traded to the seventh-place Boston Braves.

Later in life, Stengel quipped: "It's a good thing I didn't hit three homers in three games, or McGraw would have traded me to the Three-I League!"

He was joking.

Maybe.

56 EDDIE MATHEWS: MILWAUKEE MAULER SAVES SERIES

Man on second.

One out.

Scored tied, bottom of the 10th.

The New York Yankees lead the 1957 World Series, two games to one over the Milwaukee Braves.

Eddie Mathews, who would hit 512 career home runs, is due up for Milwaukee. Hank Aaron, who would hit 755, is on deck.

Mathews often batted ahead of Aaron. They would combine to hit 863 homers from 1954 to 1966, the highest total for teammates in major-league history. In the 1920s and '30s, Babe Ruth and Lou Gehrig had hit 859 as teammates for the New York Yankees.

First base is open. It is a Sunday in Milwaukee. Elvis Presley's "Teddy Bear" is the big hit on the radio. Two days before, the Soviet Union launched an unmanned space ship, Sputnik.

Aaron has been the only Brave hitting in this World Series. He gave Milwaukee an early lead with a three-run homer in the second inning.

Mathews had hit 32 homers in the regular season. He would hit more than 30 homers in nine consecutive seasons, including smacking 40 or more dingers four times, leading the National League twice in the long ball. Gehrig also had a nine-season, 30-plus homer streak. By 1957, the only person to surpass that was Jimmie Foxx, who had 30 homers in twelve consecutive seasons.

When Mathews was still a teenager, Ty Cobb, the baseball all-timer, said of him: "I've only known three or four perfect swings in my time. This lad has one of them."

But Mathews, a week from his twenty-sixth birthday, was hitting only .091 in the '57 World Series: a double earlier in Game Four, his only hit in 11 at-bats.

Yankee manager Casey Stengel, who had guided the team to six world championships in the previous eight years, elected to pitch to Mathews.

Bob Grim, the Yankee reliever who had given up the tying run, had led the American League with 19 saves.

Mathews dug in, his familiar number 41 on his back. Milwaukee's County Stadium was all bedlam and anticipation.

The Braves had moved from Boston to Milwaukee in 1953, and the city had adopted the blue-collar Mathews as its own—"The Milwaukee Mauler," they called him. He was fresh-faced, all power, and a "gamer" before the term was invented. The team's last year in Boston, it drew 281,000 fans. The Braves drew more than that in their first 13 home games in Milwaukee.

Mathews hit 47 homers in 1953, with 135 RBIs and a .302 batting average.

Hall of Famer Rogers Hornsby gave this scouting report in 1954: "Mathews is the most dangerous hitter in baseball today. And he's going to get better because he wants to learn, because he's always asking questions. He's got power and he's got rhythm, along with a fine level swing."

With one perfect swing, Mathews turned the 1957 World Series around. The ball was high, far, and gone to deep right field, tying the Series at two games apiece. He became, at the time, only the third player to hit an extra-inning, game-ending homer in Series history.

The next day, Lew Burdette, traded six years earlier by the Yankees to the Braves, outdueled Whitey Ford, 1–0. Mathews reached on an infield hit with two out in the sixth inning and was chased home by Hank Aaron and Joe Adcock singles.

In Game Seven at Yankee Stadium, Mathews doubled home the winning runs in the third inning.

In the bottom of ninth, with the bases loaded, Moose Skowron of the Yankees hit a scorcher down the third-base line. Off the bat it looked like a bases-clearing double. Mathews backhanded it and, like a little kid, joyfully jumped on third to end the game and the Series.

Mathews called that play his proudest moment in baseball.

Burdette, pitching on two days' rest, spun his third complete game and second shutout of the Series to help the Braves become the first non-New York team since 1948 to win the World Series.

After the Series, Hank Aaron would say of Mathews, "He didn't get a lot of hits, but that one was the big one. That set up the whole Series for us."

Mathews was the only person to play for the Braves in Boston, Milwaukee, and Atlanta. He played in 10 All-Star Games. He knocked in 100 runs five times. He appeared on the first cover of *Sports Illustrated* and was inducted into the Hall of Fame in 1978.

"Eddie Mathews was my hero," said Joe Torre, then the manager of the Yankees, and his Braves teammate from 1960 to 1966. "He was captain and I always called him that. He never backed off, never was tentative."

When hearing the news of Mathews's death, Aaron said, "He could hit them just as well as I could. I was there to shake his hand quite a few times when he crossed home plate. He was a better hitter than a lot of people gave him credit for. He was a good fielder and ran the bases very well, too. He was a great teammate. . . ."

Eddie Mathews was also the manager of the Atlanta Braves the night Aaron broke Babe Ruth's home run record.

55 YOGI BERRA: A PERFECT ENDING

On October 8, 1956, Don Larsen threw the only perfect game in World Series history, and he did so without shaking off one sign from catcher Yogi Berra.

That fact gets lost in the retelling of the historic event illustrated so well by a famous photograph of Berra leaping into the arms of Larsen when the game was over. But Berra would remind fans years later that, as monumental as that game was, the World Series wasn't yet finished.

The Yankees, with a three-game-to-two lead, still had to travel by bus to Brooklyn to play the Dodgers in Game Six. There, Berra would say, "the Dodgers [behind Clem Labine's seven-hit shutout] came back and beat us 1–0 in 10 innings to force a Game Seven."

In the deciding game, the Yankees, who were starting rookie Johnny Kucks, had to face Brooklyn's ace, Don Newcombe. A 6-foot-4, 220-pound right-hander, Newcombe was 27–7 in 1956. That year, he was the inaugural Cy Young Award winner, and also took home the title of National League Most Valuable Player. The next time a pitcher would win both awards would be when Detroit's Justin Verlander garnered them in 2011.

In 1949, Newcombe was the first black pitcher to start a World Series game, and in 1951, he became the first black pitcher to win 20 games. He was even better in 1956, with his 27–7 record and 18 complete games.

Kucks, a tall, slim right-hander, was 18–9 for the Yankees in his second big-league season, but hadn't won since September 3.

According to Peter Golenbock's book *Dynasty: The New York Yankees, 1949–1964,* when Kucks toed the rubber for the bottom of the first, he couldn't help but notice teammates Whitey Ford and Tom Sturdivant warming up.

He muttered to himself, "Boy, big guy, they sure got faith in you."

The Dodgers had beaten the Yankees in the 1955 World Series.

They wanted to do it a second time, but Berra would get in the way.

Craggy-faced, 5-foot-7, 180-pound Berra was signed by the Yankees in 1942 for $500, the same amount the St. Louis Cardinals had paid for his neighbor Joe Garagiola. (Branch Rickey, then general manager of the Cardinals, had offered Berra only $250.)

Berra was the son of Italian immigrants who had settled on "The Hill" in St. Louis. He never made it past eighth grade. He'd grown up playing third and outfield, and only caught occasionally, so the Yankees had their Hall of Fame catcher Bill Dickey school him in the finer points of the position.

Berra, born Lawrence Peter Berra, already bore his classic nickname, given to him by an American Legion teammate who thought that when Berra sat down he looked like a Hindu yogi.

The gunner's mate on the USS *Bayfield* during the D-Day invasion became a Yankee for good in 1946.

His was a remarkable career.

- As a player he appeared in 14 World Series, 10 of which were won by the Yankees. As a coach or manager he participated in seven more Series, on the winning side three more times.
- He hit the first pinch-hit homer in a World Series in 1947, off of Brooklyn's Ralph Branca, the same pitcher who gave up Bobby Thomson's "Shot Heard 'Round the World" in 1951.
- He was an 18-time All-Star.
- He won the American League Most Valuable Player Award three times, in 1951, 1954, and 1955. He also received MVP votes in 15 straight seasons, tied with San Francisco's Barry Bonds and second only to Hank Aaron's 19 consecutive years.
- He hit 358 career homers with a .285 lifetime average.
- Five times he had more homers in a season than strikeouts. In 1950, he struck out just 12 times in 597 at-bats.
- He managed the Yankees (1964) and the New York Mets (1973) to the World Series.
- He was elected to the Hall of Fame in 1972.
- In 1999, Major League Baseball named him to the All-Century Team.
- According to baseball historian Bill James and his Win Shares formula, Berra is the greatest catcher of all time and the 52nd-best non-pitcher.

As a hitter, Berra was known for his great plate coverage and as someone who could hit a pitch out of the strike zone.

He supposedly once said, "If I can hit it, it's a good pitch."

And, like most of his famous sayings, Berra was right. As he would quip long after his career was over, "I really didn't say everything I said."

Paul Richards, the longtime player, manager, and general manager, called Berra "the toughest man in the league in the last three innings."

Defensively, Berra was outstanding. He could handle both a pitching staff and the ball in the dirt. His arm was strong and accurate. And he was tough. In 1962, when he was thirty-seven, he caught all 22 innings in a game with Detroit.

Later in his career, when Elston Howard started catching regularly for the Yankees, Berra became a decent left fielder, which is saying something, considering how spacious the left field was in the old Yankee Stadium.

After losing to the Dodgers in 1955, the Yankees were hungry in 1956. The last time they had won a Series was in 1953. The Cleveland Indians had broken the team's string of five straight world championships in 1954. The Indians had won 111 games that season, while the Yankees took 103. No Casey Stengel–led team had won that many regular-season games. (The Indians did lose to the New York Giants in the '54 World Series.)

In 1956, Mickey Mantle and Berra powered the Yankees. Whitey Ford won 19 games.

The Yankees won the American League by nine games over the Indians.

Mantle won the Triple Crown, leading the American League in homers (52), RBIs (130), and batting average (.353).

Berra batted .298 and reached the seats 30 times. It tied his American League record for homers by a catcher, which he set in 1952. Berra finished second to Mantle in the MVP vote.

But on October 10, 1956, it was Game Seven, do or die.

Berra was batting fourth.

Yankee right fielder Hank Bauer singled to open the game. Second baseman Billy Martin struck out, as did Mantle.

With two outs, Berra launched a drive to deep right field to silence the Ebbets Field throng.

In the third inning, again with two outs and one on, Berra slammed another homer deep to right.

The Yankees led, 4–0, and didn't look back. The final score was 9–0. Kucks threw a complete-game three-hitter. He didn't shake Berra off, either.

The Yankees became World Champions for the sixth time in eight years.

"The two home runs I hit were probably one of the biggest thrills I ever had," Berra said, adding that he always told Larsen, who'd been awarded the Corvette from *SPORT* magazine as World Series MVP, "If you hadn't pitched that perfect game, I'd have won the car!"

Of course, he was kidding.

All Yogi Berra really cared about was winning the game.

54 BABE RUTH: FITTING FINALE FOR THE GAME'S GREATEST

Connie Mack considered hiring Babe Ruth to manage the Philadelphia A's in 1935.

Mack was seventy-two, taking a goodwill tour of Japan in the fall of 1934 with a boatload of future Hall of Famers: Ruth, Lou Gehrig, Jimmie Foxx, Earl Averill, Lefty Grove, and Charlie Gehringer. Also along for the trip was Moe Berg, a backup catcher who liked to take photographs and turned out to be an American spy.

Always a scout eyeing talent, Mack kept both eyes on Ruth.

Mack already had more wins than any manager in history and would finish with 3,731.

As an owner and manager, he had built teams and torn them down, selling off players piece by piece to pay the bills, then rebuilding his team one more time. He had managed five World Series champs and nine American League pennant winners. His clubs would also go on to finish last seventeen times.

When he looked into the future in the fall of 1934, he didn't see the A's as much of a contender. Mack, both a baseball man and a businessman, knew Ruth wouldn't hurt attendance as a player-manager.

In 1914 he had been offered Ruth, then a teenage pitcher from Baltimore, by Jack Dunn, the owner of the minor-league Orioles. The price was $10,000. Mack didn't have the money. The Boston Red Sox did, paying Dunn $25,000 for the Babe.

The Ruth-led New York Yankees were no strangers to Mack and the A's. By the second half of the 1920s and the early 1930s, the two teams always seemed to be battling for the American League pennant.

Mack had selected and started Ruth in right field for the first All-Star Game, on July 6, 1933, at Comiskey Park in Chicago. The Babe hit the first home run in All-Star Game history.

He finished '33 with 34 homers and 104 RBIs, batting .301. The Yankees finished second. As a publicity stunt on the last day of the season, Ruth pitched against his old team, the Boston Red Sox. He twirled a complete-game victory, his 94th career win.

Ruth would play his last full season in 1934. He was thirty-nine, and it showed. He was a liability in right field, and he couldn't run much. But he could still hit.

Ruth swatted his 700th career homer on July 13, 1934, off Tommy Bridges at Detroit's Briggs Stadium. The ball sailed over the right field wall and down a street. He finished the season with 22 homers and a .288 average. Not Ruthian, of course, but not bad for a man terribly out of shape. The Yankees again finished second.

Ruth was talking even more openly about becoming the Yankees manager. Team owner Jacob Ruppert offered him a chance to manage the Triple A Newark Bears. Ruth considered it, but his wife Claire nixed the idea. She thought it was beneath her husband.

On February 26, 1935, the Yankees released Babe Ruth.

The Boston Braves signed him the same day, with the promise he would become a team vice-president and assistant manager to Boston pilot Bill McKechnie, the first man to win pennants as skipper of three different teams: Pittsburgh, St. Louis, and Cincinnati. McKechnie was elected to the Hall of Fame in 1962.

Emil Fuchs promised Ruth a share of the team's profits and the chance to be a co-owner.

Ruppert thought this was "the greatest opportunity Ruth ever had."

Turned out it wasn't.

Ruth was forty.

But on Opening Day, with 25,000 nestled into Braves Field, he flirted with the past. He hit a two-run homer off of Hall of Famer Carl Hubbell, knocked in another with a single, and scored the final run in a 4–2 win over the New York Giants. He also made a nice catch in left.

He had two hits in game two.

It wasn't long after that Braves pitchers started bellyaching to McKechnie that they didn't want to pitch when Ruth was playing the outfield.

McKechnie listened to the pitchers, but not to any advice from his assistant manager.

By April's end, Ruth wanted to retire. Fuchs talked him out of it. He appealed to the Bambino's vanity. There were days in his honor scheduled in May in Chicago and St. Louis. He decided to play until after Memorial Day.

By the time the Braves visited Pittsburgh in late May, Ruth was hitting .155 with three home runs. He was 3 for his last 45.

May 25, 1935, was a Saturday. The afternoon was unseasonably cold. The Braves were 8–19, the Pirates, 18–17.

Ruth batted third. In the first inning, he hit a two-run booming homer to right off of Red Lucas, known as a pretty good control pitcher who had the bad luck of pitching for mostly lousy teams.

In the third, Ruth powered a home run to right off Guy Bush, who had been the Chicago Cubs lead bench jockey in the 1932 World Series. The last time Bush had faced Ruth was three years earlier. He hit him with a pitch. This time, Ruth blasted a two-run homer, his 713th. He followed with an RBI single in the fifth.

In the seventh, the Babe launched a two-run homer over everything in right at Forbes Field. Number 714. The ballpark was twenty-six years old. No one had ever hit one out of the two-tiered structure.

"I never saw a ball hit so hard before or since," Bush said. "He was fat and old, but he still had that great swing. Even when he missed, you could hear the bat go swish. I can't remember anything about the first home run he hit off me that day. I guess it was another homer. But I can't forget that last one. It's probably still going."

Claire Ruth asked her husband to retire after the game. She thought it was a perfect way to end a career. He said no.

Babe Ruth ended up going 0 for his last 9 before calling it quits on June 2.

In 1938, the Brooklyn Dodgers hired him as first-base coach. When the managing job became open after the season, the Dodgers hired Leo Durocher, Ruth's former Yankee teammate. Ruth and Lou Gehrig, after three to five years of estrangement due to misunderstandings, made up on Lou Gehrig Appreciation Day at Yankee Stadium on July 4, 1939.

In the last decade of his life, Ruth golfed and bowled a lot. He loved listening to *The Lone Ranger* on the radio.

When Ruth lay dying in the summer of 1948, his throat cancer having spread, Connie Mack was one of the Babe's last visitors. While he never hired Ruth as a manager, Mack, who had started managing in 1892, always liked him and respected how much he had transformed the game.

"The termites have got me, Mr. Mack," the Babe whispered.

Babe Ruth died on August 16. He was fifty-three.

53 FERNANDO TATIS: TWO FOR THE RECORD BOOK

The St. Louis Cardinals acquired Fernando Tatis from the Texas Rangers in July of 1998.

The Cards dealt Royce Clayton, the man who replaced Ozzie Smith at shortstop, and Todd Stottlemyre, son of former New York Yankees great Mel, for Tatis. The deal helped Texas to the American League playoffs that year.

By April of 1999, Tatis, twenty-four, was paying dividends for the Cardinals. He was also hitting cleanup. Slugger Mark McGwire was batting third. Many a scout thought the third baseman from the Dominican Republic was a budding star. Texas general manager Doug Melvin agreed. "We always thought he was going to be a 30-home run, 30-stolen base guy. He's a good defensive player, too. That's the risk that goes with trying to win. You make a decision and live with it."

Tatis showed loads of promise during his first two months in St. Louis, batting .287 with eight homers and 26 runs batted in.

His last homer of the 1998 campaign came in the final game of the season. It was a bit overshadowed as McGwire slugged his 69th and 70th.

In the off-season, the Cardinals hired Mike Easler as the team's hitting coach. He was a former big-league slugger and the man credited with turning Boston's Mo Vaughn into a terrific hitter. He had actually played with Tatis's father in the Houston organization in the 1970s.

"When he (Tatis) came over here last year, I think it was a big adjustment for him," Walt Jocketty, the Cards general manager told Murray Chass of the *New York Times*. "He left a situation that was comfortable for him. But we have a few more Latin players this year. . . . Mike has a great relationship with Fernando. . . . He found some things they started working on in spring training. He got his hands down. Mostly Fernando has gained confidence. He is a highly motivated kid."

Tatis entered the game on April 23, 1999, at Dodger Stadium, a pitcher's park, with 23 career home runs.

The Dodgers took an early 2–0 lead on that cloudy, low-60s April evening. Chan Ho Park, coming off a 15–9 season, was on the hill for the home team. The right-hander had given up three homers in his 17 previous innings.

Darren Bragg of the Cards led off the third with a single, Edgar Renteria was hit by a pitch, and McGwire singled to load the bases.

Park fell behind Tatis in the count, 2–0.

Tatis had never hit a grand slam. But that was about to change. He powered the next pitch deep to left field, high, far, and gone, 420 feet away, for a 4–2 Cardinals lead.

Park, the winningest Korean-born pitcher in baseball history (he finished his career with 124 wins), had never surrendered a grand slam until eleven days earlier, to Travis Lee of the Arizona Diamondbacks.

History was only starting to unfold.

Park retired J. D. Drew, but catcher Eli Marrero hit the second homer of the inning. Second baseman David Howard and left fielder Joe McEwing walked. St. Louis pitcher Jose Jimenez tried to bunt them over, but the sacrifice attempt was botched by the Dodgers, loading the bases. Bragg reached on another error to make the score 6–2. Renteria singled for a 7–2 lead. McGwire flied out to shallow right. The bases were still loaded.

Number 23, Fernando Tatis, a tad under 6 feet, wiry and solid at the same time, came to bat again. Park was still in the game.

No major leaguer had ever homered twice with the bases loaded in the same inning.

Pitcher and hitter worked the count to 3 and 2.

Tatis later would note that he wasn't thinking home run, saying, "It's not like I'm Mark McGwire." But on the next pitch, a hanging slider, those thoughts changed.

He drilled a line drive to left-center field and the pavilion seats, becoming the first person in baseball history to hit two grand slams in the same inning.

After giving up eight hits and 11 runs (six earned) in 2⅔ innings, Park was removed from the game. He'd just become the second pitcher to give up two grand slams in an inning, following Bill Phillips of the Pittsburgh Pirates, who'd surrendered fifth-inning grand slams to Malachi Kittrudge and Tom Burns of the Chicago Cubs on August 16, 1890.

Tatis's name was inscribed in the history books.

In 1961, Baltimore's Jim Gentile hit grand slams in back-to-back innings. Hall of Famers Tony Lazzeri (in 1936) for the Yankees and Frank Robinson (in

1970) for the Baltimore Orioles were among the ten big leaguers at the time to hit two grand slams in a game, but, in a steroid-fueled age in which home run records kept falling, Tatis had accomplished something that seemed close to impossible.

Those two grand slams also set a record for most RBIs in a single inning—eight.

Tatis would finish the season with career highs in homers (34) and RBIs (107). The following year, injuries started piling up, the worst a groin muscle pulled in April. He missed 54 games. He was never again the same player. Instead of becoming a big star, Tatis turned into a journeyman.

After the 2000 season, the Cardinals dealt him to the Montreal Expos. Because of recurring injuries, he played in only 208 games in the next three years.

Tampa Bay gave him a shot in 2004, but released him during spring training. He was just twenty-nine.

After two years out of baseball, Tatis, who'd made himself into an outfielder in his native country, caught on with the New York Mets as a bench player. Mets general manager Omar Minaya had originally signed Tatis, then seventeen, while a Texas scout in 1992.

In 2008, filling in for injured Met outfielders Moises Alou and Ryan Church, Tatis batted .297, with 11 homers. His season was cut short by a torn labrum. *The Sporting News* named Tatis the National League Comeback Player of the Year.

Tatis was selected to play for the Dominican Republic's national team in the 2009 World Baseball Classic, replacing an injured Alex Rodriguez.

His big-league career was over the following year. He was thirty-five and looking back on 113 lifetime homers.

Tatis kept his baseball dreams alive, playing in both the Dominican Republic and Mexico, hoping the phone might ring one more time.

He didn't formally announce his retirement until the fall of 2014.

52 GEORGE BRETT: HISTORIC BATTLES WITH THE YANKEES

George Brett was hitting .400 as late as September 19, 1980.

No one had hit .400 since Boston's Ted Williams batted .406 in 1941.

Brett's season had started shakily, as he hit just .259 in April. The Kansas City Royals third baseman ramped it up in May with a .329 average. He sizzled in June, raising his average to .337. But trying to swipe second in a game on June 10, he tore a ligament in his right ankle. He didn't return to the lineup until exactly one month later. When he did, Brett got hotter than ever.

In 21 July games, he batted .494, starting a 30-game hitting streak on the 18th of the month. During the streak, he hit .467 and caught the nation's attention and imagination: Could he hit .400?

On August 17, Brett went 4-for-4 at home against the Toronto Blue Jays. His last hit, a bases-clearing double, nudged his average from .399 to .401. He received a prolonged standing ovation from the crowd.

But Brett, then twenty-seven, wasn't through. He would reach .407 on August 26.

He battled injuries and slumped later in the season, but still finished the year hitting .390, the highest batting average by a third baseman in baseball history. He would win the American League Most Valuable Player Award, but, more importantly to him, led the Royals to the AL Western Division Championship and a rematch with the New York Yankees, who had eliminated Kansas City from the playoffs in 1976, 1977, and 1978.

The Royals had taken a 2–0 lead in the 1980 American League Championship Series when Game Three was played on October 10 at Yankee Stadium.

Second baseman Frank White's home run gave the Royals a 1–0 lead in the fifth. The Yankees took a 2–1 lead in the bottom of the sixth as Yankee Stadium shook with anticipation. The Yankees had won 103 games and the American League East Championship under manager Dick Howser.

Reggie Jackson had had his best season as a Yankee, with 41 homers and 111 RBIs.

The lineup also boasted Graig Nettles, Willie Randolph, and Lou Piniella. The pitching staff was headlined by Tommy John, who'd won 22 games; Ron Guidry, who'd had 17 wins; and Rudy May, with a 15–5 record.

The bullpen was anchored by future Hall of Famer Rich "Goose" Gossage.

In an age where closers pitched multiple innings, Gossage was incredibly valuable to the Yankees. On some days, Howser would tell his closer to stay home, wanting to avoid the temptation to overuse him.

Gossage was 6–2 with a 2.27 ERA in 1980, posting 103 strikeouts in 99 innings. He was 6-foot-3 and 200 pounds, all arms and legs and pure power. He was as intimidating as he was good. He'd made his big-league debut for the Chicago White Sox in 1972 and pitched his last game, for the Seattle Mariners, in 1994. He was elected to the Hall of Fame in 2008.

According to baseball historian Bill James, only Nolan Ryan threw harder than Gossage, then twenty-nine, in that era. Goose would finish third in the AL MVP voting, behind Brett and Jackson.

In Game Three of the series at Yankee Stadium, Howser summoned Gossage with two out and KC's Willie Wilson on second in the seventh.

Gossage gave up a single to Royals shortstop U. L. Washington. Men on first and third.

Up stepped Brett, number 5, in his powder-blue road jersey. Yankee Stadium was in full roar.

Brett had a history with the Yankees.

In the 1976 playoffs, Brett clubbed a three-run homer in the top of the eighth of the deciding Game Five to tie the game at six. Chris Chambliss boomed his bottom-of-the-ninth homer to win the series for the Yankees. In the 1977 postseason, Brett, after hitting a triple, brawled with Nettles, leading to a bench-clearing rumble. The following year, Brett hit three consecutive homers off Catfish Hunter at Yankee Stadium in Game Three of the playoffs. In 1980, Brett homered in Game One, but while he was 0-for-4 in Game Two, he made a terrific play to cut down the tying run. Against Game Three southpaw starter Tommy John, he was 0-for-3.

But the first pitch Brett saw from Gossage—a 98-mile-per-hour fastball—was hit into the third deck at Yankee Stadium.

You've never heard 56,588 people go so quiet so fast. The three-run dinger reclaimed the lead for the Royals, 4–2, and reinforced Brett's reputation for coming through in the clutch. In 43 postseason games, Brett, who had a lifetime regular season average of .305, hit .337. (He was actually a .286 lifetime hitter against Gossage, 10-for-35, with two homers, the other one—the infamous Pine Tar Incident—more famous than the playoff clout.)

The Yanks would load the bases with no outs in the eighth, but the great KC reliever Dan Quisenberry, who owned a unique submarine delivery and a lot of guile, worked out of the jam.

The Royals were on their way to their first World Series.

Brett hit .375 in the 1980 World Series, but the Royals bowed to the Philadelphia Phillies in six games.

Brett had to leave Game Two because of hemorrhoid pain. He had minor surgery on a day off. In Game Three, he homered to lead the Royals to a 4–3 win.

After the game, Brett was quoted as saying, "My problems are all behind me." The Yankees would fire Dick Howser after the 1980 season. He would end up managing the Royals to their first World Series championship in 1985. Brett was his third baseman. Brett was great again. He hit 30 homers, knocked in 112 runs and hit .335. He finished in the Top 10 in 10 different offensive categories. He was also voted his only Gold Glove.

Down the stretch in the regular season, he went 9-for-20 with five homers and nine RBIs while leading the Royals to five of six wins to clinch the division title. He rallied the Royals, down three games to one against the Cardinals, including a four-hit game in Game Seven.

He would win batting championships in three decades—1976, 1980, and 1990—the only player to do so. Brett is also one of four players—Hank Aaron, Willie Mays, and Stan Musial—to have 3,000 hits, 300 homers, and a career average of .300.

Brett was elected to the Hall of Fame in 1999 with 98.2 percent of the vote, a higher percentage than that of Babe Ruth, Hank Aaron, Willie Mays, Ted Williams, or Joe DiMaggio.

51 MIKE SCIOSCIA: AN UNLIKELY THUMPER

Doc Gooden had walked John Shelby, who had fought back from an 0–2 count to lead off the ninth.

The New York Mets were leading, 4–2, in Game Four of the National League Championship Series on October 9, 1988, against the Los Angeles Dodgers. They were three outs from going up in the series, three games to one.

Gooden was New York's ace.

The Mets, almost as great as they were when they won the World Series in 1986, had beaten the Dodgers 10 out of 11 times during the regular season. They had outscored the Dodgers, 49 to 18.

Mike Scioscia, the Dodger catcher, future manager of the Anaheim–Los Angeles Angels and a student of the game, would one day say, "The '86 Mets were really good but I think they were more loaded in '88. They were a great team. During my time with the Dodgers, I don't know if we played against a better team than the '88 Mets."

Gooden, 18–9 in 1988, was also 9–1 with a 1.31 ERA lifetime against the Dodgers. He had retired six of the seven batters he faced in the seventh and eighth innings. But Gooden, who had thrown 248 innings in 1988, was up to 126 pitches after the Shelby at-bat, a lot even in 1988. Met manager Davey Johnson still thought Doc was still his team's best option.

Gooden did, too.

Up came Scioscia, the Dodgers catcher. He was 6-foot-2, 220 pounds, solid as a sturdy wall. He'd been the Dodgers first-round draft choice in 1976, a high school kid out of Springfield, Pennsylvania, the 19th overall selection.

Scioscia made the big leagues in 1980 at the age of twenty-one. He was the kind of person who volunteered to learn Spanish so he could catch another up-and-coming prospect, pitcher Fernando Valenzuela.

By the time he retired in 1992, Scioscia had caught more games in Dodger history than anyone else. More than Roy Campanella, the Hall of Famer, and Johnny Roseboro, who caught Sandy Koufax.

When Scioscia made the National League All-Star team in 1989, he was the first Dodger catcher to be selected since Tom Haller in 1968.

Scioscia was never a power hitter—he'd hit 68 homers in 13 years—but a decent contact hitter. Sometimes the Dodgers batted him second, but his forte was defense.

Al Campanis, the Dodgers general manager from 1968 to 1987, said Scioscia was the best plate-blocking catcher he'd seen in his 46-year baseball career.

Scioscia caught two no-hitters, by Fernando Valenzuela on June 29, 1990, against the St. Louis Cardinals, and Kevin Gross on August 17, 1992, against the San Francisco Giants.

"When you evaluate him, you can really only describe Mike one way," pitcher Orel Hershiser, who threw a record 59 consecutive shutout innings in 1988, once said. "Irreplaceable."

In 1988 Scioscia had just three homers in the regular season, his last on September 13, against a minor-league call-up, future Hall of Famer John Smoltz.

Gooden remembers his adrenaline pumping in extremely loud Shea Stadium.

"I was sure I was going to close it out," he recalled. "Scioscia wasn't a power guy so when he comes up, I'm thinking he's going to take a strike, knowing I just walked a guy. I was thinking completely the opposite of what he was thinking. And that was a huge mistake."

Gooden was still throwing hard.

"With Keith Hernandez holding the runner on, and [second baseman] Wally [Backman] pinching the middle for a double play, I saw a big hole on the right side," Scioscia recalled, "and I was just looking to get the head of the bat out and pull one through that hole."

Instead, he struck a line drive to right field that kept carrying.

Al Michaels, calling the game for ABC-TV, said, "[Darryl] Strawberry goes back, she's gone! Mike Scioscia, with 35 home runs in eight-and-a-half-years in the major leagues. And we've talked about him throughout the series, big and strong, but really a contact hitter, a man who doesn't strike out a lot and who doesn't hit very many home runs, averaging about four per season, hits the biggest home run of his career."

One of the biggest homers in Dodgers history.

"What I remember most is how quiet it got at Shea," Scioscia said. "It was really eerie. It was the first time I could ever remember running around the bases and hearing my spikes crunching as they hit the ground. And I'm thinking, 'This is pretty cool but it's almost surreal.'"

As Sunday, October 8, turned into Monday, October 9, the Dodgers won the game in the 12th, on a Kirk Gibson home run. It broke his 1-for-16 slump. Gibson would overshadow that home run with his pinch-hit homer off of Oakland's Dennis Eckersley in the first game of the World Series.

Hershiser, who had pitched seven innings the day before and had been dazzling all season, came in to work out of a jam and record the save. He ended up winning a shelf-load of awards for his pitching in 1988.

When Scioscia retired, he coached in the Dodgers system before the Angels hired him as manager in 2000.

He skippered the Angels to their first world championship, in 2002, becoming the 17th person to win a World Series as a player and manager.

He was named the 2002 American League Manager of the Year, and even would play himself on the television hit *The Simpsons*.

But that 1988 Dodger championship season, with the upsets of the Mets and A's, was made possible by Scioscia's unlikely home run.

"I was hoping no one in the Mets bullpen would catch the ball," he said years later. "Because maybe they'd call me out or something. The guys in the dugout were kidding me about my home run trot, but I told them I was running as fast as I could."

50 ROBERTO CLEMENTE: PRIDE AND FURY OF A LATINO LEGEND

Roberto Clemente didn't like Mike Cuellar. The feeling was mutual.

In January 1971, Clemente, of the Pittsburgh Pirates, was managing the Senadores de San Juan in the Puerto Rican Winter League. Cuellar, a Baltimore Oriole, a Cuban, the first Latino to win a Cy Young Award, and a four-time 20-game winner, was one of his pitchers.

According to the 2006 book *Clemente: The Passion and Grace of Baseball's Last Hero*, by David Maraniss, Cuellar thought Clemente "was unreasonably demanding, and said so."

Clemente didn't like hearing what Cuellar had to say. He also didn't like the fact that Cuellar quit the team halfway through the season.

As usual, Clemente channeled it.

Roy McHugh of the *Pittsburgh Press* told Maraniss that Clemente used every perceived slight to his psychological advantage. "Anger, for Robert Clemente, is the fuel that makes the wheels turn in his never-ending pursuit of excellence," he said. "When the supply runs low, Clemente manufactures some more."

Clemente won a National League Most Valuable Player Award, four batting championships, 12 Gold Gloves, and two World Series titles. He stroked, lined, laced, drilled, and powered 3,000 hits, including an inside-the-park, walk-off grand slam. He owned a .317 lifetime batting average. His arm was otherworldly. He was a great humanitarian.

He died in a plane crash on December 31, 1972, as he attempted to deliver food and medical supplies to earthquake-ravaged Managua, Nicaragua. His body was never found.

He was elected into the Hall of Fame in 1973 without the prescribed five-year waiting period. He was the first Latin American player to be enshrined. The Pirates retired his number 21.

Clemente played in the age of Hall of Famers Hank Aaron, Mickey Mantle, and Willie Mays. Pittsburgh wasn't a media center. And the Pirates had been lousy for a long time. They hadn't won a World Series since 1925 or been in one since 1927.

Starting in 1949, Pittsburgh had nine straight losing seasons. But by 1960, thanks to Clemente and another future Hall of Famer, Bill Mazeroski, the Pirates won the National League pennant and stunned the powerful New York Yankees in the World Series.

Clemente hit .314 during the regular season and delivered a hit in every game of the Series.

Hall of Famer George Sisler, a lifetime .340 hitter, was the Pirates batting coach in 1961. He suggested Clemente use a heavier bat. Clemente tried it and won the NL batting title that year with a .351 average. He made his first All-Star Game and tripled in his first at-bat.

He did better in 1967, when he hit .357. In 1970, at age thirty-six, Clemente, who hit a pitcher's best pitch and was just as notorious for drilling pitches out of the strike zone, too, produced a .352 average.

By then he was a familiar figure in All-Star Games and Games of the Week. In homage, young baseball fans across the country would rotate their necks like Clemente before they entered the batter's box.

In 1971, in their first full season at the new Three Rivers Stadium, the Pirates won the National League East with 97 wins, and dispatched the San Francisco Giants in the NL Championship Series in four games.

At age thirty-seven, Clemente had a terrific season, hitting .341 with 86 RBIs, but the star of the '71 Pirates was slugging left fielder Willie Stargell, who'd powered the Pirates with 48 homers and 125 RBIs. Stargell hit his 200th homer that season and, on June 25, boomed a drive that landed in the 600 level at Philadelphia's Veterans Stadium.

The Pirates pitching was led by Dock Ellis (19–9) and Steve Blass (15–8). Dave Giusti had 30 saves out of the bullpen.

On September 1, the Pirates became the first team to field an all-minority lineup:

Rennie Stennett, second base
Gene Clines, center field
Roberto Clemente, right field
Willie Stargell, left field
Manny Sanguillen, catcher
Dave Cash, third base
Al Oliver, first base
Jackie Hernandez, shortstop

Dock Ellis, pitcher

The Pirates faced the defending champion Baltimore Orioles in the World Series. The Birds took the first two games. The Pirates obituary was being written on sports pages across the country. But in Game Three, Clemente knocked in a first-inning run off Cuellar to give the Pirates a lead they wouldn't surrender.

It was a Clemente play in the seventh that would haunt Baltimore manager Earl Weaver's dreams.

Clemente chopped a Cuellar screwball back to the mound. Cuellar waited for the ball. Clemente ran as if he were being chased. Now rushed, Cuellar threw wildly to first. Clemente was safe.

"The most memorable play of the series," Weaver said decades later to David Maraniss. "The one that I think turned it around, the key to the series, when [Clemente] ran hard after tapping the ball back to Cuellar on the mound. Cuellar took his time, looked up and Clemente was charging to first, and it surprised him and he threw off target . . ."

Cuellar walked Stargell on four pitches. First baseman Bob Robertson missed a bunt sign and hit a three-run homer. The Pirates won, 5–1. It was a Series again.

Clemente kept playing as if he had something to prove.

"How to pitch Clemente? There was no way," Weaver would say. "But we tried to pitch him inside. Jam him. But he'd hit anything. We couldn't get him out."

In Game Seven, Cuellar retired the first eleven Pirates. With two outs in the fourth, Clemente stepped to the plate. Cuellar, 20–9 in the regular season, tried to jam him. Instead, Clemente lashed the pitch 390 feet and over the left field wall at Memorial Stadium.

Clemente hit 240 career home runs, and was never considered a home run hitter, but that one put the Pirates up for good.

He was voted the Most Valuable Player in the Series, finishing with a .414 average, two doubles, a triple, and two home runs. Clemente had a hit in every game.

When interviewed after the game, he made a conscious decision to speak first in Spanish.

As Maraniss wrote, "It was one of the most memorable acts of his life, a simple moment that touched the souls of millions of people in the

Spanish-speaking world. *'En el dia mas grande de mi vida para los nenes la benedicion mia y que mis padres me echen la benedicion.*"

["In the most important day of my life, I give blessings to my boys and ask that my parents give their blessing."]

Later, with the sweet smell of champagne still in the air, as Maraniss reported, ". . . Clemente on a bench in the dressing room, surrounded by reporters, let it out one more time, a stream-of-consciousness monologue that fluctuated between pride and fury and grace. "Now people in the whole world know the way I play...."

A reporter turned to Manny Sanguillen, Clemente's best friend on the team, and said, "He's going pretty good, eh?"

Sanguillen replied, "Everything he is saying is true, you know. It's strange that he would have to remind people. Everyone should know it."

49 DUSTY RHODES: A LESS-THAN-COLOSSAL BLAST

Leo Durocher wasn't known as "Leo the Lip" because he relied on nuance.

In a more than 50-year career, he managed the Brooklyn Dodgers, New York Giants, Chicago Cubs, and Houston Astros. He played with Babe Ruth, Lou Gehrig, and the St. Louis "Gashouse Gang." He was in the third-base coaching box when the New York Giants Bobby Thomson hit "The Shot Heard 'Round the World."

He argued with umpires, players, management, and the commissioner of baseball. Marrying and divorcing four times, he ended up in big trouble with the Catholic Church, which believed he was corrupting the youth of Brooklyn. He had opinions on everything, which he usually said loudly and with a peppering of expletives.

Leo Durocher was inducted into the Hall Fame in 1994, mostly for winning 2,008 games as a big-league manager. But he'd also spent 17 years as a shortstop, always scrappy and combative.

As a rookie in 1928 with the Yankees, he nudged a runner trying to beat out a triple.

The runner was Ty Cobb.

"If you ever pull a stunt like that again," Cobb, one of the best and most notorious players in history, shrieked, "I'll cut off your legs."

Durocher replied, "Go home, grandpa! You're gonna get hurt playing at your age. You've gotten away with murder all these years, but you are through. You'll get a hip from me any time you come down my way, and if you try and cut me, you'll get a ball rammed down your throat!"

That summer, Cobb was forty-one, Durocher twenty-three.

Everywhere he went, Leo the Lip was as blunt as the business end of a hammer. He was no different when he sat down to write his 1975 memoir, *Nice Guys Finish Last.*

"[Dusty] was the kind of buffoon who kept a club confident and happy," Durocher wrote of Dusty Rhodes, the unlikely hero of the 1954 World Series. "Between Willie Mays and Dusty Rhodes there was nothing but laughter in our clubhouse all season. Pressure? They spit at it."

Durocher won two rings as a player, with the 1928 Yankees and the 1934 Cardinals, but didn't capture his first World Series as a manager until the New York Giants in 1954.

A big reason why the heavily underdog Giants beat the Cleveland Indians, who had won 111 games (out of 154), was the clutch hitting of Dusty Rhodes.

The Indians had a starting rotation including three Hall of Famers: Bob Feller, Bob Lemon, Early Wynn, and also Mike Garcia, who was 19–8 with a 2.64 ERA.

In Game One of the '54 Series, Willie Mays made that spectacular catch of Vic Wertz's shot to the deepest part of the Polo Grounds' cavernous center field.

The catch in the eighth saved two runs, at least.

But in the bottom of the 10th, the score tied, 2–2, with two men on, Durocher barked, "Dusty, get a bat."

Durocher was a manager who always played hunches. He wanted Rhodes to pinch-hit for his buddy Monte Irvin, a right-handed hitter.

Lemon, who won 20 games six times and 207 in his career, was still pitching for the Indians.

Rhodes hit .341 with 15 home runs as a part-time outfielder for the Giants in '54.

The left-handed hitter had 15 pinch hits that summer. He was also a terrible outfielder, maybe the worst Durocher had ever seen.

"I ain't much of a fielder and I got a pretty lousy arm, but I sure love to whack at that ball," Rhodes told a reporter from the *New York World-Telegram and Sun* in 1954.

And whack he did. His left-handed stroke was made for the short fence at the Polo Grounds.

Facing Lemon, Rhodes hit a fly ball to right. Cleveland right fielder Dave Pope kept drifting back and back. He leaped at the wall, but the ball landed in the first row.

While the ball Mays caught was more than 420 feet from home, Rhodes's hit barely traveled 280 feet, just inside the foul pole. But it was far enough, and the Giants won, and Dusty was hailed in New York newspapers as the "Colossus of Rhodes."

Years later, Bob Feller dismissed Mays's great play, in which he caught the ball with his back to the plate, twirled and threw to hold runners from tagging up and scoring, as something most center fielders would have done. He called Rhodes's homer "a pop-up."

The next day, Rhodes pinch-hit in the fifth and delivered a single to tie the score. He stayed in the game and, in the seventh, hit a homer off Wynn. The Giants won, 3–1.

In Game Three, in Cleveland, Rhodes delivered a two-run pinch-hit single off Garcia in a 6–2 Giants win.

Rhodes didn't play in Game Four, the result of another Durocher hunch.

"It's just as well," Rhodes said years later to a reporter. "After the third game, I was drinking to everybody's health so much that I about ruined mine."

Rhodes finished the Series with four hits in six at-bats, two homers off future Hall of Famers, and seven RBIs.

Earlier in '54, Durocher tried to have him traded.

"I decided Rhodes couldn't run or field a ball and I decided I didn't want him around," Durocher admitted after the Series. "Get rid of him. He can't do nothing. He convinced me now how wrong I was."

Rhodes had come to the big leagues in 1952 as a hard-living country boy from segregated Alabama. He hit eight home runs in his first 11 days as a Giant.

In those wary early days of baseball integration, Rhodes was also friends with black players. He, Mays, and Irvin ended up lifelong pals.

Rhodes's major-league career was over in 1959, when he was thirty-two. He finished with a career .253 average and 54 home runs, and went on to play three more years in the Pacific Coast League.

When he was asked why his big-league career lasted only seven years, Rhodes said that when Durocher left the Giants in 1955 to become a television commentator, "baseball wasn't fun anymore."

Ten years after his historic fall, Rhodes was working as a Pinkerton guard at the 1964 World's Fair in New York City. The previous year he had been mugged in the New York subway. The thief got away with his 1954 World Series ring.

A pal hired Rhodes, who lived on Staten Island, as a steerer, a deckman, and a cook on tugboats.

He loved the work.

"He never had a bad word to say about anybody," his daughter, Helane Rhodes, told the *New York Times* after Rhodes's death in 2009 at age eighty-two.

"No? Not even about Durocher?" Bruce Weber of the *Times* asked.

"Well, he'd call him an S.O.B," his daughter conceded. "But then he'd laugh."

48 GABBY HARTNETT: THE HOMER IN THE GLOAMIN'

Mace Brown was a fine relief pitcher.

Actually, he was one of the early specialists in the role.

In 1938, Brown led the Pittsburgh Pirates in wins with 15. They all came out of the pen. He was the first relief pitcher ever selected to an All-Star Game.

The right-hander, who threw the javelin while on a track scholarship at the University of Iowa, was called upon on September 28, 1938, against the Chicago Cubs at Wrigley Field.

The score was tied, 5–5, in the bottom of the ninth. It was getting dark. Too dark to play. The umpires decided that if the Cubs didn't score, the game would be replayed the following day. The Pirates, who led the National League for much of the season, were clinging to a half-game lead over the charging Cubs, who were in the midst of a 10-game winning streak.

Brown easily retired the first two Cub hitters in the ninth. Then came Gabby Hartnett, the Cubs player-manager. A future Hall of Famer considered the Johnny Bench of his time, Hartnett was thirty-seven and had led a full baseball life.

He was the National League Most Valuable Player in 1935. He was the first major-league catcher to hit more than 20 home runs in a season, which he accomplished in 1924. He slugged 37 homers in the 1930 season and batted .344 in 1935. He also regularly led National League catchers in fielding and caught-stealing percentage. When Hartnett retired after the 1941 season, he owned the records for homers, RBIs, and games played by a catcher. He was elected to the Hall of Fame in 1955, the same year as Joe DiMaggio.

Gabby Hartnett was thirty-seven in the summer of 1938, as the Cubs looked to be out of contention. They were 5½ back on July 20, when team owner Philip Wrigley fired manager Charlie Grimm and named Hartnett the skipper.

The climb from third to first place took more than two months. Hartnett did more managing than catching. But there it was, within grasp, with Gabby Hartnett at the plate on that late September day in 1938. Mace Brown was using the gathering darkness to his advantage. He got two quick strikes, both curveballs, on Hartnett.

"When he was swinging at one of them, he just looked like a schoolboy," Brown told Bob Cairns, who wrote the 1992 book *Pen Men*, which is about men who spend their careers in relief of other pitchers. "And I said to myself, 'I'll just throw him a better one and strike him out.' Well, I just made a lousy pitch. He hit it to left center up into the seats. I didn't follow it into the darkness. I knew it was gone."

So did Gabby.

"I swung with everything I had, and then I got that feeling, the kind of feeling you get when the blood rushes out of your head and you get dizzy," he recalled years later to a friend. "A lot of people have told me they didn't know the ball was in the bleachers. Well, I did. Maybe I was the only one in the park who did. I knew the moment I hit it."

Soon enough, hundreds of the 35,000 in attendance knew, too, and tried to join Gabby, who was joyously circling the bases in the twilight.

The "Homer in the Gloamin'" is the most important home run in Cubs history. The expression was a play on the popular song "Roamin' in the Gloamin'."

"I don't think I saw third base," Gabby later said. "And I don't think I walked a step to the plate—I was carried in."

47 BILL SKOWRON: VINDICATION FOR MOOSE

It really bothered Moose Skowron.

He was that kind of guy: eager to please, sensitive, a terrific teammate, friend, and so often, clutch, especially in the biggest of games.

He hated making the last out of the 1957 World Series. The thought haunted him. Skowron's given name was William. Some people called him Bill, but most, "Moose."

It wasn't that at 5-foot-11 and 200 pounds he was the biggest of the big, or that he wore a permanent scowl. It had to do with his grandfather giving him a haircut when Moose, born in Chicago in 1930, was eight.

"He shaved off all of my hair," Moose told author John Tullius for the 1987 history *I'd Rather Be a Yankee*. "I was completely bald. When I got outside, all the older fellows around the neighborhood started calling me Mussolini. At the time he [Benito Mussolini] was the dictator of Italy. So after that, in grammar school, high school and college, everybody called me 'Moose.'"

Moose was the son of a sanitation worker. He earned a football scholarship to Purdue to play fullback and punt, but decided baseball was his future. He was signed by the Yankees in 1950 as an outfielder, but had trouble going back on fly balls. Moose, who made his big-league debut in 1954, was converted to first base. He would take off-season dance lessons to help with his footwork around first. He also said those lessons helped his social life.

Early in his big-league career, he battled a variety of injuries and had to put up with Yankees manager Casey Stengel's platoon system. The right-handed slugger shared first base with left-handed hitter Joe Collins, but by 1957 Moose was getting more and more playing time there. He even made his first of six All-Star teams that year, and finished the regular season with 17 homers, 88 RBIs, and a .304 average.

"If Moose had played with [a team other than the Yankees] in his prime and batted fourth, where he should have been, instead of fifth or sixth, he'd be in the Hall of Fame," his former teammate Tony Kubek told Marty Noble of *Newsday*.

In the bottom of the ninth in the seventh game of the '57 World Series, the Yankees were trailing the Milwaukee Braves, 5–0. Lew Burdette, a former Yankee prospect who would go on to win more than 200 games in his career, had silenced his old team again that October afternoon at the original Stadium. The Yankees managed to cobble together three singles to load the bases with two outs.

Up stepped Moose.

The previous year, he had socked a seventh-inning grand slam off the Dodgers, draining the drama from Game Seven of that World Series.

"Moose could flat-out hit . . . for average, and he had real power," Mickey Mantle once said. "People used to look at our lineup and concentrate on the guys in the middle of the order. Moose might have been batting sixth or seventh, but he made our lineup deep and more dangerous. You didn't want to give him too much around the plate. He was like Yogi [Berra], he could hit bad pitches out and beat you."

Moose hadn't started Game Seven, but came in as a pinch-hitter. He was 0-for-2. Burdette was about to throw his third complete game at the Yankees. His ERA in the Series was 0.67. But Moose scalded one down the third-base line. Off the bat it looked like a bases-clearing double that would give the Yankees a chance with the top of the order coming up.

But it wasn't a double.

Braves Hall of Fame third baseman Eddie Mathews backhanded it and beat Jerry Coleman, the runner at second, to the bag. The World Series belonged to the underdog Braves.

Moose had a hard time forgiving himself for making the last out of the World Series.

In 1958, he hit 14 homers, with 73 RBIs and a .273 batting average, as the Yankees returned to the World Series against the Braves, who took a three-game-to-one lead. It was Moose who knocked in the game-winning run in the 10th inning of Game Six with a single to knot the Series.

In Game Seven, the score was tied, 2–2, through seven.

In the top of the eighth, Berra started a two-out rally with a double and scored the go-ahead run on Elston Howard's single. Two batters later, 364 days after making the last out in the 1957 World Series, up stepped Moose, who rocketed a three-run homer to left off Burdette. Making his way around the bases before a silenced Milwaukee crowd, Moose felt vindicated.

He would play on two more Yankee world championship teams, in 1961 and 1962. Then the Yankees would trade Moose to the Los Angeles Dodgers to make way for Joe Pepitone.

The Dodgers played the Yankees in the 1963 Series, winning it in four games. Moose hit .385 against his old team.

"I was miserable," he admitted years later. "Twelve years I was with New York, three in the minors, nine in the majors. I loved those guys and it killed me to beat them. My uniform might have said Los Angeles, but in my heart I was always a Yankee."

It was Moose's fifth World Series ring.

In 39 games over eight World Series, he hit .293 with eight homers (the same as Hall of Famers Joe DiMaggio and Frank Robinson) and 29 RBIs. In All-Star Games he batted a robust .429.

Moose slugged 211 career homers with a lifetime average of .282. His best year was 1960, when he knocked in 91 runs with 26 home runs. He hit 28 homers in 1961, the year teammates Roger Maris slugged 61 and Mantle whacked 54.

Though Moose had power, the original Yankee Stadium wasn't a friendly place for a right-handed slugger. Only 60 of the 165 homers he hit while a Yankee were at the Stadium.

Moose also seemed to be everybody's favorite teammate. There was no prank you couldn't pull on him. But he was also the kind of man who would never cuss around Yankee second baseman Bobby Richardson, a devout Christian.

He was also the kind of teammate who would be asked by Mickey Mantle's family to be a pallbearer at The Mick's funeral, in 1995.

He once had to explain to his grandmother that a crowd wasn't booing him, but screaming "Mooooooooose" with affection.

"She was so relieved," he noted.

46 DEREK JETER: WITH A LITTLE HELP FROM A FAN

Game One of the 1996 American League Championship Series between the Baltimore Orioles and New York Yankees was rained out on October 8 and rescheduled for the following afternoon—lucky for twelve-year-old Jeffrey Maier of Old Tappan, New Jersey, and, as it turned out, Derek Jeter.

Family friends of Maier who were Oriole fans gave him a ticket as a present, perfect for the boy who one week earlier had a Yankees/World Series-themed bar mitzvah party and who loved rookie shortstop Derek Jeter. His mother had called the principal at Charles De Wolf Middle School to ask that he be excused from last period. Maier, of course, brought to the game his glove, a black Mizuno. He wore his favorite T-shirt, an Emmitt Smith model that read "E=TD2."

And he held two wishes for the afternoon:

1. That the Yankees win.
2. That he catch the ultimate souvenir, a game-used ball.

The tickets were in right field, Section 31, Box 325 in the old stadium. It would be a short scamper down a few steps to the right field wall. And Maier, a center fielder and pitcher, was the best player on his little league team. He knew the game.

Jeter, twenty-two, was batting ninth that afternoon. He'd had a Rookie of the Year season—.314 average, 10 homers, 78 RBIs. But seven months earlier, Jeter was having a rough spring. Then Yankee infielders Tony Fernandez and Pat Kelly went down with injuries.

Team owner George Steinbrenner got nervous. He felt the Yankees needed a veteran shortstop if Jeter wasn't the real deal. The Seattle Mariners had offered veteran Felix Fermin. He'd been the Mariners starting shortstop when they'd beaten the Yankees in the 1995 American League Division Series, but he was now expendable. The Mariners had the up-and-coming shortstop Alex Rodriguez in the wings.

In exchange for Fermin, the Mariners wanted one of two relief pitchers, either Bob Wickman or Mariano Rivera.

"One of those two guys for Felix Fermin, and The Boss [as Steinbrenner was known] was honestly considering it and forced us to have some serious conversations about it," Yankee general manager Brian Cashman, then an assistant, said years later. "It was a fight to convince The Boss to stand down and not force us to do a deal none of us were recommending. And it wasn't because we knew what we had in Mo or Wickman, it was we had committed to go with young Jeter. Thankfully, we didn't do that deal. That was as close as we ever came to trading Mariano."

But no one was thinking of all that when Jeter came to bat in the bottom of the eighth in the ALCS game, the Yankees trailing, 4–3.

On the mound was the hard-throwing Oriole reliever Armando Benitez. The right-hander was only twenty-three. In 14⅓ regular season innings, he'd recorded 20 strikeouts.

Jeter already had two infield hits and a stolen base in the game. There was one out.

Benitez fired a 95-mile-per-hour fastball a tad outside, but Jeter reached out and lofted it deep to right. Deep enough that Yankee fans rose from their seats.

Baltimore right fielder Tony Tarasco, replacing Bobby Bonilla, who had banged into the wall and hurt his left shoulder an inning earlier, tracked the ball to the warning track, then the wall in front of the Nobody Beats the Wiz sign.

Jeffrey Maier was already on the other side of the wall. His father had told him Jeter tended to go to right against hard-throwing righties, and he'd listened to his father.

As the ball came closer, Maier leaned, his black glove extended. The ball bounced into it, and out. His only memory of the moment: "Being on the bottom of a large pileup in search of the ball."

Tarasco said, "It was a magic trick because the ball just disappeared out of midair."

Veteran American League umpire Richie Garcia called the hit a home run. Jeter ran the bases, touching them all, tying the score.

Yankee fans went crazy, the Orioles crazier in a different way.

Benitez ran from the mound to right field to argue with Garcia. Oriole manager Davey Johnson was ejected from the game for telling Garcia once too often there was fan interference.

"The way I saw it," Garcia said after the game, "I thought the ball was going out of the ballpark. I really don't feel he [Tarasco] was going to catch the ball, I don't think he could have caught that ball."

When Garcia saw the television replay, he did second-guess himself—to a degree.

"After looking at it, no, obviously," he said when asked if he still believed it was a home run. "I saw the fan reach out. The fan did not reach down. He reached out which in my judgment he did not interfere with the guy catching the ball."

Tarasco disagreed.

"To me, it was a routine fly ball," he said. "It just happened to be at the track. It was obvious. I was camped underneath it. It wasn't a line drive, it wasn't a blast out of the park. I had plenty of time to get over there."

The Yankees would win the game on a Bernie Williams home run in the 11th inning and beat the Orioles in five games. They'd go on to win the first of their four World Series in the next five years. Jeffrey Maier would go on to be a kind of baseball celebrity.

He also went on to play baseball at Wesleyan University in Middletown, Connecticut, where the left-handed-hitting third baseman set the school record for most hits in a career: 189.

As Joe Lapointe wrote in a 2006 profile of Maier in *The New York Times*, "For the second time in his life, Maier had made baseball history."

As a government major with a minor in economics, Maier produced a 3.4 grade point average and was awarded the Walter MacNaughten Memorial Award, first presented by the Class of 1900 in recognition of Outstanding Baseball Achievement.

Maier wrote his senior independent study project about the westward migration of baseball teams in the 1950s.

He also appeared in a student film about an Orioles fan. The title: *I Hate Jeffrey Maier.*

He worked as a researcher for Hall of Fame baseball writer Peter Gammons. He also worked at a baseball camp where Tarasco was a guest instructor.

"While anxious at first, Tony and I shared a nice conversation," Maier said. "He made it clear to me that he did not begrudge a young boy for wanting to catch a ball at a game."

Maier even played in the New England Collegiate League, for former Boston Red Sox general manager Dan Duquette's Pittsfield Dukes. There were rumors the Orioles were going to draft the 5-foot-11, 190-pound infielder. The Yankees worked him out. But he ended up becoming a salesman.

Maier married a Red Sox fan. He's now a father.

He's met Jeter just once, at a 1997 baseball card show in New Jersey.

Maier and his father had a private meeting with the Yankee shortstop. Jeter was gracious.

"I was thirteen years old and he signed a ball for me and took some pictures," Maier recalled. "He was a really nice guy. He and my father exchanged some banter. He called my father, 'Sir.' I was just so awestruck at being in front of my sports icon and my sports idol that I just couldn't come up with the words to get much more out. He's also 6-foot-3 and a hell of a lot bigger in person than he seems on TV. I was sort of overwhelmed with his sheer size as well."

Did they talk about the home run?

Yes.

Of course.

A little bit, Maier said.

45 MICKEY MANTLE: THE MICK'S LONGEST CLOUT

Journalist-author Jane Leavy sets the scene better than anyone:

> Standing in the capacious outfield at Washington, D.C.'s, Griffith Stadium during batting practice, Irv Noren glanced at the Mr. Boh sign atop the football scoreboard in left field and told Mantle: "Geez, you might be able to hit one out of here today."
>
> Noren knew all about the stadium's prevailing winds, when the ballpark held the heat and when the breeze blew through the open grandstands. He knew where the ball carried and where it had never gone before. He had played two years for the Senators before being traded to New York in May 1952 as insurance against Mantle's infirm right knee. . . .
>
> He also knew that no one in major league history had ever hit a ball over the thirty-two rows of poured-concrete bleachers erected in left field just in time for the 1924 World Series, the only one the Nats ever won. Noren thought that Mantle might be the man to do it and this might be the day. "I played there two years. I knew the ballpark pretty good. The wind was blowing out a little—not a gale. And I always thought he had more power right-handed."

It was April 17, 1953, a Friday. The skies were gray. The Yankees were coming off their fourth straight world championship.

Mantle had played well enough in the 1952 World Series against the Brooklyn Dodgers, hitting .345 with two home runs and knocking in the winning run in Game Seven, that Brooklyn general manager Branch Rickey said, "That young man's arms and legs and wind are young, but his head is old. Mantle has a chance to make us forget every ballplayer we ever saw."

And Mantle was only twenty-one.

He was also a father for the first time. Mickey Jr., had been born on April 12.

Almost a year earlier, the Yankees had traded Jackie Jensen, a prized right-handed-hitting prospect, to the Senators for Noren, who swung from the left.

On May 6, four days after that deal, Mantle's father, Mutt, died. Mickey never got over his father's death.

In 1953, the weather wasn't helping the season unfold. Rain and chilly temperatures were overstaying their welcome as 4,206 fans settled in at Griffith Stadium. The Yankees led the Senators, 2–1, in the fifth inning.

Mantle had walked in the second and grounded out in the third.

With two outs and nobody on, lefty starter Chuck Stobbs walked Yogi Berra.

Mantle dug in.

Stobbs had broken into the big leagues with the Boston Red Sox as an eighteen-year-old in 1947. He would lead the American League in losses in 1957, but finished his career with 107 wins, most of those with lousy teams. He didn't throw hard, but he had craft. He retired after the 1961 season to a coaching career at George Washington University, where, according to Leavy's 2010 book *The Last Boy: Mickey Mantle and the End of America's Childhood,* he preached to pitchers, "No two-out walks."

In 1952, Mantle had slugged a grand slam off Stobbs, then pitching for the Chicago White Sox. In 106 career at-bats against Stobbs, Mantle would hit eight dingers.

This was Stobbs's first start as a Senator.

In the fifth inning of that gray April 1953 afternoon in Washington, Mantle took ball one. He was batting cleanup and using a bat he borrowed from teammate Loren Babe, a spare third baseman and future big-league coach. Babe had two career big-league home runs.

Leavy writes that the Mick's teammate, backup shortstop Jim Brideweser, turned to pitching coach Jim Turner and blurted, "You know, I bet this kid could hit that big scoreboard."

Turner said, "Nobody could do that."

Griffith Stadium was a pitcher's paradise—most of the time. The left field foul pole was 405 feet from the plate. Sixty-five feet beyond that stood a gigantic sign for National Bohemian Beer that featured a one-eyed man with a mustache. He was dubbed "Mr. Boh" by locals.

Mantle recalled Stobbs "had a nice, easy overhand motion. . . . He threw hard but not too hard. He also had good control. He was always around the plate."

On Stobbs's second pitch of the at-bat, Mantle powered the fastball over the left-center-field fence. The ball whistled by the 55-foot-high Mr. Boh sign, nicking the mustache as it sailed past.

Ralph Houk, then a backup catcher sitting in the bullpen, said he kept waiting for the ball to come down. He wasn't alone.

As usual, Mantle jogged around the bases with his head down—he never liked showing up pitchers.

It was Mantle's first homer of the season, the 37th of his career.

By his retirement after the 1968 season, Mantle had hit 536 dingers. Hall of Fame right-hander Early Wynn surrendered the most homers to Mantle—13.

Red Patterson, the Yankees public relations man, thought he had just seen history.

While Mantle was running the bases, Patterson was trying to get the ball and measure how far it traveled. A former sportswriter with the *New York Herald Tribune*, he was present in 1939 when Lou Gehrig ended his consecutive-game streak. Patterson also came up with the idea of an Old-Timers' Game in 1949.

He said he measured Mickey Mantle's clout by his feet.

"I walked 66 feet from the 391 mark to the back where Mantle's ball cleared the bleacher limit," he said. "That would be 457 feet. Now I paced off 36 strides . . . or 108 feet to where the ball eventually landed in the backyard on Oakdale St. It's a small backyard so the ball didn't have a chance to bounce much. So add them all up it's 565 feet."

The author Leavy (who located the Donald Dunaway who found the ball that day when he was 10) and science have debunked how far the ball actually traveled, saying it landed 512 feet from home plate.

Mantle never cared.

But 565 feet—the first tape-measure homer—was written into the baseball lexicon. Every dinger since has been measured by it.

By the ninth inning, Stobbs was out of the game. In was Julio Moreno, a right-hander. Mantle turned around and batted left. He dragged a bunt and beat it out for a single.

After all, he was, when it was all said and done, Mickey Mantle.

And the Yankees, as they so often did in the 1950s, won the game, 7–3.

44 MEL OTT: SMALL MAN WITH A BIG BAT

Fritz Schulte went back and back on Mel Ott's long fly ball to center.

Schulte had tied Game Five of the 1933 World Series with a three-run dinger for the Washington Senators in the home half of the sixth; now he was trying to stop Ott, the twenty-four-year-old left-handed slugger with the distinctive leg kick stance, from putting the New York Giants ahead in the top of the 10th.

Schulte leaped at the makeshift bleacher wall, got a glove on the ball, but his momentum took him into the crowd at Washington's Griffith Stadium.

There was a pause.

Was it a double or a home run? Mel Ott rounded second and stopped.

Umpires George Moriarty and Charlie Moran talked it over. Moriarty signaled a home run, and Ott, who hit .389 in the Series, picked up his trot and came home.

His homer ended up deciding the 1933 World Series, the Giants first Series win in 11 years. And it was just another big hit in Mel Ott's often unsung career.

"Master Melvin," as he was called, led the National League in home runs six times. He finished second seven times. He was the youngest player in baseball history to reach both 100 and 200 dingers. He was also the first player in National League history to reach 300-, 400-, and 500-homer plateaus. He passed Rogers Hornsby to become the all-time National League home run leader in 1937. It took until 1966, when Willie Mays hit his 512th, for Ott's record to fall.

In each of 15 seasons, Ott slugged more than 20 homers. He led his team in home runs 18 times.

When he was elected into the Hall of Fame in 1951, he received 87 percent of the vote, the most since the first Hall of Fame class in 1936.

"I never knew a baseball player who was so universally loved," Leo Durocher, not known for throwing compliments in an opponent's direction, said. "Why, even when he was playing against [us] he would be cheered here, and there are no more rabid fans than in Brooklyn." (It was Durocher who was reputed to have said in 1946, "Nice guys finish last," referring to a Giants team Ott was managing. Ironically, Durocher ended up replacing Ott as manager of the Giants in 1948.)

Born in Gretna, Louisiana, on March 2, 1909, Ott had uncles who played baseball. His first position was catcher. He could always hit. The New Orleans Pelicans of the Southern Association thought him too small to play pro ball (he was 5-foot-9, and never weighed more than 170 pounds) when he was playing for a semi-pro team 90 miles from home. The team owner wrote to New York Giants manager John McGraw about Ott's hitting ability.

McGraw listened. Ott tried out for the Giants in September of 1925.

As Giants second baseman Frankie Frisch described it, "Mel stepped into [the] first few pitches and smashed them solidly through the infield. Then he hit several deep into the outfield, and finally he parked a number of fastballs and curves high against the advertising signs on the right field wall."

McGraw was impressed with the batting practice display.

"He's got the most natural swing I've seen in years," McGraw said. "This lad is going to be one of the greatest lefthand hitters the National League has seen."

Ott was sixteen.

McGraw decided the kid was going to play the outfield, not catch. He kept him away from the veterans who liked to play hard off the field. He didn't change Ott's swing.

Ott's stance, though, was different. He dropped his hands and lifted his right foot while the ball approached.

McGraw said, "He's like a golfer; his body moves, but he keeps his head still with his eyes fixed on the ball."

Ott was the Giants starting right fielder in 1928. He was nineteen. His breakout season came the following year. Ott's 42 homers and 151 RBIs are the most ever for a teenager playing in the major leagues. While the Polo Grounds, the Giants home, helped Ott with a wall only 257 feet down the right field line, he also proved to be a dangerous hitter on the road that year, with 22 home runs.

He would slug 323 of his career homers at the Polo Grounds and was a lifetime .304 hitter. His batting average at home was .311; on the road it was .297.

In homage to his power, pitchers worked around him. In each of four seasons, Ott walked 100 times, and walked five times in three separate games.

Ott was also an excellent right fielder, considered the best of his time, learning to play the caroms off the Polo Grounds' right field wall. In 1929, with his catcher's arm in the outfield, he threw out 26 baserunners and was part of 12 double plays.

Quiet and unassuming, with a love of crosswords and gin rummy, Ott never stopped hitting in the 1930s, helping the Giants back to two more World Series with his pitching buddy and all-time great, Carl Hubbell, known for throwing the screwball.

The Giants lost both matchups with the New York Yankees in the Series, but Ott had seven hits and a homer in 1936 and four hits and a dinger in 1937.

One of Ott's best seasons was in 1938. He led the league in home runs for the third straight year, along with knocking in 116 runs and batting .311. He also split his time between right field and third base.

The Giants, who had fallen on hard times in the late 1930s and early '40s, named Ott player-manager on December 2, 1941. Five days later, the attack on Pearl Harbor occurred.

Ott was given a lot of credit for piloting the Giants to third place in 1942. In his 18th season as a player, Ott, who never won a Most Valuable Player Award, led the league in homers with 30.

But the following year, when World War II started changing baseball dramatically, Ott had his worst season, with a .234 average and stomach woes from worrying about his club.

The Giants stuck with him. The team improved and so did he. In 1944, at age thirty-five, he was second in the NL in homers and third in slugging percentage.

On August 1, 1945, he became the third player to hit 500 home runs. His batting average on Labor Day was .320. He finished the season at .308, with 21 homers and 79 RBIs.

Ott hit his last home run, number 511, on Opening Day of 1946. In the next game, he injured his knee trying to make a catch in right field. He was never the same player again. He only had four at-bats in 1947.

Still, his 511 homers were 210 more than the man in second place in NL history at that time, Hall of Famer Rogers Hornsby.

On July 16, 1948, Ott resigned as Giants manager, and longtime Brooklyn Dodgers manager Leo Durocher took over the team, shocking the baseball world. Ott would go on to work with Hubbell in the Giants farm system.

Then he managed in the minors before working as an analyst with the Detroit Tigers.

He died in 1958 at the age of forty-nine as a result of injuries suffered in an automobile accident in his native Louisiana.

He'd become a character in the 1989 baseball film *Field of Dreams.* The U.S. Postal Service would recognize him with a stamp in 1996.

Arnold Hano, who wrote for *Sports Illustrated* and *SPORT* magazine, typed this after Ott's death: "When he died, he held fourteen baseball records, a little man with a bashful smile and a silken swing, baseball's legendary nice guy. His death was the worst that could have happened to baseball, but his playing career had been the best."

43 HOME RUN BAKER: LIVE BAT IN DEADBALL ERA

His given name was John Franklin Baker.

He was a sixth-generation farm boy from Maryland, his mother a distant relation of Confederate General Robert E. Lee.

He batted left and threw right. He was a shade under six feet tall and weighed no more than 170 pounds. He never smoked, drank, or swore. But he swung a big bat—52 ounces—and was known for most of his life as Home Run Baker.

He would lead the American League in home runs four straight years, but never would slug more than a dozen in a season. He reached double digits in home runs only three times. He had only 96 in his career. But he was considered one of the great power hitters of his time. Walter Johnson, the Hall of Fame pitcher for the Washington Senators, went so far as to say Baker was "the most dangerous hitter I ever faced."

He earned the nickname "Home Run" by hitting home runs on consecutive days, off of two Hall of Famers in the 1911 World Series, against the mighty New York Giants. The original home run king would later be a teammate of Babe Ruth.

Jack Dunn, a former big-league pitcher who owned the minor-league Baltimore Orioles, best known for developing Ruth, saw Baker play early in the twentieth century and said he "could not hit."

Hall of Fame manager Connie Mack of the Philadelphia Athletics thought differently and signed Baker, then twenty-two, in 1908.

The dividends were paid early. Baker hit the first home run at Philadelphia's Shibe Park.

Home runs were rare in the Deadball Era, when pitchers could load up the ball with anything they pleased (like tobacco juice or spit) and could also scuff it. Fences appeared to be a cab ride away. The same balls were used game after game, the life knocked out of them.

Baker finished the 1909 season with four homers, led the team with 19 triples, and batted .305. He also played sterling defense at third base, joining an infield that featured Stuffy McInnis at first, Eddie Collins at second, and Jack Barry at short. The Athletics improved by 27 games in 1909 and finished second in the American League.

The foursome were dubbed "The One Hundred Thousand Dollar Infield" because of their purported market value, and helped the Athletics win four American League Championships in five years—from 1910 through 1914—and three World Series titles.

Baseball historian Bill James wrote that the 1914 version was the best infield in baseball history, while the 1912 and 1913 infields were in the top five.

Baker was a mainstay of the team in 1910, when the Athletics captured the American League pennant and the club's first World Series championship. He hit .409 in the Series against the Chicago Cubs.

He had his breakout season in 1911, leading the American League in home runs with 11 and producing a .344 average. Home Run Baker powered the Athletics back to the World Series.

It didn't hurt that the Athletics also had a pitching staff of Jack Coombs (28–12), Eddie Plank (23–8), and Charles "Chief" Bender (17–5), in a rematch of the 1905 World Series with the Giants.

Smart, tough, and ruthless John McGraw, someone who used every tool at his disposal, managed the Giants. One tool was intimidation, and he used it on Home Run Baker.

Two years earlier, Detroit's Ty Cobb, one of the game's great heroes and villains, had spiked Baker in the arm while sliding into third. Baker called the spike deliberate. The play caused an uproar.

Mack accused Cobb of being "the dirtiest player he'd ever seen" while a sportswriter for the *Detroit Free Press* mocked Baker as a "soft-fleshed darling."

The Giants wanted to exploit that soft-fleshed darling.

In Game One, a 2–1 Giants win, center fielder Fred Snodgrass, who would become infamous the following year for missing a routine fly ball in the Series, spiked Baker while sliding into third. Snodgrass was originally called out, but then the umpire noticed the dislodged ball rolling away. Baker stayed in the game, but his left arm needed bandaging.

In Game Two, with Collins on second and two outs in the sixth inning of a 1–1 game, up came Baker.

Giants starter Rube Marquard had struck out the slugger on three pitches in the first inning and then enticed a weak grounder to second from him in the fourth. This time, Baker launched a long drive to right. The homer at Shibe Park was only the 10th in World Series history.

After Baker accepted congratulations from teammates for the homer he would call the highlight of his career—hats, gloves, and team sweaters were tossed in the air—he walked to the end of the bench for a drink of water.

The next day, the mighty Christy Mathewson was on the hill for the Giants, nursing a 1–0 lead in the ninth. Baker, who was 0-for-3 and had two strikes on him, homered to tie the game. It was only the second run Mathewson had surrendered in his last 46 World Series innings.

In the 10th inning, Snodgrass, who had 51 steals in the regular season, tried to spike Baker again while attempting to swipe third. But Baker held on to the ball. The Athletics would win Game Three in 11 innings, 3–2, with Baker singling and later coming home with the deciding run.

Six days of rain began, and all the Philadelphia newspapers could write about were the exploits of John "Home Run" Baker.

The Athletics would win the Series in six games. Home Run Baker finished the Series with a .375 average.

In 1912, he would lead the AL in home runs and RBIs. He did the same in 1913 en route to another World Series championship. The Athletics beat the Giants again that year. Baker led the way with a .450 average and a homer and seven RBIs in five games.

Despite a bout with pleurisy in 1914, Baker topped the AL in home runs, with nine, for a fourth straight season, but the Athletics lost to the Miracle Boston Braves in the World Series.

Then Connie Mack started breaking up the Athletics, selling off much of his lineup. Home Run Baker, twenty-nine, sat out the 1915 season because Mack wouldn't renegotiate his contract

American League president Ban Johnson convinced Mack to sell Baker to the New York Yankees.

In New York, Baker and first baseman Wally Pipp provided the beating heart of the lineup.

Pipp, who would be famously replaced by Lou Gehrig in 1924, led the American League in homers in 1916 with 12; Baker was second with 10. Three years later, the Yankees topped the league in home runs with 45.

Robert Ripley, a cartoonist for the *New York Globe*, came up with the term "Murderers' Row" to describe the middle of the Yankees lineup, referring to Baker, Pipp, Roger Peckinpaugh, and Ping Bodie (the Yankees wouldn't buy Babe Ruth from the Boston Red Sox until January 5, 1920).

Baker's wife died in the off-season, and he didn't play in '20 due to grief, but returned to baseball and the Yankees in 1921 and 1922, playing on the first Yankees teams to go to the World Series.

At first, Home Run Baker wasn't impressed by Ruth's power.

He complained about the "rabbit ball," noting the baseball being used in the American League traveled much farther than the ones used for much of his career.

But Baker changed his mind after the 1921 season.

"I hope he [Babe Ruth] lives to hit one hundred homers in a season," he told a reporter. "I wish him all the luck in the world. He has everybody else, including myself, hopelessly outclassed."

By 1925, Baker was retired as an active player and managing a team in the Class D Eastern State League. There he discovered one of the great home run hitters in history, Jimmie Foxx. He called his former manager, Connie Mack, to tell him about the kid with all this power.

By the time Foxx retired in 1945, he was only the second player to hit more than 500 home runs in a career.

Foxx, who played for the Philadelphia A's, Boston Red Sox, Chicago Cubs, and Philadelphia Phillies, was inducted into the Baseball Hall of Fame in 1951.

Four years later, the Hall welcomed Home Run Baker.

42 KEN KELTNER: HISTORIC CLOUT FROM A RENOWNED GLOVEMAN

For as long as Joe DiMaggio's 56-game hitting streak lives, so will the fact Ken Keltner helped stop it.

Twice.

Both times with backhanded stabs on balls that seemed destined for doubles that evening of July 17, 1941.

His two plays were so definitive and distinctive in halting the streak that he and his family were assigned a police escort after the game. And Keltner, the Cleveland Indians third baseman, had been playing at home that damp July evening.

Keltner, who batted and threw right-handed, was among the best defensive third basemen of the 1940s. He had soft hands and a strong arm. He led the league in assists four times, double plays five times, fielding percentage three times, and range factor twice. The Gold Glove Award hadn't been established yet, but his glovework was so good it overshadowed his hitting. And he was a fine hitter and a power threat.

In 1936, the New York Yankees had tried to acquire Keltner from his minor-league team, but the Indians won the bidding war with $25,000 and six players. As a rookie in 1938, Keltner hit 26 homers and knocked in 113 runs while batting .276.

The following year, he hit a career-high .325. He was selected to the American League All-Star team in 1940 and again in 1941.

In the '41 All-Star Game, Keltner started the key rally by beating out an infield hit, which set the stage for Ted Williams's two-out, game-ending, three-run home run that delivered a 7–5 victory to the American League.

Less than two weeks later, Keltner was stationed at third base with DiMaggio coming to the plate. DiMaggio had started his hitting streak on May 15 with a single off Chicago White Sox pitcher Eddie Smith. In the course of hitting in 56 straight games, he owned a .408 average with 15 homers and 55 RBIs.

On July 1, DiMaggio broke the previous hit record of 45 consecutive games set by Wee Willie Keeler in 1896–97. DiMaggio's streak became an American obsession, a distraction for a country on the brink of war.

"Did he get a hit?" That was the question.

Everyone knew who "he" was—Joltin' Joe, The Yankee Clipper.

That Thursday, the Cleveland Indians decided to shift the night game from their usual and smaller League Park, which held about 30,000, to Municipal Stadium, which could hold more than 70,000. Rain fell all morning but stopped by early afternoon. DiMaggio and his roommate, Lefty Gomez, decided to make their way to the park by cab. It was only a handful of blocks from their hotel, but they'd heard there were long lines at the box office and they didn't want to draw attention.

But the cabbie recognized DiMaggio.

"I've got a strange feeling in my bones that you're going to get stopped tonight," the cabbie said, looking at DiMaggio in his rearview mirror as he pulled up to the players' entrance.

If DiMaggio was bothered, he didn't say. But Gomez, who was starting that night, was angry.

In the top of the first, Cleveland southpaw Al Smith threw ball one to DiMaggio. On the next pitch, DiMaggio hit a curveball hard down the third-base line. Sportswriters thought it was going to be a double. But Keltner, playing deep and within a step of the line, backhanded it, the momentum of the play taking him into foul territory. Keltner straightened and threw the ball on a line to first baseman Oscar Grimes. DiMaggio was out by a step.

Returning to the dugout, DiMaggio knocked mud from his cleats. "Ground's still wet," he said to himself. "Footing's not the best."

In the fourth, Smith walked DiMaggio on a 3–2 pitch. The majority of the 67,468 in attendance, the largest crowd ever to see a night baseball game at that time, booed.

Batting second in the seventh, DiMaggio faced Smith again. The score was tied, 1–1. On the first pitch DiMaggio saw, he again ripped it down the third-base line. And again, Keltner backhanded the shot while hugging the foul line, straightened up, and threw DiMaggio out by a step.

Bob Feller, the Cleveland Hall of Fame pitcher, would say of Keltner, "Keltner was simply the best in the American League. He could go to his right better than anyone and had a great, great arm."

DiMaggio would have one more at-bat in the game, this time against Jim Bagby Jr., a Cleveland reliever. DiMaggio had extended the hit streak to 28 a month earlier off Bagby, with a home run.

This time, however, on a 2–1 pitch, DiMaggio hit a grounder to Cleveland shortstop Lou Boudreau, who started a 6–4–3 double play.

The Yankees won the game. In the clubhouse, DiMaggio said, "Well, that's over."

He started a 16-game hitting streak the next day.

Keltner missed the entire 1945 season because of World War II, but returned to the Indians in 1946 and was selected to his sixth All-Star team.

In 1948, Keltner, at thirty-one, had his best season, finishing third in the American League with 31 home runs, knocking in 119, and helping the Tribe to the team's first pennant since 1920.

The club featured a pitching staff with three future Hall of Famers: Bob Lemon, Bob Feller, and Satchel Paige. Gene Bearden, a rookie southpaw knuckleballer, who was awarded the Purple Heart during World War II, won 20 games in that year, too.

As great a season as Keltner had, Cleveland player-manager Lou Boudreau had a better one, batting .355 with 106 RBIs. The Indians were the first team in baseball history to draw more than two million fans.

Cleveland finished the regular season tied with the Boston Red Sox, meaning a one-game playoff would be played to determine the American League Championship.

At Boston's Fenway Park, in the do-or-die game on October 4, Keltner hit one of the most important home runs in team history.

With the score tied at 1–1 in the fourth, Boudreau singled. Joe Gordon followed with another base hit. The Red Sox were expecting a bunt to advance the runners, but Keltner launched a two-strike Denny Galehouse fastball high over the Green Monster in left to break the game open.

Keltner also had a single and double and recorded six assists, including the final out of the game, as the Indians put the Red Sox to bed for the season.

The Indians then beat the Boston Braves in six games for the World Series title.

Keltner struggled with injuries in 1949 and was traded to the Red Sox in 1950 before retiring.

During his career, Keltner made seven trips to the All-Star Game, slugged 163 homers, and batted .276.

In 1985, baseball historian Bill James created the Keltner List to evaluate the qualifications of players who have not been elected to the Hall of Fame but who deserve consideration. Among the 15 questions James included: Was he the best player on his team? Was he considered the best player at his position? Did he have an impact on multiple pennant races?

After both players had retired, Joe DiMaggio had one question for Ken Keltner: "Why were you playing me so deep and on the line?"

Keltner said something about never even thinking about DiMaggio's hitting streak. He just wanted the Indians to win. He knew DiMaggio wasn't going to bunt, and he wanted to prevent a double.

On the 50th anniversary of the streak, DiMaggio and Keltner made a few appearances together and talked about that soggy July night.

"I'm glad I'm remembered for something," Keltner said. "I didn't feel like a villain. Somebody had to do it. I'm glad he hit them to me."

41 JOHNNY BENCH: CLUTCH HR FROM GAME'S BEST CATCHER

By any definition, 1971 was a bad year for Johnny Bench.

He played hurt, of course—all catchers play hurt. It's part of the daily grind, the squatting, foul tips, collisions, and the exertion of it all. And Bench was involved in it all. His teammates called him "Little General," because he made every detail of the game his business.

Still, Cincinnati manager Sparky Anderson claimed it wasn't all the traveling on the 1970 postseason banquet merry-go-round that left Bench tired in 1971. Being a gentleman, Anderson said something like, "it was all the smiling."

When the Reds started skidding, Bench tried to hit five-run homers. Impossible, of course, though he did hit 27 dingers while knocking in only 61 runs and hitting a dismal .238. He was just trying too hard.

Cincinnati fans booed him every chance they could. It bothered the young catcher. Bench refused to tip his cap after the dingers he did manage to hit.

It was a marked contrast to the year before, when Bench had been the National League Most Valuable Player. He hit 45 home runs and knocked in 148 (a team record and the high-water mark for catchers) as the Cincinnati Reds captured the National League Western Division Championship with 102 wins.

Johnny Bench was twenty-two, the youngest MVP in National League history.

On July 26, 1970, he hit three consecutive homers off future Hall of Fame pitcher Steve Carlton, then with the Cardinals.

The Reds swept the Pirates in the National League Championship Series but bowed to the mighty Baltimore Orioles led by the Robinsons, Frank and Brooks, in five games in the World Series.

Even so, you could hear the ignition turning on what would become the Big Red Machine, a moniker cooked up by *Los Angeles Herald Examiner* writer Bob Hunter back in 1969, before it was a reality.

In 1967, there were fears in Cincinnati that the Reds, founded in 1869, were moving to San Diego unless a new stadium was built. Riverfront Stadium opened in 1970, and the Reds drew 1.8 million fans that year, a team record.

But the Reds and Bench slumped the following season. The Reds finished fifth with a less than mediocre 79–83 record. It was the only losing season the team would have during the 1970s.

Bench's defense was stellar. His bat was another story. Frustrated, he tried new stances, different grips, listened to all advice, suggestions, anything. He lost his confidence.

In his 1979 book *Catch You Later*, Bench wrote, "Going from MVP to MDP [Most Disappointing Player] was a crucial period for me, the closest thing to anything like an identity crisis kids my age had in college or thereabouts."

Bench was born December 7, 1947, in Oklahoma City, but grew up in the small town of Binger. His father, Ted, a propane gas distributor who had played semi-pro baseball, thought his son's quickest route to baseball success was as a catcher. Ted had Johnny throw 254 feet—twice the distance from home plate to second base.

From a crouch.

Bench once boasted that he could "throw out any runner alive."

The valedictorian of his high school class, Bench, who grew up a Mickey Mantle fan, was selected in the second round of the 1965 draft. (Future big leaguer Bernie Carbo was the Reds first-round pick. Six catchers were selected ahead of Bench, including future big leaguers Ray Fosse and Gene Lamont.)

By 1966, the 6-foot-1 190-pounder with the enormous hands (he could hold seven baseballs in one hand) was *The Sporting News* Minor League Player of the Year.

In September of 1967, Bench had his first cup of coffee in the majors when the Reds called him to the big leagues. At spring training in 1968, Hall of Famer Ted Williams signed a ball for the rookie, "To Johnny Bench, Hall of Famer for sure."

Bench put a down payment on that prediction, winning the National League Rookie of the Year Award with 15 homers and 82 RBIs, beating New York Mets starter Jerry Koosman for the honor. He also caught 154 games and won a Gold Glove Award for his defense. It was his first of 10 in a row.

The Chicago Cubs Randy Hundley introduced the one-handed catching style in 1966, but Bench adopted it as his own. With a hinged mitt, he kept his throwing hand behind his back to keep from being nicked by foul tips. Bench was also the first catcher to wear a protective helmet. He caught more than 100 games in 13 straight seasons, a National League record.

In 1969, Bench was better (26 homers, 90 RBIs), and by 1970 he was being compared to all-time greats Mickey Cochrane of Detroit, Brooklyn's Roy Campanella, and Bill Dickey and Yogi Berra of the New York Yankees.

After the disaster of the 1971 season, Bench spent his off-season clearing his head and refereeing high school basketball games. Renewed, he was a powerhouse again in 1972.

Again, Bench was compared to the greats. He was the *Time* magazine cover boy on July 10, 1972. The headline, printed on his mitt: "Baseball's Best Catcher."

Bench rebounded with 40 homers, 125 RBIs, and a .270 average. Of course, he won another Gold Glove, and the Reds captured the National League West.

They faced the Pirates again. With Hall of Famers Roberto Clemente and Willie Stargell, Pittsburgh, the defending World Series champions, was the favorite.

The National League Championship Series was extended to five games, with the Pirates clinging to a 3–2 lead into the bottom of the ninth at Riverfront. Pirates ace reliever Dave Giusti, who earned 22 saves and pitched to a 1.93 ERA, was summoned to face Bench, Tony Perez, and Denis Menke.

Giusti got ahead of Bench on the count, 1–2. Bench then powered a soaring fly ball deep, but foul, into the red seats of the upper deck. On the next pitch, Bench hit another fly ball, this one to right. It barely landed over the right field wall. The game was tied.

As many a Reds fan of that generation—and then-Cincinnati play-by-play man Al Michaels, who would become famous as a network football announcer—will tell you, it was Bench's most clutch home run. The Reds won the game, though they lost to the mighty Oakland A's in the World Series.

The Reds beat the Boston Red Sox and New York Yankees in 1975 and 1976, the first National League team to win back-to-back World Series since the New York Giants in 1921–22.

The 1975 world championship was the first for the Reds since 1940. The starting lineup in '75 and '76 was dubbed "The Great Eight," and manager Sparky Anderson would recite the names like poetry, always starting with Johnny Bench.

"Johnny Bench, Pete Rose, Joe Morgan, Tony Perez, Dave Concepcion, George Foster, Ken Griffey, and Cesar Geronimo," he'd repeat with great delight when he talked about his team.

Bench hit two homers in Game Four of the '76 Series, the clincher against the Yankees. He finished his career in 1983 as a struggling third baseman with sore knees.

The 14-time All-Star was elected to the Hall of Fame in 1989 with 96 percent of the vote.

Bench could boast 389 home runs, 327 as a catcher, at the time the most in history. That mark was later surpassed by both Carlton Fisk and Mike Piazza. He knocked in 1,376 runs and owned a lifetime .267 average.

In 1999, he was named to baseball's All-Century Team, and the same year *The Sporting News* listed him the 16th-best player in history.

Marty Brennaman, who has called more than 6,000 Reds game on radio, said, "Johnny Bench had the greatest flair for the dramatic, more than any player I've ever seen. If you needed something, he delivered."

Or, as Sparky Anderson once famously said after the 1976 World Series, "You don't compare anyone to Johnny Bench. You don't want to embarrass anybody."

40 GEORGE BRETT: PINE TAR POLEMICS AT YANKEE STADIUM

In 1983, Yankee manager Billy Martin was one of the most charismatic figures in baseball, and the Kansas City Royals George Brett was one of the game's outstanding players. Both men had mercurial personalities, but when the teams squared off in what appeared to be a benign contest in Yankee Stadium on July 24, nobody could have predicted their destinies on that fateful day.

The game was a routine midseason contest that, until the top of the ninth inning, had proceeded without incident. The Royals were at bat, trailing, 4–3, and were down to their last out. Kansas City's U. L. Washington was on first base, with Brett at the plate. In what is now part of baseball folklore, Brett is rumored to have said, "Watch this baby fly," right before he stepped into the batter's box. The formidable Yankees reliever Rich "Goose" Gossage stared at his catcher, who signaled for the pitch he wanted. Gossage concurred and served up a high fastball, but the sharp-eyed Brett promptly pummeled the ball, sending it soaring into the right-field stands. The visiting team's bench erupted in celebration, high-fiving their hero as he returned to the dugout. Kansas City now led, 5–4.

Meanwhile, Martin was at home plate having a discussion with first-year umpire Tim McClelland. The wily Martin had noticed earlier that Brett used what appeared to be an excessive amount of pine tar on his bat, but he bided his time, waiting for an opportune moment to bring it to the umpire's attention. As Brett sat bewildered in the dugout, McClelland and the rest of his staff measured the amount of pine tar and analyzed the situation in detail. McClelland then walked toward the Kansas City dugout, pointed at Brett, and threw a decisive air punch, indicating that Brett had used an illegal bat and was ruled out. Game over. Yankees win, 4–3.

Brett's reaction was instantaneous. All hell broke loose as he exploded, wild-eyed, off the bench and charged the plate area like a crazed animal. His manager, Dick Howser, as well as his teammates, attempted to restrain him, but Brett, totally out of control, thrashed and cursed at the umpire, a scene that has since been witnessed thousands of times on videotape. Meanwhile, the incredible turned into the surreal.

As a commentator was famously quoted, it appeared as if "Brett has become the first player in history to hit a game-losing home run." To complicate matters even further, Royals pitcher Gaylord Perry gave the infamous bat to the batboy so the weapon in question couldn't be examined by the American League office. The batboy then sprinted down into the depths of the stadium clubhouse until he was finally apprehended by members of the New York City Police Department.

But the story was far from over. The Royals duly appealed the ruling, and the American League President, Lee MacPhail, overturned the decision, stating that the "spirit of the restriction" was simply that of economics, and not of acquiring an unfair advantage. In reality, the only reason for the pine tar rule was that baseballs were being ruined for league play when they came in contact with the sticky substance.

As MacPhail went on to state, Brett had not "altered [the bat] to improve the distance factor." The result of the decision was that the game needed to be resumed with two outs in the top of the ninth and the Royals leading, 5–4.

After a legal battle ensued, the resumption was finally scheduled for August 18.

But before the first pitch was thrown, a still irate Billy Martin directed pitcher George Frazier to throw the ball to first base, claiming that Brett had not touched the bag as he trotted around the diamond after his home run. After first-base umpire Tim Welke signaled safe, Martin then had his hurler toss the ball to second, arguing that neither Washington nor Brett had touched that base as well, but umpire Dave Phillips also gave the safe signal. When Martin challenged that ruling, the well-prepared umpiring crew calmly produced a notarized affidavit attesting that Brett had indeed touched all four bases.

The rest of the saga is anticlimactic. Frazier struck out Hal McRae to end the top of the ninth, and Royals reliever Dan Quisenberry got the Yanks one-two-three in the bottom of the inning to end one of the most bizarre games ever played.

So what became of the infamous pine tar bat? It can actually be viewed in the Baseball Hall of Fame, where it has resided since 1987.

39 KEN BOYER: CLUTCH CLOUT FROM CARDS' CAPTAIN

In the seventh inning of Game One of the 1964 World Series, Ken Boyer struck out on Al Downing's high changeup. The K didn't hurt the St. Louis Cardinals. They went on to beat the New York Yankees, 9–5. But Boyer filed away the information on Downing's changeup.

In the twenty-three-year-old Downing, the New York Yankees thought they had another Sandy Koufax. He had pitched 244 innings in the regular season and led the American League in strikeouts, with 217. In 1963 and 1964, he almost matched Koufax in strikeouts per nine innings.

Downing once fanned three Cleveland Indians on nine pitches. He was an American League All-Star in 1967. Four years later, as a member of the Los Angeles Dodgers, he was the National League Comeback Player of the Year, winning 20 games and finishing third in the Cy Young voting, behind future Hall of Famers Ferguson Jenkins and Tom Seaver.

Downing is best known for surrendering Hank Aaron's 715th home run, which eclipsed the career home run mark of Babe Ruth, on April 8, 1974. But in St. Louis, he's the answer to another trivia question.

Soon after the 1964 World Series, Ken Boyer was voted the National League Most Valuable Player. Playing in all 162 games, the third baseman had kept the Cardinals in the pennant race. He hit .350 in May, .342 in July, and .400 in five games in September against the Philadelphia Phillies, who spent most of the season in first place. The Phillies collapsed down the stretch, and the Cards didn't miss the opportunity to win the National League crown. It was the first time St. Louis had been in the Series in 18 years.

For Boyer, who'd made his major-league debut in 1955, it was his first trip to the Fall Classic, where he would be playing against his younger brother, Clete, who manned third base for the Yankees. It was Clete's fifth straight World Series appearance.

The elder Boyer completed the regular season with 24 homers and 119 RBIs. It was his seventh straight season of knocking in 90 or more runs, tying the record of Pittsburgh's Hall of Famer, Pie Traynor, for third basemen. Boyer, the captain of the Cardinals from 1959 to 1965, finished the '64 season with a .295 batting average.

"He was the boss of our field," Tim McCarver, the Cardinals catcher in 1964, would later say. "Kenny was the guy everyone looked up to. He was the guy who really filled that role, if that role needed to be filled."

Boyer, a solid 6-foot-1, 190 pounds, smacked a home run in his 1955 big-league debut and would go on to hit better than .300 five times. He finished with a career .287 mark and 282 home runs, having been selected as an All-Star seven times.

In his statistical analysis, Bill James, writer, historian, and baseball executive, considered Boyer the 12th-best third baseman in baseball history.

But it was Game Four of the World Series at Yankee Stadium that showed the nation how clutch Ken Boyer was.

On the afternoon of October 11, the Yankees had a 3–0 lead in the top of the sixth. They were also leading the Series, two games to one. Downing, who was starting in the place of the injured future Hall of Famer Whitey Ford, was dominating, allowing only one hit and one walk. Carl Warwick, a spare outfielder batting for pitcher Roger Craig, led off the Cardinals sixth with his third pinch hit of the series (tying a World Series record), a single to left. Curt Flood followed with a single to right.

St. Louis left fielder Lou Brock flied out. Up came shortstop Dick Groat. He slapped a potential double-play ball to Yankee second baseman Bobby Richardson, who bobbled the ball, then threw wildly to shortstop Phil Linz.

The inning should have been over, but now the Cardinals had the bases loaded with one out.

Ken Boyer, number 14, was up.

Not only had he struck out against Downing in Game One, but was 0-for-2, striking out earlier in Game Four.

The first pitch he saw was a fastball outside. Yankee catcher Elston Howard called for another fastball, but Downing shook him off and threw a high changeup. Boyer turned on it, launching a line drive into the left field seats for a grand slam, giving the Cardinals a 4–3 lead.

"When he hit the home run," Clete Boyer said, "I was probably as happy as he was."

Short pause.

"You don't think that's the one that's going to beat you."

But it was.

The homer turned the Series around. Instead of the Yankees being up 3–1, the Series was knotted.

"We had them down and were just gonna whomp 'em," recalled Yankees pitcher Rollie Sheldon in Philip Bashe's 1994 book *Dog Days*. "And all of a sudden we let them back in."

In Game Seven, back in St. Louis, Boyer had three hits, including a double and homer (his brother Clete also homered, the only time brothers have homered in a World Series game), and scored three times behind Bob Gibson's clutch pitching to lift the Cardinals to their first world championship since 1946.

Boyer's 11th and final season with the Cardinals was in 1965. His back was bothering him. His batting average (.260), home runs (13), and RBIs (75) all dropped. In the off-season, the team traded him to the New York Mets. He actually helped the Mets escape last place for the first time in their history in 1966. He played for the Chicago White Sox before finishing his career in 1969 with the Dodgers.

That off-season, he returned to the Cardinals nest, hired by the club to manage in its farm system. By 1978, Ken Boyer was the manager of the Cardinals.

In parts of three years at the helm, Boyer's team compiled a 166–190 record. He was fired early in the 1980 season, replaced by future Hall of Fame manager Whitey Herzog. Boyer died of lung cancer in 1982, at age fifty-one.

Two years later, the Cardinals retired his number 14. Ken Boyer remains the only player whose number has been retired by the team but who is not in the Hall of Fame.

38 RICK MONDAY: A HOMER FOR THE RED, WHITE, AND BLUE

It was a cold and miserable day for baseball in Montreal.

The previous day was all rain and snow, and the game had been postponed, with the series between the Montreal Expos and Los Angeles Dodgers tied at two.

The Dodgers, of course, had a baseball history longer than any Main Street. In 1981, the Montreal Expos were looking to go to the team's first World Series. The score was tied in the top of the ninth in the deciding Game Five.

Dodgers pitcher Fernando Valenzuela was terrific. Ray Burris had also pitched well for the Expos. But with the game and season on the line, Montreal manager Jim Fanning summoned Steve Rogers to pitch the ninth.

Rogers was 3–0 with a 0.68 ERA in the playoffs. He recorded two quick outs.

Up came Rick Monday.

Monday had had a good year in the strike-shortened 1981 season. He never hit higher than the .315 he posted that spring, summer, and fall. He also launched 11 home runs. Once upon a time, 1965 to be exact, he was the first pick in the first major-league baseball draft. He signed with the Kansas City A's for $105,000, a pyramid-pile of money back then. But, in the open market, he could have signed for more.

He made his major-league debut in 1966, and would play until 1984. Monday hit 241 home runs in his 19-year major-league career. He also had a .264 lifetime average.

Monday played for the A's, the Cubs, and the Dodgers, batted left, and threw left. The Dodgers acquired Monday for Bill Buckner in early 1977.

While Monday had a very good season in 1981, he was, by the playoffs, being spelled by Glenn Burke and Reggie Smith. Still, there he was, facing Steve Rogers in the ninth inning of a deciding game in a foreign country.

Not only had Rogers dominated the defending World Champion Philadelphia Phillies earlier in the playoffs, but he had also silenced the Dodgers in Game Three. He was the Expos all-time win and strikeout leader.

Rogers fell behind on the count; three balls and one strike. Slugger Pedro Guerrero was on deck. Rogers decided to throw a sinker. His catcher, Gary Carter, agreed with the choice.

Monday had singled earlier in the game and had come around to score the Dodgers only run.

He'd become famous as a Chicago Cub at Dodger Stadium when, on April 26, 1976, he spotted two people, a father and a young son, with a cigarette lighter and a crumpled American flag. Monday sprinted toward them. He was a center fielder. They were in left.

At the time, Monday wasn't sure what was unfolding.

But because it was a day game, he spotted a reflection of what he thought was a can of lighter fluid.

Monday had been in the Marine Reserves for six years.

"I didn't want anyone saying, 'Marine, why did you stand by and watch those guys burn that American flag?'" he recalled.

Monday grabbed the red, white, and blue and took off for the Dodgers dugout.

"I could feel and smell the lighter fluid," he said. "They'd doused it."

He ended up handing the flag to Dodger pitcher Doug Rau. The crowd was singing an off-key version of "God Bless America."

When Monday came to bat again, he was greeted with a standing ovation. In left field, the scoreboard flashed: "RICK MONDAY . . . YOU MADE A GREAT PLAY."

Dodger catcher Steve Yeager noted Monday's deed, but added, "We're still trying to strike you out."

Monday ended up going 3-for-5 that afternoon, with an RBI and two runs scored.

The Dodgers would beat the Cubs, 5–4, in 10 innings.

But few people would remember that. Or that Monday had his best season in '76, with 32 homers, 77 RBIs, and a .272 batting average.

But they remember Rick Monday.

"If you are going to burn the flag, don't do it around me," Monday said later. "I've been to too many veterans' hospitals and seen too many broken bodies of guys who tried to protect it."

Baseball fans also remember Rick Monday because, on an October Monday in 1981, he hit a hanging sinker for a home run over the center-field wall at Olympic Stadium in Montreal, to send the Dodgers to the World Series.

In Montreal, they still refer to the day as "Blue Monday."

In a 2010 documentary about the Expos, Monday, now a Dodger broadcaster, said he was surprisingly delayed by a Canadian immigration official once, missing his connecting flight.

When Monday asked what that was all about, the official asked if he was the former Dodger outfielder. Then he smiled.

37 DAVID JUSTICE: THE ONE THAT ENDED THE BOOS

They were booing David Justice.

In pregame introductions. At home. In Atlanta.

Justice had dared to question the passion of Braves fans the day before Game Six of the 1995 World Series. He said it felt like "It's us against the world."

Braves fans weren't happy.

Even two hours before the game, Justice didn't back down.

"If we get down 1–0 tonight fans probably will boo us out of the stadium," he said. "You have to do something great to get them out of their seats. Shoot, in Cleveland, they were down three runs in the ninth and [the fans] were still on their feet."

Then Justice gave Atlanta fans something to cheer about.

He hit a solo home run in the sixth inning to back Tom Glavine's combined one-hitter with Mark Wohlers as the Braves won Game Six, 1–0, and the World Series, four games to two.

In the *Chicago Tribune*, Jerome Holtzman, who later would become the historian for Major League Baseball, wrote, "You can't boo a home run."

And in Atlanta, they had not.

"I've been booed so many times here that I look for the one or two fans I see clapping and I play for them," Justice said after the game. "They were killing me in the on-deck circle. They had me going everywhere. I understand how they feel. I made a big mistake."

The tide had started to turn in the fourth inning, when Justice ripped a double to deep left center off Cleveland starter Dennis Martinez

He led off the sixth against Indians left-handed reliever Jim Poole, with a drive out of reach in right.

It was enough for Glavine, and for Mark Wohlers, who earned the save with a nine-pitch 1–2–3 inning in the ninth.

It was the Braves first World Series win since 1957, when the franchise was located in Milwaukee.

The Atlanta Braves, the best National League team of its generation, with 14 straight division titles, lost the World Series in 1991 and 1992.

Justice had been a Brave since 1989. He'd been drafted in the fourth round in 1985 as a smooth 6-foot-3, 195-pound, left-handed-hitting outfielder. In 1990, he replaced Atlanta icon Dale Murphy, who was traded to Philadelphia, in right field. Those were big shoes to fill.

Murphy had enjoyed 12 straight years of double-digit home runs. In four consecutive years, he'd hit at least 36 dingers. In 1987, he slugged 44. Murphy finished his career with 398 home runs. Justice responded with 28 homers and a .282 average, and was named the National League Rookie of the Year. The Braves finished last.

In 1991, the Braves not only went from last to first in the National League East, but also made it to the World Series, losing to the Minnesota Twins, also a last-place team in 1990, in seven games. It was one of the great World Series, with five games decided by one run, four in the final at-bat, and three games extending into extra innings.

On New Year's Eve of 1992, Justice married movie star Halle Berry. In 1993, he hit 40 homers and knocked in 120 runs. He finished third in the Most Valuable Player vote, behind Pittsburgh's Barry Bonds and Philadelphia's Lenny Dykstra.

In 1994, he was listed as one of *People* magazine's "Most Beautiful People." But the players' strike ruined Justice's great season. He was hitting .313 when the games ended in August.

Seven months after being the hero of the 1995 World Series, Justice separated his shoulder checking a swing. He was out for the rest of the 1996 season. It also turned out to be his last at-bat for the Braves. The team traded him in a 1997 spring-training blockbuster with the Cleveland Indians.

Outfielder Marquis Grissom joined Justice in going to the American League for star center fielder and leadoff hitter Kenny Lofton, and lefty reliever Alan Embree.

Justice was shocked.

"Quite candidly, I think we made a good baseball trade that was motivated by baseball economics on both sides," said Braves general manager John Schuerholz.

The Indians wanted Justice to fill the thumping role vacated by Albert Belle, who had signed with the Baltimore Orioles in the off-season. The Braves wanted to create greater financial flexibility to keep pitchers Greg Maddux and Tom Glavine, who would be up for new contracts at the end of the season.

Justice had a great year for the Indians, leading them to the World Series in a losing cause against the Florida Marlins. Justice had 33 dingers and 101 RBIs while batting .329. He was fifth in the MVP voting. It was also the year he and Berry divorced after widely publicized allegations by Berry that Justice had been abusive. He played consistently for the Tribe in 1998 and 1999 before being traded to the New York Yankees in June 2000. Looking for power, the Yankees originally had hoped to acquire Sammy Sosa from the Chicago Cubs, or Juan Gonzalez from the Detroit Tigers. Justice delivered the offensive punch his new team needed, launching a monster three-run homer against the Seattle Mariners in that year's playoffs.

Justice finished 2000 with a combined 41 homers and 118 RBIs.

He was a useful bat for the 2002 Oakland A's, too, after he landed there for the final season of his career.

Justice played in the postseason every year but two from 1991 to 2002, the exceptions being 1994, when Commissioner Bud Selig cancelled the Fall Classic because of the players' strike, and 1996, when Justice had a bum shoulder.

He hit 14 homers and knocked in 63 runs in 112 postseason games.

But none was bigger than that homer on October 28, 1995, to win a World Series and answer the boos in the contentious and tight Fall Classic.

"They [the fans] proved me wrong," Justice said. "I was so happy to hear them screaming."

Future Hall of Fame pitcher John Smoltz, who was scheduled to start Game Seven if needed, stated that what Justice said took a lot of guts.

"In this situation, we needed our fans," Smoltz said after the game. "And the fans came through for us. David came through in a tough situation. . . . David was tremendous."

36 TOMMY HENRICH: OCTOBER HEROICS BY "OLD RELIABLE"

It was Mel Allen, the New York Yankees Hall of Fame broadcaster, who dubbed Tommy Henrich "Old Reliable."

Allen gave one of the great clutch hitters in Yankee history the name of a train that operated from Ohio to Alabama and was known coast-to-coast for always being on time. Henrich dated the nickname back to 1946 and a game against the Philadelphia Athletics.

"The score was tied in the late innings, and the Yankees had to catch a train," he told the *Chicago Sun-Times* in 1989. "I got a hit that won the game, and broadcaster Mel Allen said: 'Good old reliable Henrich. Looks like we'll catch the train after all.'"

"If we were ahead 10–1 or 10–2, he was just average," Dr. Bobby Brown, Henrich's teammate and later American League president, once said. "If we were behind 10–1, 10–2, same thing. But get him in a big game and he was terrific."

Henrich was born and raised in Massillon, Ohio, a football hotbed. There were few baseball teams, so the left-handed hitter played softball until he was old enough to join a semi-pro baseball team. He made the transition well enough that the Cleveland Indians signed him in 1933, when the lanky 180-pounder was twenty.

He raked for three straight years in the minors. In 1936, playing for New Orleans in the Double A Southern Association, he put up the kind of season that gets you noticed—a .346 average with 15 homers and 111 RBIs.

Still, he wasn't invited to spring training by the Indians. His contract was sold to the Milwaukee Millers, a minor-league team with no big-league affiliation. Henrich was left confused.

Depending on whom you believe, the Indians were trying to hide a prized prospect, or they considered outfielder Jeff Heath a better player.

In the 1936–37 off-season Henrich wrote to the baseball commissioner, Judge Kenesaw Mountain Landis, wanting to know if he was being treated fairly by the Indians.

Almost forty years before players had the right to free agency, Landis ruled that Henrich was being improperly denied a shot at the big leagues, and declared Henrich a free agent. He signed with the Yankees in April 1937 and joined the big club a month later.

"I'd been a Yankee fan since 1921 when I was eight years old," Henrich told author Donald Honig for the 1993 book *Baseball Between the Lines*. "I was a Babe Ruth man."

He was also the Yankee right fielder in 1937, replacing George Selkirk, who had replaced Ruth.

"I never thought I had a chance," Henrich admitted. "The old Judge was leaning over backwards to be impartial and he never game me a word of encouragement or any hint I had a good case. Facts, facts, facts is what he wanted. Then, an hour later, he called me with his decision and that was the greatest thrill of my life to that point."

He would have more.

Henrich made his major-league debut a month later. In 67 games that season, he hit .320 with eight homers, five triples, 14 doubles, and 42 RBIs, despite an injured left knee that never really stopped bothering him.

While Henrich was a terrific defensive outfielder from the start, the Yankees thought in 1938 and 1939 they were auditioning the player to replace the legendary Lou Gehrig at first base.

Later in his career, Henrich was converted to first base, but he was known first as part of the great Yankee outfield featuring Joe DiMaggio in center and Charlie "King Kong" Keller in left. He'd play for Yankee managers Joe McCarthy, Bucky Harris, and Casey Stengel. All sang his praises as a player and a person.

Henrich was part of seven Yankee teams that won the World Series. He was a five-time All-Star. He hit better than .300 three times and clubbed 183 home runs in his 11-year career. He scored 100 runs in a season four times, including a league-leading 138 in 1948. He twice led the AL in triples.

Bucky Harris called him "the greatest .282 hitter who ever walked up there with a bat."

"Tommy was the steadiest ballplayer I've ever seen because he's smarter than the average player," DiMaggio said. "He's a man who took advantage of everything he saw."

Stengel underlined and emphasized those comments: "He's a fine judge of a fly ball. He fields grounders like an infielder. He never makes a wrong throw, and if he comes back to the hotel at three in the morning when we're on the road and says he's been sitting up with a sick friend, he's been sitting up with a sick friend."

In a 1949 *New Yorker* profile, Henrich also talked about his defense.

"Catching a fly ball is a pleasure," he said. "But knowing what to do with it after you catch it is a business."

After his retirement in 1950, the Yankees had Henrich teach the nineteen-year-old Mickey Mantle, then a shortstop, how to play right field.

Henrich found his place in baseball history on October 5, 1941, in Game Four of the World Series against the Brooklyn Dodgers, who were leading, 4–3, with two outs and nobody on, in the top of the ninth at Ebbets Field.

Dodgers pitcher Hugh Casey was one strike away from knotting the World Series at two games apiece. His batterymate was Mickey Owen, who had made the National League All-Star team and was in the midst of a record 508 fielding chances by a catcher without an error.

Henrich swung and missed at a wicked curve by Casey.

"Even as I was trying to hold up, I was thinking that the ball had broken so fast that [Dodger catcher Mickey] Owen might have trouble with it, too," Henrich told the author Honig. ". . . saw that little white jackrabbit bouncing and I said, *Let's go*. It rolled all the way to the fence. I could have walked down to first base."

DiMaggio singled to left, and Keller followed with a high fly double to right that scored Henrich and DiMaggio to give the Yankees a 5–4 lead. They'd add two more before the inning was over.

The Yankees won the World Series the next day.

Owen later would claim that Henrich had missed the pitch by six inches.

In 1942, the year Henrich made his first All-Star game, his country at war, he enlisted with the U.S. Coast Guard. Like many major-league players of the time, he missed much of the next three seasons.

Henrich only hit .251 in 1946, but rebounded the next two seasons with averages of .287 and .308 in 1947 and 1948 respectively.

And in 1949, Old Reliable saved the Yankees season.

The Yankees had injuries at almost every position, but the biggest loss was DiMaggio, who had a tender heel that wouldn't stop hurting. He didn't play his first game until June 28.

"Henrich has never been the captain of the Yankees," *New York Times* sports columnist Arthur Daley wrote. "But the other players just gravitate to him as their natural leader. He was the captain, in fact, if not in name."

Henrich had his own injury woes in 1949: a broken transverse vertebrae, a busted toe, and a left knee that wouldn't stop hurting. But he propped the Yankees up until DiMaggio came back.

The Yankees owned first place for much of the year, but the Red Sox started roaring in September, overtaking the Bombers.

The pennant came down to the last two games of the season. The Yankees needed both to reach the World Series.

The Yankees trailed the Red Sox, 4–0, in the next-to-last game of the season, only to win the contest on an eighth-inning home run by Johnny Lindell.

In the winner-take-all game on October 2, Henrich, batting second between Hall of Fame shortstop Phil Rizzuto and DiMaggio, knocked in an early run that the Yankees nursed until the eighth, when he homered for a 2–0 lead.

The Yankees would go on to win the game, 5–3, and their 16th pennant.

Three days later, October 5, Old Reliable hit the first walk-off homer in World Series history when he boomed a drive to right field off Brooklyn's Don Newcombe. The Yankees won that World Series in five games.

Henrich retired in 1950. He was thirty-seven.

After his playing days were over, Old Reliable coached with the New York Giants, Detroit Tigers, and Kansas City Athletics. He owned a beer distributorship. He also sang in his church choir and in barbershop quartets. He rarely missed Old-Timers Day at Yankee Stadium. In 1987, he was honored by the team with its annual Pride of the Yankees Award.

Henrich died at the age of ninety-six on December 1, 2009.

He never stopped being a Yankee fan.

"I get a thrill every time I put on my Yankee uniform," Henrich once told a reporter. "It sounds corny, but it's the gospel truth."

35 CAL RIPKEN JR.: THE HOMER AND STREAK THAT HEALED BASEBALL

Cal Ripken Jr. came to bat in the bottom of the fourth inning to another standing ovation.

It wasn't an official game yet.

But everything Ripken did that hot, sultry night of September 6, 1995, drew flashbulbs and a standing ovation from the 46,272 in attendance.

It was all practice. The game wouldn't be official until the bottom of the fifth.

Those rising from their seats included President Bill Clinton, Vice President Al Gore, and the greatest living ballplayer (as he liked to be introduced) Joe DiMaggio.

For three and a half years, DiMaggio had been Lou Gehrig's teammate with the New York Yankees. DiMaggio was in Yankee Stadium on July 4, 1939, when, between the games of the doubleheader, Gehrig made his famous speech about being the luckiest man on the face of the earth. DiMaggio had gone 3-for-5 in the second game of the twin bill to help the Yankees to an 11–1 win. But in September of 1995, DiMaggio was now two months shy of eighty-one. And baseball was trying to find some light after one of its darkest hours.

The players in Major League Baseball had gone on strike on August 12, 1994, over the issue of a salary cap. A month later, then-acting Commissioner Bud Selig canceled the World Series. Clinton ordered both sides back to the bargaining table in January, with a February 6 deadline. He was ignored. All but one of the owners were planning to use replacement players.

The one who was not—Baltimore's Peter Angelos—would not go along with the plan out of respect for Ripken's consecutive-game streak and because, as an attorney, Angelos represented unions.

Sparky Anderson, the manager of the Detroit Tigers, was placed on an involuntary leave of absence because he refused to manage replacement players. The Toronto Blue Jays assigned manager Cito Gaston and his staff to the minors, where they would avoid coaching replacements.

The strike ended only when Sonia Sotomayor, a future Supreme Court justice, but then a judge with the United States District Court for the South

District of New York, issued a preliminary injunction against the owners on March 31. Sotomayor's decision was backed by the Court of Appeals for the Second Circuit, which denied the owners' request to stay the ruling.

Fans didn't come rushing back when games began on April 25, starting an abridged 144-game season. The anger was palpable.

But there was one big carrot: the possibility that Ripken would break Gehrig's cherished consecutive-game streak.

Gehrig, the Iron Horse, had played a record 2,130 straight games from 1925 to 1939, when he went to see his manager Joe McCarthy in Detroit on May 2, 1939. Although he'd hit 29 homers with 114 RBIs and had a .295 average in 1938, Gehrig had not felt right that year. He couldn't put his finger on the problem. No one could.

By the spring of 1939, Gehrig was clumsy and, when he would complain, talked about a lack of strength. But McCarthy didn't remove him from the lineup out of respect for the Yankee captain.

That Tuesday, May 2, 1939, at Briggs Stadium, Yankee captain Gehrig brought the lineup card to the home plate umpires.

As Gehrig walked back to the dugout, Tigers public-address announcer Ty Tyson told the crowd, "How about a hand for Lou Gehrig, who played 2,130 games in a row before he benched himself today."

Gehrig received as many gasps as cheers. He returned to the Yankee dugout, took a drink from the water cooler and started to cry.

Babe Dahlgren went 2-for-5 in his place and the Yankees won, 22–2. Gehrig's consecutive-game streak, starting on June 1, 1925, and considered by many to be unbreakable, was history.

After the game, McCarthy said, "I knew there was something wrong with him, but I didn't know what it was. His reflexes were shot. I was afraid of his getting hit with a pitched ball. . . . Like everybody else, I'm sorry to see it happen. Fellows like him come along once in a hundred years."

Gehrig was diagnosed with amyotrophic lateral sclerosis in June. He died two years later on June 2, 1941. Joe DiMaggio was in the midst of his 56-game hitting streak.

Gehrig's record had lasted 56 years. But on September 6, 1995, Cal Ripken Jr. was about to break it.

He popped up to the catcher in his first at-bat. He threw out Jorge Farbregas on a routine grounder in the third. He started a double play in the top of the fourth.

The Orioles had drafted Ripken in the second round in 1978 as a third baseman. The Birds used the pick the Boston Red Sox had forfeited when signing free agent relief pitcher Dick Drago. It was Orioles manager Earl Weaver who moved the 6-foot-4 Ripken to shortstop when the twenty-one-year-old Aberdeen, Maryland, native arrived in the big leagues in 1981.

By that time, Ripken's father was the team's third-base coach. Cal Ripken Sr., a career minor-league catcher, would end up managing Cal Jr. and another son, Billy.

Cal Ripken Jr. was the 1982 American League Rookie of the Year. He won two AL Most Valuable Player Awards. He was awarded two Gold Gloves. He hit more home runs than any shortstop in the game's history (345), and slugged a total of 431 overall.

Ripken's consecutive-game streak started on May 30, 1982, a Saturday afternoon, at Baltimore's Memorial Stadium. Ripken was still a third baseman and batted eighth, going 0-for-2 in a 6–0 loss to the Toronto Blue Jays.

Ripken didn't even realize he was in the midst of a streak when he sprained an ankle in the second game of 1985. In 1993, Ripken twisted a knee in a brawl against Seattle. He was sure he couldn't play the next day, but did.

Gehrig faced obstacles in building his streak, too. He played through a broken thumb and a busted toe. Later in his career, his hands were X-rayed. Doctors found seventeen different fractures that had healed while he played.

Ripken knew Gehrig's story. He knew what breaking the streak meant. There had been an unfounded rumor in early September that Ripken was content to tie the record, not break it. Facing California's Shawn Boskie in the fourth inning, he drove a 3–0 pitch deep to left field for a home run. The sound at Oriole Park at Camden Yards was deafening. It only got louder when number 8 trotted out to shortstop in the bottom of the fifth. The cheering didn't stop for twenty-two minutes.

A banner was unfurled from the B&O warehouse in right field. It read "2,131."

Baseball's healing had begun.

Ripken's streak didn't stop until he played in 501 more consecutive games.

He decided to end the streak on September 20, 1998, the last Orioles home game of the season. The Birds opponent was the Yankees. It just seemed right. There was no big announcement. He wanted to end it on his terms.

The new consecutive games-played record was 2,632 games.

On the night he passed Gehrig, Ripken said, "Tonight, I stand here, overwhelmed as my name is linked with the great and courageous Lou Gehrig. I am truly humbled to have our names spoken in the same breath. Some may think our strongest connection is because we played many consecutive games. Yet I believe in my heart that our true link is a common motivation—a love for the game of baseball, a passion for our team, and a desire to compete on the very highest level."

34 TED WILLIAMS: TEDDY BALLGAME'S ALL-STAR BLAST

Ted Williams's favorite hitting park was Briggs Stadium in Detroit.

He said the darkness between the upper and lower deck provided him with the ideal backdrop for framing the ball.

Of his 521 career home runs over 19 seasons, Williams smacked 55 in Detroit. Only Babe Ruth, with 60, slugged more in Briggs.

On Williams's first trip to Detroit in 1939 as a Boston Red Sox rookie, teammate Elden Auker spoke to Tigers pitcher Tommy Bridges. Auker recalled the conversation in his 2001 book *Sleeper Cars and Flannel Uniforms*. Bridges wanted to know the deal on Williams.

"He's good," Auker said. "I'll tell you what Tommy, I'll bet you before we leave this ballpark, he'll hit one over the right field roof."

In Teddy Ballgame's second at-bat, he drove a pitch from Roxie Lawson to right field that banged against the roof for a home run.

In his next at-bat, Williams worked the count to 3-and-0. Pitcher Bob Harris decided to throw a strike. Williams was ready. He hit it completely out of the park, becoming the first player to clear the roof there. The next time someone slugged one out of Briggs was 17 years later, when Mickey Mantle accomplished the feat.

Gerry Moore of the *Boston Globe* wrote of the dinger, "It was a climbing liner—as much of a liner as a drive could be which cleared a 120 foot barrier, straight as a string, over the whole works about a dozen feet fair. According to eyewitnesses outside the park it landed across adjoining Trumbull Avenue and bounded against a taxi company on the other side on the first hop."

Those long balls that day were the second and third of his career.

He was twenty, truly then "The Kid."

Williams clubbed 31 homers in 1939 with 145 RBIs and a .327 average. He encored in 1940 with 23 dingers, 113 RBIs, and a .344 average.

Williams started the 1941 season playing on a bum ankle he hurt sliding in a spring-training game. He didn't mind missing early April games. He loved to hit, but not so much in the cold.

Because pitcher and teammate Joe Dobson was rehabbing, too, in extended spring training, Williams got all the batting practice he needed in Florida. When Williams returned to the Sox lineup in April he hit everything, and didn't stop.

His average stood at .405 on July 8, 1941, the date of the annual All-Star Game. (He would finish the season at .406, the last man to hit .400.)

It some ways, it was no big deal.

A dozen players had hit .400 or better since 1900, the last being New York Giants first baseman Bill Terry in 1930.

The story of the day was Joe DiMaggio and his hitting streak.

By the All-Star Game, DiMaggio had hit in 48 straight games. The streak would extend to 56 games and end on July 17.

When Williams arrived in Detroit for the All-Star Game with Boston teammates Dom DiMaggio, Joe Cronin, Bobby Doerr, and Jimmie Foxx, he brought his new 8mm movie camera, wanting to film Briggs Stadium, the fans in the stands, and Joe DiMaggio.

"I want to study his style," he told reporters.

Williams added that he thought DiMaggio was the "greatest hitter I ever saw and probably will see in my career. He hits the ball hard in all directions."

DiMaggio was batting third in the American League lineup. Williams was in the cleanup spot. He was aware that his mother, May, was listening to the game.

May was a member of the Salvation Army. Ted grew up loving her, but also being embarrassed that she was always in the street asking for donations. It was her brother, Saul, who had once pitched against Babe Ruth and Lou Gehrig in a series of exhibition games in the 1920s, who taught Williams how to play baseball.

As a kid growing up in San Diego, Williams idolized Bill Terry of the New York Giants and Pepper Martin of the St. Louis Cardinals.

He wanted to be a star. And it was no wonder Teddy Ballgame loved being invited to All-Star Games.

This was an era in which these games counted, the best playing the best for pride.

Williams was 6-foot-3 and all sinewy muscle. Even Babe Ruth was a fan.

"When I first saw Ted Williams swing a bat, I knew he'd be one of the best," Ruth told legendary sportswriter Grantland Rice. "He's loose and easy with a great pair of wrists. Just a natural. Williams ought to be one of the first hitters in many years to pass .400."

Williams knocked in the American League's first run with a long double to right in the fourth.

But the American League was down, 5–4, in the bottom of the ninth because Pittsburgh's Hall of Fame shortstop Arky Vaughan hit two two-run homers.

There were men on first and third and two out for the American League, and Williams was due up.

Cincinnati Reds manager Bill McKechnie was piloting the National League. He was the first manager to win the World Series with two teams, the 1925 Pittsburgh Pirates and the 1940 Cincinnati Reds. (He also skippered the 1928 pennant-winning St. Louis Cardinals, who lost to the Yankees in the World Series.)

Nicknamed "Deacon" because he sang in the church choir, the National League skipper went to the mound to confer with Chicago Cubs pitcher Claude Passeau, who had struck out Williams in the eighth. The right-hander would win 162 games in his career. In the 1945 World Series he threw a one-hitter as the Cubs beat the Detroit Tigers in Game Three.

McKechnie asked Passeau how he felt about walking Williams to load the bases and face Dom DiMaggio.

The decision was made not to walk him and Passeau toed the rubber while Williams dug in and gave himself a pep talk.

Williams had taken strike three in the eighth. He thought the pitch was low. He also believed he wasn't as aggressive as he should have been in the at-bat, so he decided he wasn't going to have any "cut-down protect swing."

Williams recalled he unleashed his home run swing "probably with my eyes closed" and it soared deep into the right field upper deck.

The only question was: Fair or foul?

Halfway down the first-base line Williams realized it was gone. Instead of running, he started leaping about and clapping.

Joe DiMaggio greeted him at home plate.

"I was just so happy," Williams said. "I laughed out loud. I had never been so happy. . . . I had hit what remains to this day the most thrilling hit of my life."

Back at his hotel after the game, Williams told a reporter, "Do you know the biggest kick I get out of this whole thing? I'm tickled for my mom's sake, because she was listening."

33 BABE RUTH: A DINGER FOR AN AILING KID

Their 27 world championships, Hall of Fame legends, and bottom-of-the-ninth heroics, are just a few reasons for New York Yankees fans to love their team. But the magic of Pinstripes lore is what makes this very special team's history so remarkable.

Consider the antics of the here-again, gone-again, here-again Billy Martin, Babe Ruth's memorable pose before parking a dinger into the outfield stands, the legendary carousing of Mickey Mantle and Whitey Ford, the controversial team owner George Steinbrenner, or the "Yogi-isms" that made the Yankee catcher so lovable. These anecdotes and many, many more have been passed from parents to children, from generation to generation, and are as much a part of the historic franchise as its stellar records.

One of these tales is that of John Dale "Johnny" Sylvester who was born on April 5, 1915, in Caldwell, New Jersey. Like many children in the tri-state area, little Johnny was a huge fan of the New York Yankees. In 1921, the Sylvester family moved to the neighboring town of Essex Fells, where young Johnny earned the nickname "The Babe Ruth Kid" because of his devotion to the Great Bambino.

During most of his childhood, all was well for Johnny and his family. But on a life-altering day in the summer of 1926, fate took a dark and violent turn. While horseback riding on the Jersey Shore, Johnny was thrown from the saddle as the horse took a nasty tumble. In the mayhem that ensued, the horse kicked the youngster in the head, resulting in something similar to an osteomyelitis of the skull. The rare condition, caused by an infection, can lead to bone deterioration, and to make matters worse, Sylvester was also suffering from blood poisoning that got so bad that his doctors thought the eleven-year-old might die.

In an effort to boost the young man's spirits, the Sylvester family sent a telegram to Ruth, who was playing in the World Series. In response, Johnny received a package containing two baseballs. One was signed by members of the Yankees and the other by the St. Louis Cardinals, New York's opponent. Also included was a thrilling note written by Ruth himself stating, "I'll knock a homer for you on Wednesday," which just happened to be the day of Game Four of the Series.

On that Wednesday, October 6, 1926, the Ruth hit not one, not two, but three dingers to carry the Bombers to a 10–5 victory. And in a script that not even Hollywood could conjure up, as an apparent result of the Babe's gallant efforts, Johnny's spirits were so bolstered that his condition began to immediately improve, so much so that New Jersey's biggest Yankee fan eventually made a full recovery.

The 1926 World Series would conclude with a heartbreaking Yankee loss as Ruth was caught stealing for the final out. But in a fitting end to the story, Ruth visited Sylvester at his house, where little Johnny consoled the Babe by saying, "I'm sorry the Yankees lost."

There have been several different versions told of the Sylvester story. According to some hard-hearted skeptics, the whole incident never occurred and was fabricated. But in the hearts of Yankee fans, Babe Ruth's heroics on that fateful day in the fall of '26 led directly to the miraculous recovery of little Johnny Sylvester, the kid from New Jersey who was his most devoted fan.

32 SCOTT SPIEZIO: LIKE DAD HAD TAUGHT HIM

Scott Spiezio started switch-hitting when he was three.

You read that right.

By the time he was five or six, Spiezio's baseball routine included taking 500 to 600 swings a day.

Batting practice would be heading into the evening with situational hitting drills conducted by his father, Ed, a former big leaguer who'd gone on to own a furniture store, and who would call out before he threw his final pitches: "Man on third, one out."

Then he'd throw a high strike or maybe something in the dirt. The kid had to be aware and react.

In good weather, the drills were held in the family's Morris, Illinois, backyard, which held two pitching mounds, one with Little League dimensions, the other 60 feet, 6 inches, big-league regulation size.

Ed Spiezio would throw fastballs from the Little League mound and a variety of breaking pitches from the big one.

When the Illinois weather turned, baseball was played in the basement, Scott swinging at tennis balls hung from the ceiling, taking his cuts off tees, and at a rug-covered pole (to help hit with power).

Regardless of the conditions, the workout would always end with these words from Ed Spiezio: "Son, pretend it is Game Seven of the World Series, bottom of the ninth, your team is down, guys on base, you at bat."

Of course, usually baseball doesn't work like that.

Scott Spiezio hit the most important home run in the history of the Los Angeles Angels en route to the team's only world championship in the bottom of the seventh of Game Six of the 2002 World Series, when hope was merely a rumor. The San Francisco Giants were leading 5–0. They were eight outs from being the best team in baseball.

In the mid-1960s, Ed Spiezio was supposed to have been the heir apparent to Ken Boyer, the great St. Louis Cardinals third baseman. No less than Cardinal Hall of Famer Red Schoendienst once told *The Sporting News* that Ed Spiezio was "the finest looking young hitter" he had ever seen.

But injuries limited his playing time. He played parts of nine years. He was on two Cardinals teams that won the World Series. Ed retired with 39 lifetime homers at age thirty, six days after his only son, Scott, was born in September 1972.

At age thirty, Scott was the first baseman for the American League's Wild Card winning Angels. After a stellar career at the University of Illinois, he had been drafted in the sixth round in 1993 by the Oakland A's.

He broke into the big leagues three years later and played mostly second base for the A's before signing with the Angels as a jack-of-all-trades in 2000. Extremely versatile, he kept five gloves in his locker in case he had to play first, second, third, or the outfield.

Scott spent much of his Angel career believing the organization didn't think he was an everyday player. In 2001 he hit .303 with 11 homers over the last 10 weeks playing first base, but the team toyed with the idea of moving center fielder Darin Erstad there.

In 2002, Scott won the first-base job. He played 153 games and knocked in 82 runs.

Angels hitting coach Mickey Hatcher thought he was the MVP of the team, a club that had Garret Anderson and his 123 RBIs.

"He's been picking us up offensively and defensively all year," Hatcher said of Spiezio.

Scott Spiezio was something else again come playoff time.

Entering Game Six of the World Series, he was hitting .347 with 16 RBIs in 14 postseason games, the best hitting stretch of his career coming in the biggest games. But how big was hitting in the bottom of the seventh down 5–0? No team in World Series history had ever come back from so far behind in a potential deciding game.

San Francisco manager Dusty Baker was so confident that he made a point of handing the game ball to Giants starting pitcher Russ Ortiz when he walked to the mound to take him out of the game.

There were two on and one out. The Rally Monkey video was playing on the Edison Field scoreboard. The capacity crowd in Anaheim was on its feet, banging together inflatable red plastic rally sticks.

Spiezio dug in from the left side to face Felix Rodriguez, a hard-throwing right-hander, who had held opponents to a .163 batting average in the postseason but had also surrendered the game-winning home run to Tim Salmon in Game Two.

Spiezio took ball one, outside.

He then fouled off three straight 97-mile-an-hour fastballs.

Ball two.

He fouled off another heater straight back.

Tim McCarver, the Fox broadcaster and former Cardinal teammate of Spiezio's father, said after the last foul: "If you make a mistake away, it's a single. If you make a mistake in, it's 5–3."

Then Spiezio took ball three, a fastball away. The count was three balls and two strikes.

"I'm sure this is a bit like déjà vu for him," Ed Spiezio would later say. "He feels like he's been there before."

On the eighth pitch of the epic at-bat, Spiezio lifted it high and deep into the California night.

He wasn't sure he got all of it. He would later say it was the first time he hit a home run "where I was actually past first base waiting for the ball to travel over the fence . . . I was praying on the way to first base."

When Spiezio got back to the dugout he sat by himself. He closed his eyes and bowed his head. He said he was thinking of the feeling he had at the plate. He was trying to remember what he did right.

For the next at-bat, just like his father taught him.

31 BABE RUTH: A TRIO FOR THE BAMBINO

Everybody talks about the 1927 New York Yankees, the team to which every other great club is compared.

"Are they as good as the '27 Yankees?"

Of course, the answer is always the same: No, and with good reason.

The 1927 Yankees were 110 and 44. Babe Ruth hit 60 homers that season. They won the American League pennant by 19 games. The World Series was almost an afterthought, an exclamation point.

For the record, the Yankees beat the Pittsburgh Pirates in four games. Babe Ruth hit two more home runs.

But the '28 Yanks?

They're almost baseball's orphans. That team featured nine future Hall of Famers:

Right fielder Babe Ruth
First baseman Lou Gehrig
Shortstop Tony Lazzeri
Center fielder Earle Combs
Catcher Bill Dickey
Infielder Leo Durocher
Pitcher Waite Hoyt
Pitcher Herb Pennock
Pitcher Stan Coveleski

Add Yankee manager Miller Huggins and general manager Ed Barrow, both of whom also would be elected to the Hall of Fame.

Coveleski really made the Hall for his work with the Cleveland Indians. But he was 5–1 for the '28 Yanks. A right-handed pitcher who was allowed to throw a spitball even after it was outlawed in 1920, he won 215 games and retired with a 2.89 ERA. In 2001, Bill James, the baseball historian, considered him the 58th-best right-handed pitcher in history.

Leo Durocher, twenty at the time, made the Hall as a manager. He won three pennants and a world championship. He managed Jackie Robinson with the Brooklyn Dodgers and nurtured the young Willie Mays with the New York Giants.

It didn't hurt that he was colorful, profane, and controversial, worth a shelf-load of books unto himself.

And Babe Ruth never liked him.

According to Robert Creamer's book *Babe: The Legend Comes to Life*, Ruth saw Durocher, a rookie, sporting a tuxedo in the lobby of a spring-training hotel in 1927.

He already didn't like Durocher's arrogance. The tuxedo didn't help Ruth's mood. He later accused "Leo the Lip," as Durocher was known, of stealing an expensive watch. Creamer says that accusation wasn't true. Durocher would later say, "Jesus Christ, if I was going to steal anything from him it would be his god-damned Packard."[12]

Still, Babe was Babe, the sun in the baseball universe.

After hitting 60 homers with 165 RBIs (teammate Gehrig led the league in runs batted in with 175) in 1927, Ruth was almost as good in '28, with 54 homers and 146 RBIs.

So were the Yankees.

They were nine games off their 1927 pace, but still finished 101–53.

New York faced the St. Louis Cardinals in the World Series. But they entered the Series a bit gimpy.

Gehrig had been beaned in the final game of the regular season. Combs had a badly sprained wrist. Lazzeri was trying to get by with a shoulder that needed surgery. Pennock, who won 17 games, had a sore arm and wouldn't pitch in October.

The Cardinals, featuring Frankie Frisch and Pepper Martin, captured the National League pennant with 95 wins.

Frisch, "The Fordham Flash"—he earned the nickname for being so fast in track—played second base. He was originally a New York Giant, tutored by Hall of Fame manager John McGraw. In his New York accent he called his new club the "Cawd'nals." They would win three of the next four National League pennants. Frisch was named the National League Most Valuable Player in 1931.

12 For the record, Ruth didn't like Detroit's Ty Cobb, either. He found the "Georgia Peach," according to Creamer, "cruel and humorless."

Martin would be best known for being a member of the "Gashouse Gang," the 1931 Cardinals team that upset the Philadelphia A's in the World Series. In 1928, Martin was a utility man.

The biggest name on the Cards was pitcher Grover Cleveland Alexander. He would win 373 games, tied with New York Giant Christy Mathewson for the third-highest total of all time. In 1999, *The Sporting News* named Alexander the 12th-best player in baseball history. Named for nineteenth-century Democratic president Grover Cleveland, he was played by future Republican president Ronald Reagan in the 1952 movie *The Winning Team.*

Alexander, known to friends as "Pete," served on the front lines in World War I. He suffered from shell shock. He also ended up liking his drink and was later diagnosed as an epileptic.

Alexander, in disputable sobriety, famously shut down the Yankees after being called out of the bullpen in the seventh game of the 1926 World Series, with the Cardinals loosely holding a 3–2 lead.

He was 16–9 in 1928. He was also forty-one years of age. Alexander tossed his 90th career shutout that summer. He would be elected to the Hall of Fame in 1938.

The Cardinals, according to Leigh Montville's book *The Big Bam: The Life and Times of Babe Ruth*, were 5–3 favorites.

Even "The Big Train," Walter Johnson, by then retired with 417 wins, wrote, "To me, the St. Louis Cardinals should make short work of the New York Yankees. The Yankees don't look good. They haven't looked good for a while."

By the fourth game of the '28 World Series at St. Louis, the Yankees were dominating, three games to none.

Ruth was 7-for-11, with no home runs. He hit into an inning-ending double play in the first. In the fourth, he knotted the score at one with a line-drive homer to right off southpaw Bill Sherdel.

Nicknamed "Wee Willie," because he stood about 5-foot-8, Sherdel was 21–10 that year. Known for his slow curveball and for rarely walking a hitter, he won the pennant-clinching game, as he had in 1926.

In the seventh inning, with the Cardinals leading 2–1, Sherdel quick-pitched Ruth on an 0–2 count. Quick pitching, not waiting for the batter to be set in the box, was still allowed in the National League, but not in the American League. Commissioner Kenesaw Mountain Landis had outlawed it in the World Series. Sherdel's pitch didn't count as strike three.

There was an argument between the Cardinals and the umpires, while Ruth stood with a delinquent's smile.

Ruth had life.

With the count 2–2, he rifled a shot deep to right, and scampered around the bases as happy as a child on a snow day. Ruth's home run ignited a four-run inning, giving the Yankees a 5–2 lead.

Ruth batted again in the eighth, this time against Alexander.

In 1926, with the Yanks trailing by a run in Game Seven of the World Series, Ruth had led off the bottom of the ninth against Alexander. The Yanks were behind by a run. Two outs later, he decided to try to steal second, believing there was more of a chance the Yankees could tie the score with one hit, than getting two off of Alexander.

Ruth was thrown out. The 1926 Series was over.

But this was 1928.

This time, Ruth powered a home run off Alexander, the second time he had hit three homers in a World Series game.

Playing left field, he also caught Frisch's foul fly for the last out of the game, ensuring the Yankees third world championship.

Ruth finished the World Series with a .625 average.

Leaving Sportsman's Park, Montville writes, someone shouted, "Hooray. Ruth for president."

"I told my friends out there in the bleachers I'd hit two homers in this game," Ruth said. "Wow! And I hit three."

30 JIMMIE FOXX: TAPE-MEASURE HOME RUN

In the 1992 film *A League of Their Own*, Tom Hanks plays a washed-up former baseball star named Jimmy Dugan. The character is said to be loosely based on either Hack Wilson or Jimmie Foxx.

Philip K. Wrigley, the owner of the Chicago Cubs and the chewing gum company, helped establish the league. Wilson, a slugger with a drinking problem, once hit 56 homers and knocked in 191 runs in a season for the Cubbies. He was considered by sportswriters, the arbiters of sports during the roaring twenties and the Great Depression, the right-handed Babe Ruth.

It took sixty-eight years for his National League home run record to be broken. His 191 RBIs—no one has come close.

Drink got the best of Hack Wilson. He was forty-eight when he died in 1948. He was buried in a donated suit. His son didn't claim his body. Wilson was elected to the Hall of Fame in 1979.

Foxx actually managed the 1952 Fort Wayne Daisies of the All-American Girls Professional Baseball League. In his years with the Philadelphia A's and Boston Red Sox, he was considered Wilson's American League counterpart when it came to swinging from the right-hand side. He was also considered the right-handed Ruth.

He was known as "The Double X" and "The Beast."

Hall of Fame pitcher Ted Lyons of the Chicago White Sox recalled Foxx "had great powerful arms and he used to wear his sleeves cut off way up, and when he dug in and raised that bat, his muscles would bulge and ripple."

Foxx, known for his kindness, generosity and gentle ways, credited farmwork for his physique.

The legendary slugger Home Run Baker discovered the son of tenant farmers in the wilds of Maryland. Foxx, born October 22, 1907, dropped out of high school and was playing pro ball by the time he should have been going to the junior prom.

He was in the big leagues by 1925, at age seventeen, drilling a single in his first at-bat a month before he should have graduated from high school.

By 1929, Foxx was on the cover of *Time* magazine, when that still meant the world. That summer, he hit .354 with 33 home runs.

The A's won the next three American League pennants and two straight World Series.

Foxx usually batted fifth, after Hall of Famers Al Simmons and Mickey Cochrane. He was a catcher when he made the big leagues, but the A's had Cochrane behind the plate so Foxx played first, third, and the outfield.

Hall of Fame catcher Rick Ferrell, who played with the Washington Senators, St. Louis Browns, and Boston Red Sox, called Foxx "the greatest all-around athlete I ever saw play major league baseball. If it wasn't for Cochrane, Foxx would have developed into a great catcher."

Regardless of the position, Foxx mostly mashed, high, far, and gone. He was six feet tall, about 200 pounds with massive forearms. He always cut a stocky figure. He hit 30 homers or more for 12 straight years. The record wouldn't be broken until 2007 by Alex Rodriguez.

Foxx also knocked in 100 runs for 13-straight seasons. Only Babe Ruth, Lou Gehrig, and Rodriguez have matched that streak.

In 1932, Foxx plated 169 runs for the A's. His batting average was .364, three points shy of the batting title, which would have ensured him his first Triple Crown. (Dale Alexander, a first baseman for the Detroit Tigers and Boston Red Sox, won the batting title in '32 with a .367 average. He wouldn't have under current rules because he didn't have enough at-bats.)

Foxx also boomed 60 homers in 1932, which would have tied Babe Ruth's 1927 record, but two were washed away in games that ended up being rained out.

He did win the Triple Crown the following season, with 48 dingers, 163 ribbies, and a .356 average.

Foxx was voted the American League Most Valuable Player three times. He was the next player after Ruth to reach 500 career home runs, and the first right-handed hitter. The next right-handed hitter to reach that plateau was San Francisco's Willie Mays, in 1965.

Lefty Gomez, the New York Yankees Hall of Fame ace southpaw during the 1930s, said of Foxx, "He had muscles in his hair."

Gomez would know. Foxx whacked a pitch off him into the third deck in left field—97 feet up, about 475 feet from home plate—at the original Yankee Stadium.

When Gomez was asked how far it had gone, he said, "I don't know, but I do know it took forty-five minutes to go up there and get it back."

By the time Foxx launched that ball, he was playing first base for the Boston Red Sox.

Foxx had built his reputation as part of the back-to-back World Series-winning A's of 1929 and '30. His teammates not only included Cochrane, but slugger Al Simmons in the lineup. Hall of Famer Lefty Grove led the rotation.

His most important dinger came in Game Five of the 1930 World Series in St. Louis at Sportsman's Park.

The Cardinals and A's were tied at two games apiece when Foxx powered a long home run in the top of the ninth off future Hall of Famer Burleigh Grimes to break a scoreless tie, giving the A's a 2–0 win behind Grove.

The A's won the Series two days later.

As the Great Depression ground on, Connie Mack, the manager and owner of the Philadelphia A's, could no longer keep his team intact.

He traded Foxx to the Red Sox, owned by Tom Yawkey, on December 10, 1935, for $150,000 (approximately $2.6 million in 2015) and two players.

Foxx's best year in Boston was 1938. Again, he was the American League MVP. He had 175 RBIs with 50 homers and a .349 average, missing another Triple Crown as Detroit's Hank Greenberg powered 58 home runs.

He was so feared that he was walked six times on June 16, 1938, against the St. Louis Browns.

The closest Ted Williams ever came to the 175 RBIs Foxx had was 159 in 1949.

Double X's Red Sox team home run record would last until 2006, when David Ortiz broke it with 54 homers.

Hall of Fame catcher Bill Dickey said of his contemporary, "If I were catching blindfolded, I'd always know when it was Foxx who connected. He hit the ball harder than anyone."

Foxx was beaned and knocked out in a 1935 barnstorming game. After that, he suffered sinus problems. It was also said that's when his hard drinking started.

Foxx finished his career in 1945, as a part-time corner infielder and pitcher for the Philadelphia Phillies. He was 1–0 with a 1.59 ERA in 22⅔ innings.

Foxx retired with 534 home runs, 1,992 RBIs, and a .325 average.

His post-baseball life was a rough one. Investments went bad. He was drinking. He took all kinds of jobs, meatcutter to truck driver to being a glad-hander at a restaurant.

While he managed the Daisies for a year, he also found baseball work later in the 1950s, coaching the University of Miami team.

He died at age fifty-nine on July 21, 1967, after choking on a piece of meat. A year earlier his wife, Dorothy, had died in the same fashion.

In 1999, *The Sporting News*, the longtime baseball bible, selected Foxx as the 15th-best player in the history of the twentieth century, ranked higher than Johnny Bench, Mickey Mantle, Roberto Clemente, and Josh Gibson.

29 JOE DIMAGGIO: THE ONE THAT BEAT KEELER'S STREAK

"Wee Willie" Keeler had that nickname for a reason.

He was 5-foot-4, 140 pounds. Maybe.

But he was one of the great hitters in baseball's Deadball Era.

Born in Brooklyn on March 3, 1872, to Irish immigrant parents, Keeler choked about halfway up his bat (at 30 inches and 46 ounces, the shortest and the heaviest in the big leagues) and, as he said more than once to *Brooklyn Daily Eagle* sportswriter Abe Yager, "I try to hit 'em where they ain't."

And he did.

He had a record streak of eight consecutive seasons of 200 hits or more from 1894 to 1901 with Baltimore, Brooklyn, and the New York Highlanders (now the Yankees) that stood for more than 100 years. Seattle's Ichiro Suzuki broke the record with 10 straight seasons of 200 or more hits from 2001 to 2010. (A student of the game, Ichiro actually visited Keeler's grave at Queens's Calvary Cemetery after breaking the record.)

Keeler also owned a string of 13 straight years of hitting .300 or better. He won two batting championships and three times led the league in hits. He was part of the brawling, bawdy Baltimore Orioles of the 1890s, although Keeler didn't drink or swear and had a reputation for being amiable.

The right fielder's best season was in 1897 as a member of the Orioles, when he produced a .424 average. No left-handed hitter in history recorded a higher average. (Foul balls weren't counted as strikes in this era.) In that season of 1897, Keeler stroked 27 doubles and legged 19 triples. He stole 64 bases and scored 145 runs.

Those numbers may imply power, but Keeler was mostly all nuanced maestro with the bat. He was a great bunter and an expert at chopping at the ball to produce a high hop, later called a "Baltimore chop." When fielders would move in, he'd try to loft the pitch over their heads.

"Keeler could bunt any time he chose," Pittsburgh's Hall of Fame shortstop Honus Wagner remembered. "If the third baseman came in for a tap, he invariably pushed the ball past the fielder. If he stayed back, he bunted. Also, he had a trick of hitting a high hopper to an infielder. The ball would bound so high that he was across the bag before he could be stopped."

Despite being a man who never led the league in handing out compliments, John McGraw, first Keeler's teammate in Baltimore, later his manager with the New York Giants, said, "Keeler had the best batting eye I have ever seen."

Keeler did hit 33 homers in his career, but only three went over a fence.

He singled in his last at-bat in 1896, and then rapped hits in the first 43 games of 1897 for a 44-game hitting streak that ended on June 19.

His streak outlived him (he died in 1923) and his induction into the Hall of Fame (1939), but became the topic of conversation in the summer of 1941.

New York Yankee Joe DiMaggio, a star since 1936 and the American League Most Valuable Player in 1939, had started a hitting streak on May 15 with a solid single off Eddie Smith that drove in a run. The Yankees lost to the White Sox, 13–1.

The Yankees were scuffling, still mired in fourth place. DiMaggio wasn't helping, either, batting .194 in his previous 20 games.

On May 16, DiMaggio hit a long home run and a triple that sparked New York past Chicago.

It wasn't until the hitting streak was past 20 games that the nation picked up on the fact that something special was happening. As spring gave way to summer, the streak became something of a national obsession.

"Did he get a hit?" was the question asked with the hope of a positive response.

A little more than a month after the streak started, DiMaggio, twenty-six, broke the Yankee hitting-streak record of 29 shared by Roger Peckinpaugh in 1919 and Earle Combs in 1931.

But as Richard Ben Cramer noted in his 2000 book *Joe DiMaggio: The Hero's Life,* "The Streak was formed not of months or weeks, but moment to moment—this at bat, that pitch, this swing . . . and every instant, every instance, with its own fingerprint unique."

On June 29, in the second game of a doubleheader against the Washington Senators, DiMaggio singled to break St. Louis Browns George Sisler's record 41-game-hitting streak, considered the modern record. The all-time record remained Wee Willie Keeler's, at 44.

As DiMaggio inched toward the record, Ty Cobb, then baseball's hit leader, chimed in. He said DiMaggio was wonderful, but he didn't care for hitting streaks.

"When a team's leading hitter is after a batting streak record," said Cobb, who had a 40-game streak in 1911, "I don't care how good a competitor he is, he's thinking about himself more than usual."

The Yankees disputed that assertion, climbing from fourth place to first three days before DiMaggio passed Sisler. By the time DiMaggio set the 56-game hitting streak on July 17, the Yankees had gone from 5½ games behind the Cleveland Indians to seven games ahead.

But first, DiMaggio had to pass Keeler.

Both were son of immigrants (DiMaggio's parents had come from Italy) and both would end up in the Hall of Fame. At 6-foot-2, 190 pounds, DiMaggio was physically a bigger man. He swung a 36-inch-long bat weighing anywhere from 33 to 37 ounces. His favorite Louisville Slugger was stolen with his streak at 43 games. Despite the contours of Yankee Stadium that didn't benefit him as a right-handed hitter, DiMaggio didn't rely on bunts or chops. He was a line-drive hitter with power.

DiMaggio tied Keeler's record on a hot and hazy Tuesday in the second game of a doubleheader on July 1 before 53,832 fans at Yankee Stadium. He drilled a single off Black Jack Wilson, a hard-throwing Boston Red Sox right-hander, right over the head of shortstop Joe Cronin. Much of the crowd headed home. They saw what they wanted to see: a little history.

The next day, in the bottom of the fifth, against Red Sox rookie hurler Dick Newsome, who would win 19 games in 1941, DiMaggio parked a two-run homer to left field over the head of Boston's Ted Williams. Williams didn't think it was going out. He was playing for a carom. DiMaggio had established a new consecutive-game hit streak.

He wouldn't be stopped until July 17 in Cleveland, when third baseman Ken Keltner took two hits away from him with sterling backhanded plays.

DiMaggio hit .408, going 91-for-223 in his 56-game run, slugging 16 doubles and 4 triples. He only struck out five times. The Yankees went 41–13–2.

The Yankees continued on to win the pennant and World Series.

DiMaggio beat out Boston's Ted Williams (who hit .406) to win his second American League Most Valuable Player Award.

In 1978, Cincinnati's Pete Rose tied Keeler with a 44-game hitting streak, still the National League record.

In 1999, *The Sporting News* selected Keeler as the 75th-best player in history. The publication picked DiMaggio as number 11.

When DiMaggio passed Keeler with a long homer on that hot July afternoon, DiMaggio's friend and Yankee pitcher, Lefty Gomez, quipped with a wink and a nod to Keeler, "You hit 'em where they ain't."

28 WILLIE STARGELL: POPS GOES THE "FAMILY" MAN

Pops.

What a great nickname for Willie Stargell.

His own father walked out on him and his mother before Stargell was born. He had a kind of *Grapes of Wrath* childhood, always moving, from Oklahoma to California to Florida, then back to California. Stargell attended high school in Alameda, California, where, after future big leaguers Tommy Harper and Curt Motton, he was only the third-best player on his high school baseball team.

Stargell didn't meet his father until Willie was nineteen and already a professional player in the Pittsburgh Pirates system.

"I accepted my father as he was," Stargell would say years later. "I didn't offer judgment on what he had done and eventually I grew to love him for what he was."

That's Willie Stargell, real name Wilver, a combination of his father's first name, William, and his mother's maiden name, Vernell. He signed autographs as Wilver, not Willie.

Another example of his spirit and grit: he was still a teenager, a scuffling minor leaguer, when approached by two men at the entrance to a ballpark in Plainview, Texas. A racial epithet was slurred menacingly by one of the men, a revolver pulled, and a threat made: "I'm gonna blow your brains out if you play today."

Stargell was frightened.

"But by the time the rest of the team got there, I decided that if I was gonna die," he said in great deep voice, "I was gonna die doing exactly what I wanted to do. I had to play ball."

And that's who he was in the Pirates clubhouse, a man of power and grace, toughness and forgiveness, building bridges regardless of ego, race or ethnicity.

It was never more evident than in the 1979 season when, at his suggestion, the Pirates adopted as their theme Sister Sledge's "We Are Family."

Stargell, a left-handed hitter with the familiar number 8 on his back, had five game-winning hits, including four home runs, as the Pirates dashed to the

1979 National League East Championship, winning the title on the final day of the regular season. He belted an 11th inning home run in Game One of the NL Championship Series to start a sweep of the Cincinnati Reds.

Pittsburgh fell behind the Baltimore Orioles three games to one in the World Series, only to overcome the deficit and win it all.

Stargell, playing on wobbly and painful knees, put them ahead to stay in the sixth inning of Game Seven with his third home run of the Series. The blow that sealed it for the Pirates came off crafty Baltimore southpaw Scott McGregor. At one time in his career, Stargell didn't hit lefties well.

At thirty-nine, he was voted the NL's MVP, the oldest player to be so honored. He shared the prize with St. Louis first baseman Keith Hernandez.

Stargell was also the MVP of the NLCS and the World Series, becoming the first player to win that Triple Crown.

At 6-foot-4 and 225 pounds, Stargell, who started his career as a left fielder before moving to first base, was a physically imposing man. He looked just like the cleanup hitter he was.

Often, Stargell would swing a sledgehammer instead of a weighted bat in the on-deck circle. He also had a distinctive way of pinwheeling his bat in rhythm to the pitcher's delivery. It all paid off. He led the National League in homers in 1971 and 1973, and hit 475 dingers (tied with St. Louis great Stan Musial on the all-time list) in his 21-year career, all with the Pirates.

And, he didn't just hit home runs; he launched them, just like New York Yankees Babe Ruth and Mickey Mantle did. Stargell clubbed seven homers over the right field roof at Pittsburgh's Forbes Field, which happened only eighteen times (Ruth was the first) in sixty-one years. He rocketed four homers into the right field upper deck at Pittsburgh's Three Rivers Stadium.

Stargell was also the first player to hit a homer out of Dodger Stadium. Then he did it again.

Hall of Fame pitcher Don Sutton, who saw him often while on the mound for the Dodgers, once said of Stargell, "He just doesn't hit pitchers, he takes their dignity."

Stargell's first wife, Delores, kept statistics on how far her husband hit his home runs. She estimated Stargell would have had 22 more home runs in 1969 if the Pirates had played in the soon-to-be-opened Three Rivers Stadium instead of the cavernous Forbes Field.

Even so, Stargell still knocked 29 homers in 1969.

"Nobody could hit a ball as far as Willie," said Chuck Tanner, who managed the Pirates from 1977 to 1985. "In 1979 in Montreal, he hit a ball so far there they painted the seat gold. I went up there the next day and sat in that seat, and everybody on the field looked like puppets, that's how far it traveled."

Stargell came to the big leagues late in the 1962 season. Pirates star Roberto Clemente took him under his wing.

"The things he taught me about the game, and about being a man, were a big part of my life," Stargell said.

When Clemente was killed in a plane crash on New Year's Eve in 1972 while attempting to bring supplies to earthquake-broken Managua, Nicaragua, Stargell became the team leader.

"I had an education, being a ballplayer, anyone would envy," he would later say. "Rubbing shoulders with good folks I learned it all boils down to how you treat people."

The Pirates hierarchy occasionally complained about Stargell's weight and strikeouts (he finished with 1,936 strikeouts) but he loved to quote Pie Traynor, the Hall of Fame third baseman, who told him, "'If the Pirates left me alone and quit worrying about my weight so much, I'd become the greatest home run hitter in Pirate history.' Pie was a wise old son-of-a-gun."

As was Stargell.

In 1979 he started awarding stars for deserving players to attach to their caps. The criteria were something not found in box scores: hustle, moving a runner over, a gutsy pitch in a tight situation.

Stargell came up with the idea after hearing about a man who used to pin roses on people doing good work of some kind.

"He would walk up to that individual and say, 'I just saw what you did and I think you deserve a rose for your efforts,'" Stargell said at his induction into the Hall of Fame in 1988, at the time the 17th player to be elected on the first ballot. "I was so impressed with that. He had a catalogue of different things you could stick on. We got to the page with the stars, and I thought about them being the first four letters of my last name."

The Pirates retired his number 8 on September 6, 1982. Stargell, a seven-time All-Star, retired three weeks later. Along with his 475 home runs he finished with a .282 career average and 1,540 RBIs.

Stargell was sixty-one on April 9, 2001, when he died from complications of a stroke. His obituary even ran in *The Guardian*, a London-based newspaper. It read, in part, "The image of Stargell, ringed cap balanced precariously atop his bushy afro, bulging out of his double knit orange and black Pirates kit [uniform], is for many as enduring as any of the disco era.

"He was renowned for the enjoyment he took from the game.

"The umpire says 'play ball,'" was a favorite Stargell phrase. "He doesn't say 'work ball.'

"He may have acquired the nickname 'Pops' for his resemblance to the singer Pops Staples or simply because he was a father figure who held the Pirates team together."

27 MICKEY MANTLE: MUTT'S SON BECOMES A MAN

On December 11, 1951, Joe DiMaggio announced he was retiring from the New York Yankees.

He was thirty-seven. His shoulders were on the bum and his right knee barked. The heels, with their stabbing pains that had haunted him since 1946, felt better, but DiMaggio said, "I was full of aches and pains and it had become a chore for me to play. When baseball is no longer fun, it's no longer a game."

At the press conference, Yankee manager Casey Stengel was asked who would be replacing DiMaggio in center. The answer was Mickey Mantle.

"Whether the kid can do it or not, I don't know," Stengel said. "He has speed, a good throwing arm, and he hits both ways, so he can be in there every day. But he's very green. Remember, he has played only one year in the outfield."

Mantle had just turned twenty.

His father and hero, Elvin "Mutt" Mantle, forty, was dying of non-Hodgkin lymphoma. He would not last to Memorial Day 1952.

During the 1951 Series, Mickey had found out that his father was ill.

In Game Two of that series, at Yankee Stadium, Mantle famously ran after New York Giants rookie Willie Mays's soft line drive heading toward right-center field. Mantle's cleat got caught in an exposed outfield drainage pipe, forever damaging his right knee. He was taken off the field on a stretcher. When he left the stadium for the hospital, his father tried to help Mickey into a cab. Mantle put all his weight on his father, who collapsed on the curb. In their shared room at the Lenox Hill Hospital, father and son watched the Yankees win the 1951 World Series.

The year had started out with promise. Mantle, then nineteen, hit his way onto the Yankees roster with monster spring training. Originally, team general manager George Weiss hadn't wanted to invite the teenager to spring training because he didn't want to rush him. But Tom Greenwade, the scout who signed the switch-hitter out of Oklahoma's Commerce High School in 1949, kept insisting Mantle was ready.

Signed as a shortstop, Mantle was converted to the outfield by Stengel, who had former Yankee right fielder Tommy Henrich teach the finer points of right field to the blond-haired boy who had never used sunglasses in a game.

As Peter Golenbock wrote in his 1975 book *Dynasty: The New York Yankees, 1949–1964,* "Mantle's hitting overshadowed any lack of refinement in his fielding. Mantle, who stood about 5-foot-10 and weighed about 165 pounds, was not a large person, but he had the shoulders and arms of a blacksmith. When it was his turn to bat during training, the veterans would stop to watch him hit. They just couldn't believe the long, arching drives which clattered against the distant outfield bleachers."

Mantle hit .402 in spring training and was in the Opening Day lineup, batting third. He hit his first homer in May. By June, he was being platooned. In July, Stengel sent Mantle back to the minor-league Kansas City Blues.

Mantle was crushed. All he seemed to do was strike out from both sides of the plate. He thought hard about quitting. He called his father, starting the conversation with, "I don't think I can play baseball anymore."

Mutt Mantle drove from Commerce to Kansas City. At his son's hotel room, he started packing Mickey's clothes into a cheap suitcase.

"I thought I raised a man," Mutt said, hardly controlling his fury. "I see I raised a coward instead. You can come back to Oklahoma and work the mines with me."

Mickey Mantle changed his mind about quitting.

He also started hitting, batting .361 with 11 homers and 50 RBIs for Kansas City. The Yankees brought him back to the big club, changing his uniform from number 6 to number 7, a number he never liked, just as he never liked its implication of luck. Mantle finished his rookie season with 13 homers and a .267 average.

He was batting leadoff and playing right field when the Yankees hosted the New York Giants on October 4, the day after Bobby Thomson had hit the home run known as the "Shot Heard 'Round the World," which capped the remarkable comeback by the Giants to win the National League pennant.

Both Mutt and Mickey's mother, Lovell, made their first trip to New York to watch their son.

The Yankees lost the opener to the Giants, 5–1. In his World Series debut, Mantle went 0-for-3 with two walks.

In Game Two, he led off the second inning with a drag bunt single. He struck out in his second at-bat. Then he got hurt pulling up, not trying to run into DiMaggio, who made a late "I got it" call on the fly ball by Mays in the fifth inning.

The Yankees won Game Two and were on their way to winning the World Series without Mantle in six games. While his teammates were celebrating, Mantle learned his knee would get better and his father was dying.

Mantle turned twenty just days after leaving the Lenox Hill Hospital. Two months and three days later, he married his high school girlfriend, Merlyn Johnson, on December 23, 1951. Mutt was there. He was gone by early May.

According to Jane Leavy, author of *The Last Boy: Mickey Mantle and the End of America's Childhood,* "Mantle found his father laid out in an open casket in the front parlor of the home he had purchased with his 1951 World Series check . . . Mutt was buried in the Grand Army of the Republic Cemetery along Route 66 between Miami and Commerce. When it was time to leave him in the ground for good, Mickey refused to go with the rest of the family. He stayed behind, berating himself for never having told his father he loved him."

Mutt Mantle had named his first child after Detroit's Hall of Fame catcher Gordon "Mickey" Cochrane, and raised his son to be a baseball player. And after the funeral, Mickey Mantle returned to that job, with a heavy heart, and a knee that worried the Yankees.

Four days before Mutt Mantle died, the Yankees had traded another promising outfielder, Jackie Jensen, to the Washington Senators for outfielder and first baseman Irv Noren.

The Yankees were hedging their bet on Mantle.

They were no lock to win the World Series for the fourth straight season. DiMaggio was gone. Pitcher Whitey Ford was in the army, as were infielders Jerry Coleman and Bobby Brown. Eddie Lopat, another starting pitcher, had a sore arm. The Yankees needed Mantle. And, not for the last time, he responded.

Catcher Yogi Berra led the 1952 team with 30 homers and 98 RBIs, but Mantle battled .311. He launched 23 home runs and knocked in 87 runs. He made his first All-Star team and was third in the American League Most Valuable Player voting. Stengel was calling him the greatest switch-hitter in history.

The Yankees, who survived a ferocious late-season run by the Cleveland Indians, met the Brooklyn Dodgers in the World Series. The Dodgers owned a three-games-to-two lead when Mantle slugged his first World Series home run deep to left center at Brooklyn's Ebbets Field in Game Six to build a 3–1 lead. The Yankees held on to win, 3–2, and knot the series.

The homer was hit from the left side, the first of Mantle's 18 World Series home runs. Billy Loes, a slight twenty-two-year-old right-hander, who went 13–8 with a 2.69 ERA, surrendered the bomb. After the game he said of Mantle, "He fell away from the pitch when he hit it out. Imagine if he had taken a full swing."

The next day, in Game Seven, Mantle muscled a sixth-inning homer over everything at Ebbets Field onto the sidewalk of Bedford Avenue. It gave the Yankees a lead they wouldn't relinquish.

It was their fourth straight World Series title.

Mantle returned to Commerce for a huge parade. Everybody was there, except the man he would spend the rest of his life looking for.

26 JIM LEYRITZ: THE SHORT-LIVED KING OF A NEW DYNASTY

In the late 1970s and early 1980s, Jim Leyritz was probably the second-best high school baseball player in Greater Cincinnati.

The best? Barry Larkin, who would go on to have a 19-year career with the hometown Cincinnati Reds on his way to the Hall of Fame.

The two played together on summer leagues and on all-star teams.

When Leyritz was eighteen, he broke his left foot in a tennis match two days before the 1982 draft. The injury would alter his batting stance forever. He can remember a scout from the Atlanta Braves phoning his home to inquire about Leyritz's college intentions, and having the youngster tell him he had a foot in a cast.

No team called on draft day.

Leyritz enrolled in Middle Georgia Community College, and then transferred to the University of Kentucky. He was eligible for the 1985 draft, but his name was never called.

It was only after he played in the Jayhawk Collegiate League in Kansas that the New York Yankees offered him a contract.

They thought he could catch and hit a little. He was never considered a big-time prospect, but he always could hit.

At Oneonta in 1986: .363

At Fort Lauderdale in 1987: .307

At Albany-Colonie in 1989: .315

At Columbus in 1990: .289

Leyritz had a little pop, too. He could reach the seats. But mostly the Yankees saw him as the 23rd, 24th, or 25th player on the roster—a backup catcher, a spare at third, maybe an occasional corner outfielder, a right-handed bat off the bench.

He didn't see himself that way. When Leyritz looked in the mirror, he saw a star. He favored cowboy hats and designer sunglasses. His forearms were cartoon-character big.

His first Yankee nickname was "Elvis," then "King." That last one stuck.

Leyritz, who bore a swagger, a confidence, affability, and not a little arrogance, made the big leagues in 1990 with the Yankees.

In 1993, the first year the Yankees started to improve after more than a decade of mediocre seasons, he played a lot of first base when Don Mattingly was battling back woes. Leyritz finished the season with 14 homers, 53 RBIs, and a .309 average in a super-sub role.

He thought he should be the everyday catcher.

The Yankees didn't agree.

In 1995, the team made the playoffs for the first time since 1981. As the wild card, they played the Western Division champion Seattle Mariners in the American League Division Series and hung on to win Game One, 9–6.

Leyritz started behind the plate in Game Two. He had become pitcher Andy Pettitte's personal catcher. In the bottom of the 15th, more than five hours after the game had started, Yankee Stadium was still roaring. Midnight passed and the score remained tied, 5–5. Pat Kelly walked with one out and Leyritz came to the plate in the rain.

Tim Belcher, normally a starter, was pitching for the Mariners in relief.

Leyritz worked the count to 3–1. After every pitch he would twirl his bat at his hip the way former Yankee Mickey Rivers had taught him. Opponents hated that. With the rain falling, Leyritz launched a Belcher fastball high and deep to right field.

"In the heat of the moment, everybody thinks it's gone," Leyritz said after the game, "I knew that I hit it far and I was hoping it had enough to make it over. It was a great feeling."

Jack Curry wrote in the *New York Times*, "The scene was incredible, as the Yankees piled on Leyritz and tumbled around like a rugby scrum and most of the 57,126 fans who had remained through the long evening serenaded the team with 'New York, New York.'"

The winning pitcher that night was a rookie making his first postseason appearance with 3⅓ innings of scoreless relief.

His name: Mariano Rivera.

The Yankees lost the next three games to the Mariners in Seattle.

Yankee owner George Steinbrenner then pretty much cleaned house.

In the off-season they signed Joe Girardi to be their catcher and Joe Torre to be their manager for 1996.

The Yankees made it to the World Series that year but fell behind the Atlanta Braves, two games to none. David Cone pitched the Yankees back into the Series in Game Three, but Kenny Rogers had just about pitched them out in Game Four.

Leyritz had spent much of that game in the clubhouse, lifting weights and watching the game on television. Just in case.

Torre decided that Paul O'Neill would pinch-hit for Girardi. Leyritz was in the game. The Yankees had crawled back into the game, but were still behind.

In the eighth, Atlanta's Hall of Fame manager Bobby Cox decided to close out the game, asking his overpowering closer Mark Wohlers to get the final six outs. The Braves owned a 6–3 lead.

Wohlers could throw a fastball as hard as 103 miles per hour. He also had 39 saves in '96.

Yankees third baseman Charlie Hayes led off the eighth with a ground single. Right fielder Darryl Strawberry slapped a single to left. Second baseman Mariano Duncan grounded to short, leaving men on first and third.

Leyritz was next. He dug in, thinking fastball, settling into his funky stance, front foot straight and stiff while his back leg was bent at the knee, a style he created when taking batting practice in high school while wearing that cast on his foot.

After four pitches the count was 2–2.

Leyritz was still thinking fastball; Wohlers threw a slider.

"In 1996 we had the Yankees right where we wanted them," Atlanta general manager John Schuerholz recalled. "But it didn't happen. All of a sudden the Yankees climbed back in. Mark Wohlers was our best reliever, and up comes this guy Jim Leyritz. Wohlers throws a slider, Leyritz fouls it back. This guy is a guy with a 98-mile-an-hour fastball. But he throws another slider and Leyritz fouls that one back. Bat head right on it. Good speed. He throws another slider and you know those cartoons where the ball is hit so hard that its eyes bug out? I think that ball looked like that."

Leyritz wasn't so sure the ball was heading out of Atlanta-Fulton County Stadium.

"I didn't style or anything at the plate because I didn't know if it was going to go out of the park," he said. "But I didn't run hard to first because I knew the ball was going to be either over the fence or caught. I just watched to see what would happen."

The ball soared over the left-field fence to tie the score. The Yanks would win in 10 innings, then take the next two games.

The 1996 world championship was the start of the next Yankee dynasty.

The Yankees traded Leyritz to the Anaheim Angels in the '96 off-season.

When he returned to Yankee Stadium for the first time as an Angel, Leyritz slugged a two-run homer one night and won the next game with a two-run double in the ninth inning off Rivera.

One time later in the season, Angels manager Terry Collins pinch-hit for Leyritz.

"I was steaming. I walked by him and said, 'Have you ever heard of Mark Wohlers?'" Leyritz said. "I probably shouldn't have done that."

25 TONY PEREZ: THE BIG DOG BARKS

As the Boston Red Sox went over their scouting reports on the Cincinnati Reds prior to the start of the 1975 World Series, manager Darrell Johnson believed the key to beating the Big Red Machine was stopping Tony Perez.

The Reds had used the regular season as almost a tune-up for October. They won 108 games, and the National League West by a whopping 20 games before sweeping past the Pittsburgh Pirates in the NL Championship Series. The Reds hadn't won a World Series since 1940 and appeared poised to break the drought.

The Reds boasted Joe Morgan at second, Dave Concepcion at short, Pete Rose at third, Ken Griffey in right, George Foster in left. Johnny Bench was behind the plate.

First baseman Tony Perez hit cleanup. He was known as "Doggie" or "The Big Dog," and as one of the best clutch hitters of his time. He'd just finished his ninth straight regular season with 90 or more RBIs. His final regular season stats were 20 homers, 109 RBIs and a .282 average.

Perez, who was 6-foot-2, 190 pounds, and batted and threw right-handed, had sizzled against the Pirates, hitting .417 with a home run and four ribbies in the three games.

But he was iceberg cold against the Red Sox.

In the first four games of the World Series, Perez was 0-for-14 with one RBI and one run scored.

Cincinnati manager Sparky Anderson told him he was being dropped to fifth in the batting order for Game Five, behind Bench.

Anderson also added, according to Mark Frost in his 2009 book *Game Six: Cincinnati, Boston, and the 1975 World Series: The Triumph of America's Pastime*, "Tony, if we let this go seven games and you don't get a hit, your children can tell their children that their grandfather had an all-time World Series record: most at bats without a hit."

Tony Perez probably smiled at that line. He was always smiling.

He went on to launch two bombs off Boston starter Reggie Cleveland in Game Five. The first, in the bottom of the fourth, tied the game at 1–1.

In the sixth, Perez hit one just as far to left center in Riverfront Stadium, a three-run shot. The Reds won, 6–2.

After the game, Anderson said, "You can't keep the Big Doggie down."

It was on to Boston, where it rained and rained. Game Six was postponed until Tuesday, October 21. It probably could have been played Monday, but Fenway Park was still squishy. It was also rumored that baseball Commissioner Bowie Kuhn didn't want to put the game up against ABC's *Monday Night Football*, or the CBS hit *All in the Family*.

The Reds tried to stay game-sharp by working out at Tufts University's gym. When asked why that location, Sparky Anderson replied, "I think Harvard would be a little over my head."

When the rain stopped and they did get to play Game Six, Boston's Carlton Fisk hit his famous home run in the bottom of the 12th to win it. It was 12:34 a.m., Wednesday.

Perez remembers the game for finally getting a hit off his Cuban countryman, Boston starter Luis Tiant, who held him hitless in eight at-bats including three strikeouts in Games One and Four. They had never faced each other in Cuba: Perez was raised in the country, while Tiant was reared in the suburbs of Havana. Both grew up under the spell of Saturnino Orestes Armas Minoso Arrieta, better known in America as Minnie Minoso, a Hall of Fame outfielder, mainly with the Chicago White Sox.

Minoso, who also played in the Negro Leagues, hit better than .300 eight times in the big leagues. It was every Cuban baseball player's dream to go to America and do what Minnie Minoso had done

Perez was a tall, skinny shortstop, good enough to make a Cuban travel team as a teenager in the late 1950s.

Reds scout Tony Pacheco saw enough potential to invest $2.50 of the Reds money for a visa.

When Perez arrived in Tampa for spring training in 1960, he knew two words of English: yes and no. But he had a smile and a great disposition, and he could hit, and that was language enough to begin with. He was assigned to Geneva, New York, where early spring felt like winter, or worse, for a Cuban.

One time Perez was hurt and put on the DL. The player who replaced him was a kid named Pete Rose.

Perez made the Show in 1964 as a first baseman and played there until 1967, when he was installed as the team's third baseman.

He hit his first home run for the Reds in the second game of the 1965 season. He would end up with 379 in his career.

"Johnny Bench said that with that engaging attitude, booming baritone and wide, contagious smile, Perez cast a net over the entire team and wouldn't let them wander," Frost wrote in his book about the Reds and the Red Sox. "He was the man you could always count on to come through when the game was on the line."

Bench and Rose, and later Morgan, received the bold-faced headlines, all deserved, but Perez was the foundation.

Before there was a Big Red Machine, there was Tony Perez.

Bill Lee had thrown Perez the Eephus pitch in the second inning of Game Seven. It was a slow, high lob that hurler Rip Sewell had come up with decades earlier. Sewell was a pretty good pitcher, who ended up being shot in a hunting accident. He was 4-F when it came to serving during World War II but could still pitch in the big leagues with their watered-down lineups. Sewell was selected to the 1946 All-Star Game. He threw his Eephus pitch to Boston's Ted Williams, who hit it a mile and a half for a home run.

Lee called his pitch the "Leephus."

The Boston left-hander, a free spirit, serious yet full of mirth, threw the Leephus pitch three times to Perez in the Series. The first time, Perez looked bad, swinging at air. The second time, he took it for a ball. But Perez noticed a tiny hitch in Lee's motion before he unleashed it. Perez was going to be the fourth batter in the sixth. He prayed Lee would throw it again.

According to John Erardi and Greg Rhodes in their book *Big Red Dynasty*, Perez approached the bat rack and noticed Anderson pacing after smoking a cigarette in the tunnel. It was the sixth inning and the Reds were down, 3–0.

"'What's wrong with you, Sparky?' Perez asked in the high-pitched squeal he uses when he wants to loosen somebody up. Perez's normal voice is a deep, thick bass.

"'Damn, Doggie!' said Sparky, 'We're down three to nothing!'

"'Don't worry about it,' said Perez. "Get somebody on base. I'm going to 'heet' one. I'm going to 'heet' a bomb.'"

And he did, off of the Leephus pitch, deep into the Boston night, bringing the Reds to within a run, 3–2.

The Reds tied the game in the seventh, and won it in the ninth. The Red Sox were again denied their first World Series championship since 1918. Boston would have to wait until 2004 to become champions.

The breakup of the Big Red Machine started when the Reds traded Perez to the Montreal Expos after the 1976 season. He actually ended up a member of the Red Sox, playing for Boston from 1980 to 1982.

In 1984, at the age of forty-two, he became the oldest player at the time to hit a walk-off pinch homer. A year later, he became the era's oldest player to hit a grand slam.

His last home run came on the next-to-the-last game of the 1986 season. Back with the Reds, Perez was NL Player of the Week because he went 8-for-19 and, along with the homer, delivered three doubles and knocked in six runs.

His number 24 was retired by the Reds. The seven-time All-Star was elected to the Hall of Fame in 2000, in a class that included his manager, Sparky Anderson, and his 1975 opponent Carlton Fisk, the Boston Red Sox catcher.

At his induction, Perez said, "I doubt a king at his coronation feels better than me today."

24 BABE RUTH: THE BAMBINO BREAKS HIS OWN RECORD

All summer they went back and forth. Back and forth.

If one hit a home run on Saturday, the other would slam one on Sunday. Seven times in the course of the 1927 season they hit homers in the same game.

Newspapers called it "The Great American Home Run Derby," and it starred Babe Ruth and Lou Gehrig.

Only two homers would separate them from April into September.

Ruth batted third in the New York Yankees lineup, Gehrig fourth.

They got used to shaking each other's hands at home plate.

The 1927 New York Yankees were arguably the best team in baseball history. Six players—Ruth, Gehrig, second baseman Tony Lazzeri, center fielder Earle Combs, and pitchers Waite Hoyt and Herb Pennock—were elected into the Hall of Fame. Their manager, Miller Huggins, became a Hall of Famer, too.

They won the American League pennant by Labor Day and would finish with 110 wins and 44 losses.

Combs, the leadoff hitter, owned a .356 average. Lazzeri and left fielder Bob Meusel knocked in more than 100 runs each. Hoyt won 22 games, Pennock earned the W in 19.

A decade earlier, the top home run hitters were Dave Robertson of the New York Giants and Gavvy Cravath of the Philadelphia Phillies. They had 12 each. (Lazzeri had 18 in 1927, third in the league and third on the Yankees.) Wally Pipp, who famously would lose his first-base job to Gehrig in 1925 after being hit by a pitch and then complaining of a headache, was third in all of baseball in 1917, with nine homers.

On August 9, Gehrig actually nudged past Ruth, 38 homers to 35.

"It was the first time anyone had directly challenged Ruth's preeminence," Robert Creamer wrote in his 1974 book *Babe: The Legend Comes to Life.*

Ruth, of course, was no surprise.

In 1920, his first year as a Yankee, he launched 54 bombs and changed baseball forever. The following year he slammed 59. In 1926, he rounded the bases 47 times. He failed to win the home run crown in 1922 and 1925 because he missed six and seven weeks of those respective seasons.

Gehrig was a different story.

In 1927 he was only twenty-four, eight years Ruth's junior, in the midst of his third full season in the big leagues. He was as quiet as Ruth was loud. Coming out of Columbia University, he had pounded 20 homers in 1925 and followed up with 16 in 1926, using his gap power to also leg out 20 triples.

In his 2005 book *Luckiest Man: The Life and Death of Lou Gehrig*, Jonathan Eig described Gehrig's approach at the plate: "He lowered his center of gravity when he swung so that his left knee almost scraped the ground. He didn't need to flail. Ruth, with his wild, up-from-the-heels swing, hit soaring rockets that disappeared high in the air and fell to earth often in bleachers. Gehrig swung from the shoulder, as if wielding an ax. His home runs seemed to zip just over the second baseman's head and continue rising until they banged off a seat in the right field bleachers. His shots almost seemed to whistle."

Gehrig told *Baseball Magazine* in 1927 he didn't consider himself a home run hitter.

"I have as much respect for a home run as anybody, but I like straightaway hitting. I believe it's the proper way to hit. If a fellow has met the ball just right on the nose, he's done what he set out to do."

In 1927, while competing against his hero and friend Ruth for the home run championship, and maybe even a new home run record, Gehrig also delivered 52 doubles, piled up 173 RBIs, and put up a .373 average.

Ruth and Gehrig were tied in homers on September 6 when the Yankees played the lousy Boston Red Sox (they'd lose 103 games, the third straight season of 100 or more losses) in a doubleheader at Fenway Park.

Leigh Montville, in his 2006 bestseller *The Big Bam: The Life and Times of Babe Ruth,* set the scene: "In the fifth inning of the first game, Tony Welzer on the mound for the Sox, Gehrig unloaded a shot into the right field bleachers to take the lead at 45. . . .

"In the sixth, Ruth came back at him. With two men on base, Welzer tried a change of pace on the Bam. The Bam was waiting for it. He ran up on the ball and, according to the *New York Times*, 'dealt the sphere a fearful blow,' a shot instantly considered the longest homer in Fenway history. . . .

"In the next inning, poor Welzer still on the mound, Ruth connected again. This was a tall fly ball that sneaked into the stands close to the right field pole.

Ruth 46, Gehrig 45. Finally, in the seventh inning of the nightcap, Ruth broke up Charlie Russell's shutout with another fly ball down the right field line that snuck into the stands. Gehrig, the next batter, followed with a shot to left center, longer and harder hit than Ruth's homer that stayed in the park for a triple.

"And, yet somehow just like that the chase was done."

There were 22 games left in the season. Ruth needed 13 home runs to break his record. When he hit his 50th on September 11, he said he thought he could break his old record of 59.

It was good copy, but no one quite believed Ruth.

But he launched a grand slam off Philadelphia A's future Hall of Famer Lefty Grove on September 27. It was number 57, with four games to play.

Number 58 was off Washington's Hod Lisenbee, a skinny rookie right-hander with a funky delivery. He'd once struck out Ruth three times in a single game. In 1927, he led the American League with four shutouts and was 18–9.

None of that mattered to Ruth. In the first inning of the 152nd game of the season, Ruth, with two strikes, whacked a Lisenbee pitch into the right-field bleachers.

In the fifth, with the bases loaded, Washington manager Bucky Harris called upon twenty-five-year-old Paul Hopkins to make his major-league debut against Babe Ruth.

Ruth hit two long foul balls. The count was 3 and 2. Hopkins' next thought was that he'd snap off a deceptive curveball.

"Real slow and over the outside of the plate," Hopkins said almost seventy years later to a *Sports Illustrated* reporter. "It was so slow that Ruth started to swing and then hesitated. He hitched on it and brought the bat back. And then he swung, breaking his wrists as he came through. What a great eye he had! He hit it at the right second. Put everything behind it. I can still hear the crack of the bat. I can still see the swing."

Ruth had tied his record of 59 home runs.

The following day, September 30, a Friday at Yankee Stadium, Ruth knocked in both Yankee runs on singles. The game was tied 2–2 in the eighth.

Tom Zachary was pitching for the Senators. He was left-handed and he threw hard. He would win 186 games in his 19-year big-league career. And he would give up nine career homers to Ruth.

Mark Koenig, a terrific Yankee shortstop, was on third. Zachary's first pitch to Ruth was a strike. The second pitch was high. The third was stroked high and deep to right.

Zachary threw his glove to the ground and barked at the umpires that the ball was foul.

Ruth had bopped his 17th homer of the month and 60th of the season. He delighted in making his way around the bases waving his cap to the 8,000 or so in attendance.

At home plate, Gehrig was there to congratulate Ruth with a hearty handshake and a pat on the back.

The next day, October 1, the last game of the regular season, Ruth went homerless.

Gehrig hit his 47th. No one made a big deal of it.

Gehrig was named the American League Most Valuable Player.

But Ruth had become only more legendary.

23 AARON BOONE: CURSE OF THE BOONEBINO

Aaron Boone didn't even start the game.

Enrique Wilson did.

Wilson had managed some success in the past against Boston's Pedro Martinez, and the New York Yankees needed whatever edge they could muster against Martinez on October 16, 2003, in the do-or-die Game Seven of the American League Championship Series.

Boone entered the game in the eighth inning, to pinch-run for pinch-hitter Ruben Sierra, who had batted for Wilson.

At the July trading deadline that year, the Yankees had acquired Boone from the Cincinnati Reds for their top pitching prospect, Brandon Claussen. It had been a tough week for the thirty-year-old third baseman. His father, Bob, a former All-Star catcher, had been fired as manager of the fifth-place Reds. And the Reds were the only organization for which Aaron Boone had ever played. He was greeted at every at-bat by the fans with an enthusiastic "Boooooone." What sounded like booing felt like a hug.

On September 22, 2002, Aaron Boone had hit the last homer in Cincinnati's Riverfront Stadium, which was to be closed at season's end. He had made the National League All-Star team and was in the midst of another complete season—18 homers, 65 RBIs, .273 average, and 15 steals.

But Boone wasn't as great with the Yankees. He hit only six dingers in the final two months of the season, with 31 RBIs. His defense was shaky, too.

Still, he was a third-generation major leaguer. The Boones are the only family to have three generations of family members make the All-Star Game, play in the World Series, and hit 100 career home runs. Ray Boone, Aaron's grandfather, was a two-time All-Star infielder with Cleveland and Detroit. He drove in 114 runs for the Indians in 1953 and knocked in 116 runs for the Tigers in 1955. In retirement, he became a scout for the Red Sox. One of his signings was pitcher Curt Schilling, who was traded from the Red Sox early in his career, only to return with historic results.

Aaron's father, Bob, was a four-time All-Star catcher and known for his seven Gold Gloves with Philadelphia, California, and Kansas City.

Aaron's older brother, Bret, was a three-time All-Star second baseman, who in 2001 clubbed 37 homers, with 141 RBIs, and hit .331. He was best known as a member of the Cincinnati Reds and Seattle Mariners.

In the playoffs against the Red Sox, Aaron Boone was pressing. He was 2-for-16 in the series. He watched much of the most remarkable game of the series from the bench. It was a matchup between Boston's Pedro Martinez and New York's Roger Clemens, the former Boston ace. The two teams didn't like each other. The series had included a bench-clearing brawl in Game Three.

The Sox built an early 4–0 lead. Mike Mussina relieved Clemens in the fourth inning with no outs and men on first and third. Mussina struck out catcher Jason Varitek and induced Johnny Damon to ground into a double play, keeping the faint Yankee hopes alive.

Martinez was big-game great, mixing his pitches like only Pedro Martinez could.

New York's Jason Giambi hit two solo homers to inch the Yankees closer, but then David Ortiz homered to give the Red Sox a 5–2 lead heading into the bottom of the eighth.

Martinez had already thrown more than 100 pitches when he started the eighth. New York's Nick Johnson popped out to lead off the inning. Shortstop Derek Jeter lashed a line-drive double to right. Center fielder Bernie Williams followed with a single to center, scoring Jeter.

It was the 115th pitch by Martinez. Sox manager Grady Little walked to the mound. In the Sox bullpen, right-hander Mike Timlin and left-hander Alan Embree were warming up.

Left-handed-swinging outfielder Hideki Matsui was due up next. He had doubled off Martinez earlier in Game Seven.

Little talked with Martinez and walked back to the dugout. Martinez got ahead of Matsui with two quick strikes. Then Matsui rifled a ground-rule double down the right-field line.

Up came Yankee catcher Jorge Posada, who had exchanged heated words with Martinez in Game Three.

Martinez was now up to 118 pitches.

With the count 2 and 2, Martinez tried to bust Posada inside. Posada didn't take a great swing, but floated a fly ball into no-man's land in center, sending home two runs, tying the game at 5–5.

"Pedro wanted to stay in there," Little would say after the game. "He wanted to get the job done just as he has many times for us all season long and he's the man we wanted on the mound."

After Posada, Little replaced Martinez.

The score remained tied into the bottom of the 11th. Mariano Rivera had pitched three innings of scoreless relief. There was no guarantee he could come out to pitch a fourth.

Boone was to lead off the bottom of the 11th.

Tim Wakefield, the knuckleballer who had pitched so brilliantly in the series that he was a candidate for the ALCS MVP, was on the mound. Boone was thinking about taking a pitch, getting his timing in sync with the jitterbug nature of a knuckleball, then looking to take one good swing. But he paused, took another practice swing. *Why wait?* he thought. He knew what pitch was coming.

Boone swung and didn't miss. It was already Thursday, October 17.

The ball hadn't even come down and tears were flooding Yankee manager Joe Torre's eyes.

By the time Boone was rounding third, the voice of Frank Sinatra invited all to "Start spreading the news . . ."

Boone had punched his team's ticket to the World Series and prolonged Boston's Curse of the Bambino for another year.

The next day's New York *Daily News* back-page headline: "Curse of the Boonebino."

ESPN's *Baseball Tonight* would rank his long ball the ninth greatest home run of all time.

Boone said that when Martinez was dealing and the Yankees were trailing 5–2, things weren't looking good, "but the bullpen came in and held them and we just pecked away and like Derek told me, 'The ghosts will show up eventually.' And they did. This is . . . this is stupid."

The Yankees lost to the Florida Marlins in the World Series. Boone finished the postseason 9 for 53 (.170), with 15 strikeouts.

In 2004, Boone was set to be the Yankees starting third baseman. But he tore a knee ligament during a pickup basketball game in the off-season. The Yankees would need a third baseman.

They acquired Texas star Alex Rodriguez, who'd looked like he was going to the Red Sox in a December deal, but the Major League Baseball Players Association wouldn't agree to the contract concessions. The Yankees voided Boone's contract, and A-Rod agreed to play third base in New York.

At thirty-two, Boone would come back from knee surgery. At thirty-six, he came back to play after open-heart surgery. He retired in 2010.

He was always being reminded of his home run.

"Willie Randolph [then the Yankees third-base coach] told me that I was his sleeper pick," Boone recalled. "I remember Mo getting out of the 11th inning, I knew running off the field that inning, I had a feeling like I was gonna do something.

"When I made contact I knew almost instantly that it was gonna be a home run. I knew I got a really good piece of it. Just wanted to make sure it was gonna be fair and once I knew it was gonna be fair . . . stuck my arms out, and really just tried to embrace as much as I could.

"All of us that played ball when we were little kids, all lived out that moment in our backyard: two outs, bottom of the ninth, 3–2 count, Aaron Boone at bat . . . and you hit the home run. To actually get to live that out on a major league field in Yankee Stadium against the Red Sox was something that . . . I feel really blessed to be in that situation."

22 BERNIE CARBO: A SHOT FOR HOPE AND FAITH

When Boston Red Sox manager Darrell Johnson told Bernie Carbo to get ready in the eighth inning of Game Six of the 1975 World Series, Carbo wasn't drug-addled enough to actually think he was getting into the game.

Carbo was wrecked, but not *that* wrecked, according to him.

"I probably smoked two joints, drank about three or four beers, got to the ballpark, took some [amphetamines], took a pain pill, drank a cup of coffee, chewed some tobacco, had a cigarette and got up to the plate and hit," he would tell Stan Grossfeld of the *Boston Globe* in 2010.

Despite all that, Carbo was used to playing under the influence.

He had been doing it since he was a teenager. It was just part of the carnival that was his life.

Carbo, as a left-handed hitter, knew . . . *knew* . . . his former manager Sparky Anderson of the Cincinnati Reds wasn't going to let him face right-hander Rawly Eastwick.

Anderson went by the book, righty on righty, lefty on lefty.

If Carbo were announced into the game, Anderson would summon southpaw Will McEnaney and Johnson would counter with right-handed-hitting Juan Beniquez.

Carbo had spent much of Game Six in the dugout, whittling his bat. He took a lathe and stripped the polish. He had done such a good job that teammate Rick Wise said, "You know, you can't use that bat. It doesn't have an emblem on it."

So Carbo took a Magic Marker and wrote "Louisville Slugger" on the wood.

"That's how I kept myself amused," he said.

All the while, the Reds were building a 6–3 lead.

A Reds win would mean the team's first World Series championship since 1940. By the bottom of the eighth, Boston's Fenway Park was cemetery-silent. Fans knew the score.

Boston center fielder Fred Lynn beat out an infield hit and third baseman Rico Petrocelli walked. There was life. But Anderson called on Eastwick, who had won two previous games and saved the other. He had 22 saves in the regular season.

Eastwick struck out Boston right fielder Dwight Evans, and by the time Red Sox shortstop Rick Burleson lined out to left, it looked like the Cincinnati fireman was going to be the Series MVP.

Carbo was still on deck when Burleson made the second out.

And he stayed there, waiting for Anderson to summon left-hander McEnaney.

Carbo had hit a pinch homer in Game Three off Cincinnati right-hander Clay Carroll. It was a towering smash to deep left in Riverfront Stadium.

When Game Six was pushed back three days because of rain, most players on both sides had taken batting practice at Tufts University in Medford.

Carbo didn't participate. His reason: "I didn't know where Tufts was. I don't think I'd had batting practice in a week."

The Reds drafted Carbo as a high school third baseman with the 17th pick in the first-ever baseball draft, in 1965. Carbo would say years later that he was already an alcoholic. (Cincinnati used their second pick to select catcher Johnny Bench.)

Carbo made the big leagues for good in 1970, as an outfielder. He hit .310 and was *The Sporting News* Rookie of the Year. The Reds traded him to the Cardinals in 1972. And the Cardinals traded him to the Red Sox for Reggie Smith in 1974, in a deal that included pitcher Rick Wise.

He became a part of a clique of Red Sox iconoclasts called the Buffalo Heads, which included pitchers Bill Lee and Ferguson Jenkins. Carbo also had a habit of traveling with a stuffed gorilla he named Mighty Joe Young, who always had the middle seat on team charters.

His antiestablishment stance and idiosyncrasies were all part of Carbo's "charm," a charm fueled, he said, by cocaine, Dexedrine, Benzedrine, Darvon, sleeping pills, chasing women, and drinking beer.

"And I never played a game without them," he told Grossfeld.

When the Red Sox were being chewed up by injuries early in 1975, Carbo's bat played a major role in keeping them in the pennant race. But before he launched his pinch homer in Game Three, deep to left at Riverfront Stadium, Carbo hadn't homered since August 1.

It was National League umpire Satch Davidson, the man behind the plate when Atlanta's Hank Aaron hit his 715th home run a year earlier, who summoned Carbo to the plate.

He wasn't ready to hit.

As he told Grossfeld, "I played every game high. I was addicted to anything you could possibly be addicted to. I played the outfield sometimes when it looked like the stars were falling out of the sky."

October 21, 1975, the season in the balance, was no different.

"So I go into the batter's box. I ain't ready to hit," he told Grossfeld. "Next thing, strike one, strike two, ball one, ball two. Then he threw me a cut fastball, a little slider and I took it right out of [catcher Johnny] Bench's glove—the ball just dribbled out. I step out and I'm thinking, 'Aw man, I almost struck out. I was lucky.'

"Bench said after the game it looked like a Little Leaguer learning how to hit. Pete Rose said it was the worst swing he ever saw. Rico Petrocelli [standing on first] said [the swing] looked like a pitcher who hurt his arm, trying to make a comeback as a hitter."

Hall of Fame writer Peter Gammons wrote in his 1987 book *Beyond the Sixth Game*, that a "fastball befuddled Bernardo as if it were a Pythagorean Theorem."

Carbo told writer Peter Golenbock in his 2005 book *Red Sox Nation: An Unexpurgated History of the Boston Red Sox*, "I stepped out of the box. I figured, 'He's going to be thinking I'm going to be looking for a slider, so instead I'm going to be looking for a fastball.' I knew I would be swinging. I wasn't going to be taking."

The pitch came and Carbo rocketed a shot deep to right center, well over the 420 sign for a game-tying home run.

"I started running to first base," he said. "I didn't know if the ball was going to go out of the park, because I knew center field was a long ways . . . I could see [Cincinnati center fielder Cesar] Geronimo turn his back, and that's when I knew the ball was gone. The game was tied.

"I'm yelling to Pete Rose [at third], 'Don't you wish you were this strong?' And Pete is yelling back, 'Ain't this fun, Bernie?! This is what the World Series is about. This is fun!'"

Red Sox catcher Carlton Fisk would break the tie with a homer in the bottom of the 12th inning to win the game, 7–6. Church bells would peal in its honor, poems would be scribbled in haste, and fans would exclaim they could now die happy.

But the following day the Red Sox would lose Game Seven.

Fisk, who spent more time as a Chicago White Sox (13 seasons) than a member of the Carmine Hose (11), would be voted into the Hall of Fame in 2000.

Bernie Carbo would be out of baseball by the time he was thirty-three. Charm eventually would not be enough.

He went to cosmetology school. Started his own hair salon. But cocaine wouldn't take no for an answer. It ruined his marriage, his life for so long.

In 1994 at age forty-seven, Carbo had a conversion experience. He started to go to 12-step meetings and returned to baseball via running clinics around the country.

"I threw away my career," Carbo told Grossfeld. "If I knew Jesus Christ was my savior at seventeen, I would have been one heck of a ballplayer, a near Hall of Famer. Instead, I wanted to die."

And then, he decided to live.

Now he is remembered as the man who gave the Red Sox hope in one of the greatest games in baseball history.

21 HAL SMITH: THE "FORGOTTEN" ONE

In June of 1949, two days after graduating from a Detroit high school, Hal Smith, then a third baseman, signed with the New York Yankees for $5,000.

He had received thirty-six college football scholarship offers. But baseball scouts had told the lean 6-foot 190-pounder that after four years in school he'd be too old to make the majors.

Smith's father was a coal miner from southern Illinois who, when Hal was eleven, had moved his family to Detroit to become a house painter. Dad thought five grand in hand and a baseball career sounded like the better deal, too.

The Yankees saw their investment as a catcher, not an infielder, and put Hal Smith, like they had with Yogi Berra, under the tutelage of Hall of Fame catcher Bill Dickey. Smith thrived. In his first full season in the minor leagues he hit .363. By the end of spring training 1954, he was set to be Berra's backup with the big club. But Smith contracted mononucleosis. His fever spiked to 103. He spent ten days in the hospital. When released, he was thirteen pounds lighter. Instead of getting his first at-bats in New York, he was shipped to extended spring training to build strength and sharpen his timing. Johnny Blanchard became Berra's backup, and future All-Star catcher Elston Howard would soon be on his way.

Hal Smith hit .350 the summer of 1954—in Triple A. Instead of being called up to the Yankees that year, the team traded him to Baltimore in a seventeen-player swap, the largest transaction in baseball history.

The Yankees haul included Bob Turley, one of the game's top young pitchers, and Don Larsen, who had led the majors with 21 losses in 1954. The Yankees wouldn't have won the American League pennant or World Series in 1958 if not for Turley, known as "Bullet Bob" due to his 98-mile-per-hour fastball. Turley won 21 games and the Cy Young Award in the regular season and two games in four days in the World Series. In 1956, Larsen threw the only perfect game in World Series history.

In 1955, Smith was the starting catcher for the Baltimore Orioles. He played 135 games and hit .271. By 1957, he was playing for the Kansas City Athletics and was the only catcher in the American League to hit more than .300.

All that was a preamble.

At the winter meetings of 1959, the Pittsburgh Pirates acquired Smith in a minor deal. He was seen as the right-handed-hitting platoon and defensive replacement for Smoky Burgess, a terrific hitter but a defensively challenged catcher who would become best known as one of the greatest pinch-hitters of all time. It turned out to be a good plan put together by Pirates general manager Joe L. Brown, the son of the actor and comedian Joe E. Brown.

Smith and Burgess combined to hit 18 homers and knock in 84 runs while batting nearly .300 the next year.

On a team that featured two future Hall of Famers—Roberto Clemente and Bill Mazeroski—the Pirates, who hadn't been to the World Series since 1927 (when they were swept by the Yankees), and hadn't been world champions since 1925, won the National League pennant by seven games.

With Mickey Mantle, Roger Maris, and Whitey Ford not yet thirty, the American League champion Yankees were considered heavy favorites to win the 1960 World Series.

Despite public opinion and the oddsmakers, the Series went to a Game Seven on October 13, 1960, at Forbes Field in Pittsburgh, the site of where Babe Ruth, as a member of the Boston Braves, had hit his last three home runs in 1935.

In the 1960 World Series, when the Yankees won they dominated, rolling up lopsided scores of 16–3, 10–0 and 12–0. When the Pirates won, the games were closer, 6–4, 3–2, and 5–2.

In Ford's two complete-game shutouts, Smith went 2-for-7, both singles, against the southpaw. He was on the bench for much of Game Seven.

The Pirates had a 4–1 lead after five innings of the decisive contest. The Yankees scored four times in the sixth, pulling ahead, 5–4—Berra's three-run homer the big blow.

In the Pirates half of the seventh, Burgess opened the inning with a single, the potential tying run. He was hitting .333 in the series, but he was also a painfully slow runner. Shadows were falling. Pirate manager Danny Murtaugh decided on Joe Christopher to pinch-run. Pirate third baseman Don Hoak then flied out and Bill Mazeroski hit into an inning-ending double play.

Hal Smith entered the game as the Pirates catcher in the top of the eighth.

With two outs, the Yankees scored twice to build a 7–4 lead.

Hope stirred in the Pirates half of the eighth when Gino Cimoli opened the inning with a pinch single. Pirates center fielder and leadoff hitter Bill

Virdon followed with what looked like a routine double-play ball to Yankee shortstop Tony Kubek. But the ball took a bad hop, hitting Kubek violently in the throat. He had to leave the game with runners on first and second, no outs.

Dick Groat, the National League Most Valuable Player, singled to pull the Pirates to within two, 7–5. Yankee manager Casey Stengel replaced left-hander Bobby Shantz with right-hander Jim Coates, who was 13–3 as a spot starter, to face two left-handed hitters.

Pirate left fielder Bob Skinner dropped down a sacrifice bunt, moving the runners into scoring position. Pirates first baseman Rocky Nelson, playing in place of Dick Stuart, the team's home run leader, hit a fly ball to Maris in medium right. Virdon, on third, didn't challenge the arm of Maris.

Up came Clemente. With two strikes, he flailed at an outside pitch and hit a chopper wide of first. Coates and Yankee first baseman Moose Skowron went for the ball. No one covered first. Clemente was safe as Virdon scored. The Yankees now led, 7–6, with two Pirates on.

Hal Smith, number 5, was at the plate. He took strike one. Then ball one. On the third pitch he swung hard—a home run cut—and missed, for strike two. Next, he checked his swing on ball two. Smith had always been considered a pretty good hitter, but the knock on him was he didn't have enough power. He would hit 58 homers in his 10-year career.

Then Smith struck a low fastball high and far over the 18-foot-high ivy-covered wall for a 9–7 Pirates lead.

People there that day swear they could feel the foundation at Forbes Field shiver. Joe L. Brown, who had assembled the team, and later the 1971 world champion Pirates, called it "the most memorable play of my life."

Mel Allen, the longtime Yankees broadcaster calling the game for NBC, said it was "One of the most dramatic hits in the history of the World Series . . . that base hit will *long* be remembered."

According to Groat, Smith hit "the most forgotten home run in baseball history."

The Yankees would tie the score in the top of the ninth, thanks to alert baserunning by Mantle. Bill Mazeroski would hit his famous home run in the bottom of the ninth to win the World Series.

Hal Smith's homer was famous for about fifteen minutes. But he never really felt that way.

"It hasn't been forgotten by the people that know baseball," he once said to a reporter on the 50th anniversary of his home run. "I still get letters where fans tell me they never forgot my home run. One guy will tell me he was overseas; another guy will tell me he took his radio with him to listen from class to class. I've had people write me who never even saw the home run, but who have heard stories told by their grandfather.

"I haven't been forgotten," Hal Smith said. "I got all the attention that I needed."

20 BABE RUTH: THE CALLED SHOT

George Herman "Babe" Ruth Jr. was born on February 6, 1895, in Baltimore, Maryland.

By almost all accounts, Ruth would go down in the annals of history as the greatest baseball player to ever put on cleats. The Bambino started his major-league career in 1914, when he pitched for the Boston Red Sox, but would make his true mark on the game as a power-hitting outfielder with the Yankees of New York. After 22 seasons, when all was said and done, Ruth walked away from the game with a then-record 714 home runs, .690 slugging percentage, 2,062 bases on balls, and was one of the original five inductees in the National Baseball Hall of Fame in 1936.

Through Ruth's illustrious career, he created moments that made him a legend. And one such moment occurred in the 1932 World Series against the Chicago Cubs. The date was October 1 and the Yankees were leading the Series two games to none when the combatants faced off at Wrigley Field. The Sultan of Swat was known for a lot of things, but his white-glove etiquette was not one of them. With the Cubs bench riding the great Ruth, he was giving it right back to the Chicago players with a few choice words and gestures of his own. But this is where things really got interesting . . . and debatable.

In the fifth inning, the score was tied at four apiece. Cubs hurler Charlie Root was on the mound as Ruth took strike one. As the Chicago players continued to give the Ruth the business, the slugger pointed at what looked like a spot deep in center field. After taking strike two, Ruth pointed at the spot again. And incredibly, in a moment out of a Hollywood movie, Ruth swung at Root's next pitch, a curveball, and delivered it to the deepest part of center field . . . apparently right to where he had pointed just moments earlier. Had Ruth just called his shot? Could it have possibly happened?

Some pundits have postulated that Ruth had been gesturing toward the Cubs dugout. Others have said that perhaps he was pointing at Root. But many of the thousands in attendance that day, and the millions more who have heard the story secondhand, will swear that Ruth, had indeed, called his shot!

What many historians fail to remember about this historic day was that on the next pitch, the great Lou Gehrig launched one into the right field seats.

The Yankees would go on to win the game 7–5 and sweep the Cubs the next day to take home the championship. But as the years pass, and the legend of Ruth continues to grow, his homer is remembered by many as one of the Babe's most defining moments—the day when the greatest baseball player in history called his shot.

19 DEREK JETER: A 3,000TH HIT FOR THE AGES

Many of baseball's greatest players have worn New York Yankee pinstripes: Babe Ruth, Lou Gehrig, Joe DiMaggio, Yogi Berra, and Mickey Mantle. And more recently, Reggie Jackson, Don Mattingly, and the sensational reliever, Mariano Rivera.

All of them giants to be sure, but let us not forget a shortstop named Jeter.

While most pundits proclaim Ruth to be the greatest Yankee ever to make his living in the Bronx, Derek Jeter ranks right up there with the best.

Derek Sanderson Jeter was born on June 26, 1974, in Pequannock, New Jersey. He and his family lived in North Arlington, New Jersey, until Jeter was four years old. They then moved to Kalamazoo, Michigan, where the future star grew up to be recognized as a baseball prodigy. His .557 batting average as a high school sophomore had a bevy of major-league scouts checking out flights to the Great Lakes State. During Jeter's senior season he received a scholarship offer from the University of Michigan but turned it down when the Yankees drafted him. He was the sixth pick in the first round that year.

But it wasn't all roses and rainbows at the start. Jeter went hitless in his first seven minor-league at-bats, with an eye-popping five strikeouts. The determined youngster was undeterred, however, and three years after his first minor-league game he broke into the majors. The date was May 29, 1995. As he did in the minors, he got off to a slow start, going 0-for-5 in his first game, although this time he struck out only once. Still, in time, the new kid began to grind out hits.

Jeter collected 190 or more hits 11 times in his 20 years in the major leagues. Only Pete Rose and Ty Cobb have bettered him in that category. And there's much more:

- He won the American League Silver Slugger Award five times (2006–09 and 2012).
- On May 26, 2006, he stroked his 2,000th hit with an infield single off Scott Elarton of the Kansas City Royals. With it, Jeter became the eighth Yankee to reach that milestone.

- On September 14, 2008, he tied the legendary Lou Gehrig's team record for total hits at Yankee Stadium, surpassing it two days later.
- On August 16, 2009, he racked up his 2,674th hit and became the all-time hits leader as a shortstop in the history of the major leagues.
- On September 11, 2009, his 2,722nd hit moved him past Gehrig to become the club's all-time leader in hits.

Jeter was getting closer to Baseball's Holy Grail of 3,000 hits. Yet as the number crept closer, Captain Clutch began to feel the pressure. For the first time in his career the hits weren't coming. Then, finally, he pulled himself to within striking distance.

On July 9, 2011, before a packed house at Yankee Stadium seeking a chance to watch history in the making, he singled in his first at-bat. That brought his hit total to 2,999. In his next at-bat two innings later, the fans were on their feet. As Jeter stepped to the plate, the pressure was on. Could the talented Yankee star deliver?

Tampa Bay Rays pitcher David Price stared in at Jeter. The count was 3–2. The lefty let loose with a curveball that looked like it might be a third strike, so Jeter had to dig down to reach it . . .

C-r-r-ack!

As the ball jumped off the thickest part of the bat, it catapulted up from around Jeter's ankles and out, landing deep in the left field bleachers. Derek Jeter had become the 28th player in the history of the sport to reach the milestone of 3,000 hits, and only the second to do it with a home run.

But the story was not complete. In what can only be considered a game for the ages, the man with the number 2 on his back actually went 5-for-5 and had the game-winning hit. As Joe Girardi, his Yankee manager, said afterward, "I don't think you could script it any better. It's movie-ready to get your 3,000th hit on a home run that ties the game and then to get [number] 3,003 a game-winner. It's just remarkable the day he had."

If anything, Girardi's comments were an understatement.

18 BARRY BONDS: A TAINTED RECORD-BREAKER

Barry Lamar Bonds was born on July 24, 1964, in Riverside, California, and grew up in San Carlos, California. He is the son of former big-league All-Star Bobby Bonds, and it soon became evident that the apple didn't fall far from the tree.

As a youth, Barry excelled in baseball, basketball, and football, but it would be his seemingly destined path on the diamond that would pave his future. And what a career Bonds would have.

When all was said and done, he would play 22 seasons, from 1986 to 2007. For his first seven years he was a member of the Pittsburgh Pirates before spending his last 15 with the San Francisco Giants. And it would be as a member of the Giants, in 2001, that Bonds would hit one of baseball's most memorable home runs.

After Bonds tied Mark McGwire's single-season record of 70 home runs, the Giants, who were fighting for their playoff lives, were at home at Pac Bell Park, facing off against the Los Angeles Dodgers. It was a Friday night, October 5, and the capacity crowd could sense history. But when the visitors scored five runs in the top of the first, the air seemed to come out of the stadium, if just for a moment.

However, the fans were back on their feet when Bonds faced Dodgers pitcher Chan Ho Park in the bottom of the inning. Park's first pitch was down and away for ball one. Yet the very next pitch was hittable, and as every baseball fan knew, in 2001, Bonds missed very few balls over the plate.

Bonds took a mighty swat and left no doubt. His 445-foot bomb sailed over the right-field fence to the delight of all in attendance. As he rounded the bases for his record-setting 71st dinger, his eleven-year-old son Nikolai and all of his teammates were there to greet him at home plate. Bonds hoisted his son into the air and pointed to the heavens.

Although Bonds would hit another homer in his next at-bat, the Giants would lose the game in a heartbreaker, 11–10, and were eliminated from the playoff race. But the home crowd got what it came for, a moment of history.

Unfortunately, the career of Bonds is remembered as a mixture of greatness and controversy. Although there is no question that Bonds put up statistics that would light up the back of a baseball card, there were doubts about how he had done it since he competed during baseball's steroid era.

On the one hand, Barry Bonds was a 14-time All-Star, an 8-time Gold Glove Award recipient, and a record 7-time National League Most Valuable Player. Furthermore, Bonds retired with the most career home runs (762), the most home runs in a single season (73 in 2001), most career walks (2,558) and, in testament to the fear he put into opposing pitchers, the most career intentional walks (688). At the time of his retirement, Bonds led all active players in RBIs (1,996), on-base percentage (.444), runs (2,227), games played (2,986), extra-base hits (1,440), at-bats per home run (12.92), and total bases (5,976). Bonds is also the only member of the 500 home run–500 stolen base club.

On the flip side, in 2007, Bonds was indicted on charges of perjury and obstruction of justice for lying to a grand jury. During a government investigation of BALCO, a San Francisco-area business that supplied anabolic steroids to a variety of athletes, Bonds testified that he never knowingly took illegal steroids and was eventually convicted of the obstruction of justice charge on April 13, 2011.

Although Bonds never served jail time, his legacy was forever tarnished. Bonds, who retired in 2007 and was arguably one of the best baseball players of all time, has yet to be inducted into Baseball's Hall of Fame.

17 DAVE HENDERSON: FROM GOAT TO HERO

David Lee Henderson was born on July 21, 1958, in Merced, California.

The man who grew up to be nicknamed Hendu was originally a two-sport high school star, excelling in baseball and football. Eventually, Henderson's high school would retire his number 42 football and number 22 baseball jerseys for his exceptional play.

But after graduating from high school, there was little debate on what sport to pursue once Henderson was selected in the first round of the 1977 amateur draft by the Seattle Mariners. Henderson broke into the bigs with the Mariners on April 9, 1981, and played for Seattle until 1986, when he was traded to Boston in August. And although he would play for the Red Sox only a little over one season, it was in the Hub where he hit the dinger that defined his career.

Henderson became an immediate fan favorite in Boston when he helped lead the Red Sox to the American League Championship Series against the California Angels. As most every baseball fan was well aware, the Sox had not won a World Series title since 1918, and the Boston faithful were desperate to break the Curse of the Bambino. However, things did not look good for Boston when California, which was hoping to reach its first World Series, took a commanding three-game-to-one lead in the ALCS. Furthermore, Game Five was being played in Anaheim, and the Angels could smell victory.

The Red Sox, however, were a scrappy bunch, and they continued to fight and claw, holding a 2–1 lead going into the bottom of the sixth inning. But then the unthinkable occurred. California's Bobby Grich launched a deep fly ball that was headed toward the warning track. Henderson, an excellent outfielder, got there in time to make the catch, but the ball hit the palm of his glove just before he collided with the fence. The force of the blow dislodged the ball and sent it over the wall for a two-run homer. The Angels would later tack on two more runs to take a 5–2 lead into the ninth inning.

The Red Sox fought back with a two-run blast by former Angels slugger Don Baylor. There were two outs and Rich Gedman was on first after being hit by a pitch when Henderson came to the plate. The count was two balls and two strikes. The Red Sox were down to their final strike. The pitcher on the mound, Donnie Moore, looked in, took the sign, and delivered. The result: a two-run blast by Henderson that shocked the home crowd, gave the Sox the lead, and saved the season for Boston.

The Angels came back to tie the game at 6–6 in the bottom of the ninth, but Boston regained the edge with a Henderson sacrifice fly in the 11th inning that proved to be the game-winner. With this wave of momentum, Boston returned to Fenway Park and easily took the final two games, 10–4 and 8–1, to power its way to the World Series.

Unfortunately, as most of the baseball world knows, the Red Sox, who snatched victory from the precipice of defeat against the Angels, would have the tables quickly turned against them in New York by the Mets. With a three-game-to-two advantage by Boston in the World Series, Henderson was set to be the hero yet again when he hit a 10th-inning dinger to give his club the lead in Game Six. The Mets, aided by a crucial error by Red Sox first baseman Bill Buckner, scored two in the bottom of the inning for the win. The Mets would go on to win Game Seven and the Series.

Hendu would go on to reach a total of four World Series in his career (1986 with Boston and 1988–90 with Oakland) but ultimately took home only one title when the Athletics swept the San Francisco Giants in 1989.

Henderson would play 14 seasons in the major leagues. He ended his career with a .258 batting average, 708 RBIs, 710 runs scored, 286 doubles, 50 stolen bases and 197 homers. In four ALCS and four World Series appearances, he hit .298 with 20 RBIs, 24 runs scored, a .570 slugging average, and seven long balls. But for all of his heroics, it would be Hendu's home run in the 1986 ALCS against Donnie Moore and the California Angels that would go down as one of the most memorable dingers of all time.

16 DICK SISLER: WHIZ-KID MAGIC

Dick Sisler's father was one of the greatest baseball players of all time.

George Sisler, the St. Louis Browns first baseman, batted .407 in 1920, the year Dick was born. Two years later, George finished the season with a .420 batting average. He hit better than .300 for nine straight seasons. Twice he led the American League in triples, four times in stolen bases.

George Sisler had started out a pitcher, but ended up a slick-fielding first baseman with a sweet left-handed swing for the Browns in their pre-Baltimore Orioles days. He finished his career with a .340 batting average and was elected to the Hall of Fame in 1939.

When Branch Rickey wanted to sign a black player for the Brooklyn Dodgers, George Sisler was one of the scouts he sent to Negro League games. He respected Sisler's judgment.

In 1945, Jackie Robinson was a shortstop for the Kansas City Monarchs. The Dodgers already had Pee Wee Reese at shortstop. So Rickey decided Robinson should play first. He asked George Sisler to teach him the finer points.

George Sisler was still a scout for the Brooklyn Dodgers in 1950 when his son Dick was the starting left fielder for the Philadelphia Phillies. Dick had attended Colgate University and served in the navy. He had originally signed with the St. Louis Cardinals after World War II. The Cardinals sent him to Cuba to learn how to play first base.

He was a big hit, launching two homers in his first game there. In another, he hit three home runs. He was also the first player to blast a home run out of Havana's Tropical Park.

"You'd have thought I was president or something," he would later say. "Every morning when I came out of the rooming house, in which I lived, there were at least 100 Cubans waiting for me. I got suits, show tickets, just about anything I wanted free. All I had to do was pose with someone for a picture."

In Havana, he also became friends with novelist Ernest Hemingway, a baseball fan who mentioned him in the 1952 novel *The Old Man and the Sea*.

"In the other league, between Brooklyn and Philadelphia I must take Brooklyn," the old man tells a boy. "But then I think of Dick Sisler and those great drives in the old park.

The boy replies, "There was nothing ever like them. He hits the longest ball I have ever seen."

In 1950, Dick Sisler was having his best season in the big leagues, for the Philadelphia Phillies.

He was selected to the All-Star Game and his batting average flirted with .300 all season. The Phillies had switched him from first base to left field. He often batted third. Hall of Fame center fielder Richie Ashburn hit in front of Sisler and right fielder Del Ennis, who averaged over 100 RBIs a season during his 11-year career in Philadelphia, hit behind him.

The Phillies hadn't won a National League pennant since 1915, George Sisler's rookie year. But the Phillies spent most of 1950 in first place. They were dubbed "The Whiz Kids" for being the youngest team in the league.

Dick Sisler was one of the older players. He was pushing thirty.

In September, the Phillies started losing and the Brooklyn Dodgers started winning.

On Sunday, October 1, the last game of the regular season, the Phillies clung to a one-game lead over the Dodgers. A Dodger win over the Phillies would mean a three-game playoff to decide which team would go to the World Series.

Brooklyn's Ebbets Field was packed. The Dodgers started their 19-game winner Don Newcombe. The Phillies opted for Hall of Famer Robin Roberts, also seeking his 20th win.

Though playing with a sprained right wrist, Dick Sisler had three singles in four at- bats and had scored his team's lone run in a game that went into the ninth tied 1–1. His father was sitting behind the Brooklyn dugout.

Brooklyn had a chance to win in the bottom of the ninth. Left fielder Cal Abrams was on second with no outs when Duke Snider hit a single to shallow center field. Abrams was waved home by third-base coach Milt Stock but thrown out by Ashburn. (After the season, Stock would be fired for the transgression.) Roberts worked out of a bases-loaded jam to send the game into extra innings.

In the top of the 10th, Philadelphia manager Eddie Sawyer let Roberts bat for himself. He singled to center. Ed Waitkus, the team's leadoff hitter, followed with another single. Ashburn moved them up with a sacrifice bunt.

It was Dick Sisler's turn.

He was hoping Newcombe wouldn't bust him with an inside fastball. His wrist, heavily taped, hurt too much. Newcombe got ahead in the count, one ball and two strikes.

The next pitch was a touch outside, and Dick Sisler, a month shy of his thirtieth birthday, slammed it deep to left field.

By the time he reached second he was jumping as he made his way around the bases. He was mobbed at home and replaced in left field for the bottom of the 10th.

Roberts retired the Dodgers 1–2–3 in the ninth. The Phillies won their first pennant in 35 years.

When George Sisler was asked how he felt when his son beat the Dodgers, he said, "I felt awful and terrific at the same time."

Dick finished the season with 13 homers, 83 RBIs and a .296 average.

The Phillies would lose the World Series to the New York Yankees in four games, but Philadelphia would never forget Dick Sisler.

He died at age seventy-eight in 1998. His obituary by Richard Goldstein in the *New York Times* included this story:

"When the taxi he was taking to Ebbets Field with his teammates Del Ennis, Russ Meyer and Willie (Puddin' Head) Jones stopped for a light, a car with a priest pulled alongside. The priest recognized the players and offered Sisler a rose, saying it had been blessed.

"Sisler said, 'Father, I'm not a Catholic.'

"The priest replied: 'Take it anyway. Maybe it will bring you good luck.'

"Sisler kept the rose with him during the game and, as he remembered it: 'When I came up to bat in the 10th inning, I thought of the rose in my pocket. I reached in with my hand and touched it. I doubt that it had anything to do with what happened afterward, but who knows?'"

15 TED WILLIAMS: THE "GREATEST HITTER" ENDS CAREER HIS WAY

They called him "The Kid," "The Splendid Splinter," "Teddy Ballgame," and "The Thumper." He was also arguably the greatest hitter who ever lived.

Theodore Samuel "Ted" Williams was born on August 30, 1918, in San Diego, California. A prodigious talent, he spent his youth on a baseball field, broke into the majors in 1939, and played out his entire 19-year career as the left fielder of the Boston Red Sox.

In 1941, in just his third year in the major leagues, Williams batted .406, making him the last player to bat over .400. In 1943, at the height of his talents, Williams left the game to serve in the navy and marine corps during World War II. But when he returned from military service he didn't miss a beat. In 1946 he led the Sox to the World Series, won his first American League Most Valuable Player Award, and his second Triple Crown.

Williams would have his professional baseball career interrupted again when he spent portions of the 1952 and 1953 seasons as a marine aviator in the Korean War. But the man who many consider the greatest hitter of all time came back yet again to win the American League batting title for the fifth and sixth times, in 1957 and 1958, at the ages of thirty-nine and forty.

And he didn't only hit for average. Williams led the American League in home runs four times, as well as in runs batted in four times.

However, things didn't always go smoothly for Williams in Boston. His every move was closely monitored and sometimes criticized by the press, and because he was an intensely private and proud person, this annoyed him. Furthermore, because he was booed early in his career by the Fenway Park faithful, Williams vowed to never tip his cap to the home crowd.

In the twilight of his career, a bad back resulted in a .254 batting average in 1959. Although urged by Red Sox management to retire, the proud Williams came back for one more season in 1960 and, at the age of forty-two, hit .316 with 29 home runs. But it was number 29 that sailed into history.

It was the last game of Williams's outstanding career. In the bottom of the eighth inning, with Baltimore Orioles pitcher Jack Fisher on the mound, Williams stood at the plate for his final at-bat. The count was one and one. On the third pitch, Williams took his classic swing, and *crack!*—the ball jumped off his bat and soared into the Red Sox bullpen. The crowd roared its approval, but true to form the stubborn Williams once again refused to tip his cap.

When all was said and done, Williams would end his stellar career with a lifetime .344 batting average, 2,654 hits, 521 home runs, and 1,839 runs batted in. He was also a 17-time All-Star and a first-ballot Hall of Fame selection in 1966, garnering 93.38 percent of the vote.

Williams was noted for once famously saying that it was his goal in life to "walk down the street [and have] folks say 'There goes the greatest hitter who ever lived.'" And although it may be debatable, many argue that he achieved that dream.

14 OZZIE SMITH: THE WIZARD MAKES THEM "GO CRAZY"

Osborne Earl "Ozzie" Smith was born on December 26, 1954, in Mobile, Alabama.

Smith was a gifted athlete who excelled in baseball. After playing high school ball at Locke High School in Los Angeles and college baseball at Cal Poly, San Luis Obispo, "The Wizard," as he would come to be known for his defensive prowess, was drafted by the San Diego Padres. He made his big-league debut in 1978. Smith won his first Gold Glove in 1980 and was selected to his first All-Star Game in 1981. But it was after he was traded to the St. Louis Cardinals in 1982 that Smith's career would really take off.

In his first year with St. Louis, Smith was an integral piece in their 1982 World Series title. Yet it would be just three years later, in 1985, when Smith would have one of his most memorable moments. During the 1985 season, Smith hit .276 with 31 stolen bases and 549 assists at shortstop. St. Louis won 101 games during the regular season and would go on to face the Los Angeles Dodgers in the best-of-seven National League Championship Series. After splitting the first four games with the Dodgers, the pivotal Game Five would take place at Busch Stadium in St. Louis.

In a nip and tuck contest, the score was tied 2–2 in the bottom of the ninth. Dodgers right-handed closer Tom Niedenfuer was on the mound when, with one out, the switch-hitting Smith came to the plate batting left-handed. Smith, never a power hitter, had never hit a home run in 3,009 left-handed at-bats. Niedenfuer delivered an inside fastball and Smith turned on it, launching the ball over the right field wall to give the home team a 3–2 walk-off victory.

The moment was best voiced by the legendary broadcaster Jack Buck when he said, "Smith corks one into right, down the line! It may go. . . . Go crazy, folks, go crazy! It's a home run, and the Cardinals have won the game, by the score of 3 to 2, on a home run by the Wizard! Go crazy!"

The moment proved to be so iconic that it was later voted the greatest moment in the history of Busch Stadium by Cardinals fans.

St. Louis would go on to defeat the Dodgers in Game Six, when Jack Clark hit a late-inning homer of his own. Despite the heroics in the NLCS, the Cardinals went on to lose a controversial World Series in seven games to the Kansas City Royals.

Smith would finish his first-ballot Hall of Fame career in St. Louis, thrilling fans until his retirement at the end of the 1996 season. Although he will always be thought of, first and foremost, for his incredible fielding ability, it was his shocking left-handed dinger in the 1985 NLCS that will be remembered as one of the most incredible, and unlikely, long balls in the history of the sport.

13 CHRIS CHAMBLISS: CROWD CONTROL

Carroll Christopher Chambliss was born on December 26, 1948, in Dayton, Ohio.

Chris, as he was known, was the third of four boys born to Carroll and Christine Chambliss. His father was a chaplain in the navy and consequently the family moved often. Eventually, the Chambliss family settled in Oceanside, California, and all four brothers played baseball for the Oceanside High School team, where Chris was the star.

Although Chambliss was drafted by Cincinnati in both 1967 and 1968, he decided to forgo turning pro and instead enrolled at MiraCosta College. In 1969 Chambliss transferred to UCLA and that season he led the Bruins with 15 dingers and 45 RBIs. His prowess on the diamond led to the Cleveland Indians making him the first overall pick in the January 1970 amateur draft.

A year later, in 1971, he would make his splash in the Show when he was named the American League Rookie of the Year. Despite his success with the Indians, Chambliss was traded to the New York Yankees in April of 1974 in a multiplayer deal.

After a couple of years with the Bombers, Chambliss seemed to really come into his own. In 1976, he was an All-Star, and would live up to that billing in the American League Championship Series against the Kansas City Royals. During the series, he hit an ALCS record .524, with two homers and eight RBIs. But the magic really occurred with the best-of-five series tied at two games apiece.

With the decider knotted up in the bottom of the ninth, Chambliss drove a high fastball off of Mark Littell over the wall for the game-winner. In a scene not witnessed in our post-9/11 society, the crowd poured onto the field as Chambliss fought his way through. In one of the most memorable home runs in the history of the sport, the Chris Chambliss dinger launched the Yanks into the World Series.

Chambliss would have many high points in his playing career that lasted from 1971 until 1988. He was a key part of New York's 1977 and 1978 world championship teams, and won a Gold Glove in 1978. Chambliss would go on to be a part of four more Yankee titles, in 1996, 1998, 1999, and 2000, as a hitting coach for the Bombers. But it would be his 1976 ALCS heroics that would leave a mark in the hearts of Yankee fans.

12 REGGIE JACKSON: "MR. OCTOBER" EARNS HIS TITLE

For many fans, an athlete's performance is best measured by the numbers, so much so that statistics have emerged as a major force in sports. What was once a soft science has become an industry that thrives on itself, offering precise numbers that range from something as simple as career strikeouts to as nuanced as batting average with two men out and one man on base when facing a left-handed pitcher.

There are more numbers out there than one can access in a lifetime, but it is often a singular moment that launches a reputation. And this can separate the truly historic from just the very good. As Bobby Thomson, Bill Mazeroski, and even Bill Buckner can attest, one moment in time can forever define a career.

Reginald Martinez "Reggie" Jackson was born on May 18, 1946, in Abington, Pennsylvania. At the age of four, when his parents divorced, little Reggie was raised by his father, Martinez Jackson, who was a former second baseman for the Newark Eagles of the Negro Leagues. The son inherited his father's aptitude for baseball, and on June 9, 1967, just after Reggie's twentieth birthday, he made his major-league debut with the Kansas City Athletics. It was while playing for the A's—first in Kansas City and later in Oakland after the team relocated—that Jackson's knack for greatness under pressure was first noted. In fact, Jackson and the A's won five straight American League West division titles and three straight American League pennants and World Series. He was named the 1973 AL MVP and World Series MVP.

But apparently the lights were not bright enough in Oakland. After a one-year stint with the Baltimore Orioles in 1976, Jackson made his way to the Big Apple to play for the New York Yankees. And it was under the intense spotlight of New York where the young man from Wyncote shined the brightest.

With the Bronx Bombers, Jackson won four American League East division titles, three American League pennants and two straight World Series. But it was the 1977 World Series matchup against the Los Angeles Dodgers that cemented Jackson's greatness.

It was Game Six of the Series, played before Jackson's home fans at Yankee Stadium. The Yankees had built three-game-to-two lead and were looking to close out the Series. In Jackson's first at-bat in the second inning he walked on four pitches. But the next time up he cracked Dodgers pitcher Burt Hooton's first pitch into the lower right-field seats. In his third at-bat, Jackson faced Elias Sosa, but the result was the same, a first-pitch offering that was once again delivered into the lower right-field seats.

So far, three plate appearances, with one walk, then back-to-back homers. And then came number four, when he launched a knuckleball offering from Charlie Hough *deep* into the bleachers—an estimated 475 feet—for his third straight home run of the game. As the adoring crowd chanted, "REG-GIE! REG-GIE! REG-GIE!" the hero emerged from the dugout with a tip of the cap. Incredibly, because Jackson had hit a home run on his final at-bat in game five, he actually hit World Series home runs on four consecutive swings of the bat. Not surprisingly, his heroics earned him a second World Series MVP title.

Over his 21 major-league seasons, Jackson put up some impressive numbers. Although only a career .262 hitter, he racked up 563 home runs, 2,584 hits, and 1,702 RBIs. Certainly enough to get anyone's attention, but when you consider that in 27 World Series games Jackson belted 10 home runs, knocked in 24 runs, and had a .357 batting average, the numbers are astonishing. He was also the first player to win the World Series MVP Award with two different teams.

Never one to shy from the spotlight, Jackson raised lots of eyebrows when he pronounced himself "the straw that stirs the drink." But if you can do it, it ain't braggin', and this guy earned his accolade, "Mr. October."

11 MARK MCGWIRE: A TAINTED SEASON SAVES BASEBALL

Mark David McGwire was born on October 1, 1963, in Pomona, California.

The 6-foot-5 McGwire was aptly named "Big Mac" due to his tremendous strength and power. McGwire broke in with the Oakland Athletics, and during his rookie year of 1987 he made an immediate impact, stroking 33 home runs by the All-Star break. He ended the season with 49 homers, a record for a rookie. McGwire also recorded 118 RBIs and a .289 batting average, leading to his unanimous selection as American League Rookie of the Year.

In the years that followed, the power numbers continued. During the next three seasons McGwire totaled 32, 33, and 39 home runs and in doing so made history again by becoming the first major-league player to hit 30-plus home runs in each of his first four seasons.

As noteworthy as his early years were, it was a decade later when the baseball world would become truly focused on McGwire.

The year was 1998 and it would have a baseball summer like no other. As the season progressed, McGwire (now a member of the St. Louis Cardinals), Sammy Sosa, and Ken Griffey Jr. were all on pace to break the single-season home run mark of Roger Maris set in 1961. The 61 dingers Maris hit that year established one of the most hallowed records in all of sports and exceeded the previous mark of 60 by Babe Ruth set in 1927. The baseball world was riveted and it appeared that the home run chase was reviving the sport's dwindling popularity.

As the three men jockeyed for the home run lead, balls continued to fly out of parks across the nation. Finally, and fittingly, with Sammy Sosa and the Chicago Cubs playing McGwire's Cardinals at Busch Stadium on September 8, McGwire ripped a Steve Trachsel offering over the left field wall for his record-breaking 62nd home run of the season. To make the moment even more magical, the family of the late Roger Maris was in the stands to celebrate with McGwire. Sosa came in from right field to offer his hearty congratulations.

After the game, in a feel-good moment, the stadium worker who snatched the home run ball returned it to the slugger free of charge. When all was said and done, McGwire would end the season with 70 dingers to cap off what was, at the time, considered one of the most exciting seasons in all of sports.

However, McGwire's accomplishment was soon brought into question by a 1998 article by Associated Press writer Steve Wilstein, who reported that McGwire admitted to taking androstenedione. Although Major League Baseball did not, at the time, ban the substance, the World Anti-Doping Agency, the National Football League, and the International Olympic Committee had banned it.

And after the fallout from Jose Canseco's 2005 book *Juiced: Wild Times, Rampant 'Roids, Smash Hits, and How Baseball Got Big*, where Canseco wrote that he had personally injected McGwire with performance-enhancing drugs, on January 11, 2010, McGwire finally admitted to using steroids intermittently for a decade and stated, "I wish I had never touched steroids. It was foolish and it was a mistake. I truly apologize. Looking back, I wish I had never played during the steroid era."

But the damage had been done. Although he is eligible, baseball writers have not voted McGwire into the Baseball Hall of Fame.

10 SCOTT BROSIUS: BROSIUS THE FEROCIOUS

Scott David Brosius was born on August 15, 1966, and grew up in Milwaukie, Oregon. After an impressive career on the diamond at Rex Putnam High School, Brosius went on to play at Linfield College. He continued to excel and was taken by the Oakland Athletics in the 20th round of the 1987 amateur draft.

Brosius made it to the major leagues on August 7, 1991, and homered in his first game. After an up-and-down career in Oakland, Brosius was traded to the New York Yankees for pitcher Kenny Rogers after the 1997 season. But under the bright lights of the Big Apple, where many players wilt, he found new life. In his first year with the Bombers, Brosius batted .300 with 19 home runs and 98 RBIs, and was selected to his only All-Star team. The man who was picked up from Oakland as a mere afterthought hit .471 with two home runs and six RBIs in the 1998 World Series against the San Diego Padres, earning Series MVP honors.

Over the next three years, Brosius's productivity declined, but due to his workmanlike attitude he remained a fan favorite. And with the man ESPN sports announcer Chris Berman would nickname "Brosius the Ferocious" in the lineup, the Yankees would win the World Series every year from 1998 to 2000.

Yet it would be in the 2001 World Series against the Arizona Diamondbacks that Brosius would take his most memorable swing.

First, in Game Four of the Series, Yankees first baseman Tino Martinez was the hero when he blasted a ninth-inning, two-out, two-run homer off of Diamondbacks reliever Byung-Hyun Kim to tie the game. And then, the next night, with the Series tied at two games apiece, Brosius was put in the same position. Once again, the Yankees were trailing by two runs with Kim on the mound. This time it was Brosius's turn to play the hero as he blasted a two-out, two-run dinger to tie the game, a contest the Yankees would go on to win 3–2 in 12 innings.

Interestingly, it was the first time in World Series history that two-out, bottom-of-the-ninth home runs had occurred in successive games.

Unfortunately for Brosius and the Yankees, they would go on to lose Games Six and Seven.

After the season, Brosius retired from the game that he loved. Several years later, he would become the head baseball coach at his alma mater, Linfield College. He is currently a minor-league hitting coach in the Seattle Mariners organization.

9 KIRBY PUCKETT: "AND WE'LL SEE YOU TOMORROW NIGHT"

Anthony Kirby Puckett was born on March 14, 1960, in Chicago, Illinois, and was raised in the Robert Taylor Homes, a housing project located on Chicago's crime-laden South Side. After graduating from Calumet High School, there were no college scholarship offers awaiting the 5-foot-8 young man, so he began to work on an assembly line at the Ford Motor Company.

But Puckett's fate changed when he was given the opportunity to attend Bradley University. After one year, he transferred to Triton College where his game would take off. He quickly became a standout and was selected by the Minnesota Twins with the third overall pick in the January 1982 amateur draft.

After signing with the Twins, Puckett would immediately impress his new organization, batting .382 with three home runs, 35 RBIs and 43 steals in 65 games with the Elizabethton Twins of the rookie Appalachian League. Puckett would quickly work his way through the minors, and after being brought up to the Class AAA Toledo Mud Hens to start the 1984 season, he was promoted to the major leagues after only 21 games.

Puckett thrived in Minnesota, turning into one of the all-time greats. His signature moment came in the 1991 World Series, after Puckett and the Twins had beaten the Toronto Blue Jays in five games to win the American League Championship Series, where Puckett was named the ALCS MVP.

In the '91 World Series, the Twins faced off with the Atlanta Braves in one of the most tightly contested Series ever played. Four of the seven games were decided on the final pitch, and three of the contests went to extra innings. But the defining moment occurred in Game Six. With the Twins down three games to two, and with the home teams victorious in each game, Game Six would go into extra innings.

In the bottom of the 11th, with the game tied 3–3, Puckett led off the inning. He was facing Charlie Leibrandt, and the count was 2–1. With the home crowd already in a frenzy, Puckett belted Leibrandt's offering into the left-center-field seats for a walk-off home run. The lasting image was that of

Puckett rounding the bases with his arms raised over his head, and the great broadcaster Jack Buck saying, "And we'll see you tomorrow night!"

After the game, the Twins would replace the blue seat where the walk-off home run was caught with a gold-painted one. Game Six served as the appetizer to a dramatic Game Seven, where Twins right-hander Jack Morris would throw a complete-game, 10-inning shutout. With their 1–0 win, the Twins claimed their second Series title in five years.

Puckett retired with a career .318 batting average, which was the highest batting average by any right-handed American League hitter since Joe DiMaggio.

Unfortunately, Puckett's career was shortened by illness. After waking up on March 28, 1996, without vision in his right eye, he was diagnosed with glaucoma. Three surgeries could not abate the condition, forcing Puckett to announce his retirement at the age of thirty-six on July 12, 1996.

On March 5, 2006, Puckett suffered a massive stroke and died the following day, eight days shy of his forty-sixth birthday.

But Puckett, who was elected to the Baseball Hall of Fame in his first year of eligibility in 2001, will always be remembered for his historic blast to win Game Six of the 1991 World Series.

8 BUCKY DENT: THE CURSE CONTINUES

Russell Earl "Bucky" Dent was born on November 25, 1951, in Savannah, Georgia. Dent spent his formative years in Sylvania, Georgia, and Hialeah, Florida, as a baseball standout. After graduating from Hialeah High School, Dent was tabbed by the Chicago White Sox in the first round as the sixth overall pick in the June 1970 secondary draft.

By the age of twenty-one, Dent was playing shortstop for the White Sox. After four seasons in Chicago that included an All-Star Game selection in 1975, Dent was traded to the New York Yankees in 1977. And it would be under the Big Apple lights that he would make his mark.

Dent's contribution to the Yankees was immediate as he helped the Bronx Bombers win the Series in 1977. And just a year later, in 1978, the Yankees were back in the hunt. The rival Boston Red Sox and Yankees had finished the regular season with 99–63 records, necessitating a one-game playoff. The Red Sox won a coin toss over who would host the game, setting the stage for the Yankees arrival at Fenway Park.

Left-hander Ron Guidry started on the mound for the Yankees, with right-hander Mike Torrez hurling for the Red Sox. The Sox took an early lead on a homer by Carl Yastrzemski and an RBI from slugger Jim Rice. But then, in the top of the seventh, with one out, Chris Chambliss and Roy White singled off of Torrez. Pinch-hitter Jim Spencer flied out for the second out. And then it happened, seemingly out of nowhere. Dent, a light-hitting infielder with little power, took Torrez's offering over the Green Monster and into the netting for a three-run blast to give the Yankees the lead. It was only Dent's fifth long ball of the season. He would conclude his 12-year career with a total of 40 home runs.

The Yankees would go on to win the game by a final score of 5–4, and would end up defeating the Los Angeles Dodgers in the World Series, four games to two. Dent, who hit .417 against the Dodgers, was named the Most Valuable Player of the World Series.

Dent's heroics and the Yankees victory were seen as another painful chapter in what was known to Boston fans as the "Curse of the Bambino." And due to his improbable blast, Dent would forever be referred to as Bucky "Bleeping" Dent by the Boston faithful.

7 ROGER MARIS: 61 IN '61

Numbers hold a unique status in the world of sports.

A few examples:

100—representing Wilt Chamberlain's 100-point production in a single game of professional basketball.
18—The number of majors won by golfer Jack Nicklaus.
200—Richard Petty's NASCAR wins.

In baseball, one of those numbers became 61.

Roger Eugene Maris, the son of Croatian immigrants, was born on September 10, 1934, in Hibbing, Minnesota. He would grow up in Fargo, North Dakota, where he was an exceptional all-around athlete, so gifted that his baseball career was preempted by being recruited to play football for the Oklahoma Sooners. But after less than a semester on campus, Maris decided to leave school and sign a minor-league baseball contract with the Cleveland Indians in 1953.

Maris played four minor-league seasons before breaking into the Show with the Indians on April 16, 1957. A year later he would be traded to the Kansas City A's, where his stock began to rise. In 1959, he was chosen for his first All-Star Game, but he was traded to the New York Yankees following the season, and his life would never be the same.

Playing in the big city spotlight alongside legends like Mickey Mantle, Yogi Berra, and Whitey Ford, the quiet Maris struggled to fit in emotionally. But he had no such problem on the field.

In his first year in New York he led the league in RBIs, extra-base hits, and slugging percentage, and was named the American League MVP. He also found his power stroke, slugging 39 home runs, second in the American League to Mantle. The 1960 season would only serve as a prelude to the historic 1961 campaign in which Maris and Mantle would push each other toward one of the most storied records in sports: Babe Ruth's single-season home run mark of 60.

At the beginning of the 1961 season, Major League Baseball went through some dramatic changes. First, the number of teams in both the American and National Leagues expanded from eight to 10. The other major adjustment was to alter the 154-game schedule to 162. While the powers that be had no way of knowing it at the time, these modifications would have an immediate and profound impact. As the '61 season got under way, many contended that the additional personnel in baseball had the effect of diluting the talent. So as Maris and Mantle began to churn out home runs and chase a hallowed home run record, the skeptics were having a field day. Not only was the "lack of talent" issue duly noted, but many argued that the ball was livelier than in the past, making home runs easier to come by. And to make matters even worse for Maris, Mantle seemed to be the darling of the press, whereas the sportswriters were increasingly rough on Maris because of his reclusive nature and aversion to interviews.

As the two sluggers continued to chase Ruth's thirty-four-year-old record, Mantle caught a bit of bad luck when he incurred a hip infection late in the season. With only Maris left to pursue the great Sultan of Swat, many in the sporting world appeared to actually be rooting against him. So after 154 games, when a previous regular season would have come to an end and Maris was still short of the record, they insisted that even if he reached the Babe it would be a tainted achievement, citing the extra games needed. But Maris trudged on and finally, on October 1, 1961, in front of only 23,154 home fans, he hit a fourth-inning blast off of Boston Red Sox hurler Tracy Stallard to set a single-season record of 61 home runs. Despite the lack of support and the immense pressure, Maris had accomplished a feat once thought insurmountable: he passed the Babe and laid down his claim to Yankee greatness.

Maris was a two-time AL MVP (1960 and 1961), a three-time World Series champion, and would be honored by having the Yankees retire his iconic number 9.

But the number that will be forever associated with the career of Roger Maris is his hard-fought and hard-won 61.

6 CARLTON FISK: BODY ENGLISH

Carlton Fisk was born on December 26, 1947, in Bellows Falls, Vermont, but grew up on the other side of the Connecticut River in Charlestown, New Hampshire.

"Pudge," as he was known for being a chubby child, excelled in both baseball and basketball, and it was actually Fisk's hoop talent that earned him a scholarship to the University of New Hampshire. While at UNH, Fisk played both basketball and baseball, but when he was drafted in the first round, with the fourth overall pick, by the Boston Red Sox in the January 1967 amateur draft, the decision was an easy one. As Fisk would later state, "I could never be a 6-foot-2 power forward and play for the Celtics."

After impressing in the minors, and playing in a few major-league games in 1969 and 1971, Fisk made his splash in 1972, when he played his first full season in Boston. During his initial campaign, Fisk hit .293 with 22 home runs, 28 doubles, and nine triples, tying him for the American League lead. Along with his impressive offensive onslaught, Pudge also won the AL Gold Glove as a catcher. The season culminated in winning the American League Rookie of the Year Award.

As the kid from the Granite State continued to impress, and it looked like nothing could stop him. But as fate would have it, a home plate collision with Leron Lee of the Cleveland Indians on June 28, 1974, left Fisk with torn knee ligaments. Fisk was told that he would never play baseball again. But after reconstructive knee surgery, he was back behind the plate just twelve months later, hitting .331 in the 1975 campaign. And it would be during this magical season that baseball's sixth most memorable home run would occur.

The Hub's beloved team had not won a World Series since 1918, and the fans were more than eager for a championship. The talented 1975 team that featured Luis Tiant, Carl Yastrzemski, Jim Rice, Fred Lynn, and Dwight Evans battled into the World Series, where the Sox would face Cincinnati's Big Red Machine. After five games, the Red Sox were down three games to two, but the teams were returning to Boston for Game Six and, if the Sox could keep things going, a Game Seven.

Game Six would prove to be one of the most famous World Series games ever played. The scoring started early with the home team plating three runs in the bottom of the first. But the Reds would fight back, and after scoring three in the fifth, two in the seventh, and one in the top of the eighth, the visitors had a commanding three-run advantage and could taste the title. But as history would prove, this game was far from over.

In the bottom of the eighth, Bernie Carbo, a former first-round pick of the Reds but now playing for the Red Sox, hit a three-run blast to tie the game. And in the bottom of the ninth, it was Boston's turn to get a whiff of victory when the team had the bases loaded with no outs. But when the Sox failed to score, the thriller headed into extra innings. A magnificent catch by Evans in right field on a drive by Joe Morgan in the top of the 11th inning only added to the excitement. And then in the bottom of the 12th, history would occur.

Fisk stepped up to the plate against right-hander Pat Darcy, Cincinnati's eighth pitcher of the night. Pudge launched Darcy's second offering down the left-field line toward the Green Monster. The capacity crowd held its collective breath, not knowing if the ball would end up fair or foul. In a now-iconic scene, Fisk was jumping up and down and waving his arms fair, in an apparent attempt to use his body English to coax the shot into a game-winner. As the ball struck the foul pole, the crowd erupted. Fisk had sent the Red Sox fans home happy with a 7–6 victory. Interestingly, the iconic image of Fisk waving at the ball was almost not to be. It was later discovered that NBC cameraman Lou Gerard was instructed to follow the flight of the ball. But Gerard, stationed inside the scoreboard in left field, was distracted by a nearby rat. The menacing rodent caused the cameraman to lose track of the ball, and in a moment of spontaneity he kept the camera on Fisk.

Although the MLB Network would later rank this contest as number one in their list of the 20 greatest games ever played, it was not a storybook ending for the Sox. The next day, Joe Morgan's run-producing bloop single in the ninth inning of Game Seven turned into the Series winner for the Reds.

By the time Fisk retired in 1993, he held the record for most home runs by a catcher with 351 (since broken), and he would end up enshrined in the Baseball Hall of Fame. Yet he never hit a home run more memorable than the Game Six World Series blast.

5 KIRK GIBSON: WOUNDED WARRIOR

Kirk Harold Gibson was born in Pontiac, Michigan, on May 28, 1957, and grew up in Waterford, Michigan. As a youth, he was an outstanding all-around athlete. Gibson's baseball career was more of an afterthought than an original goal.

After attending Michigan State University and playing wide receiver for the football team, his All-American status gave him a real chance at the National Football League. At the suggestion of his football coach, Darryl Rogers, Gibson decided to play collegiate baseball as well. And while Gibson played only one year of college baseball, he hit .390 with 16 dingers and 52 RBIs in only 48 games. Eventually, this dual threat was drafted by both the Detroit Tigers baseball team (first round), and the St. Louis Cardinals football team (seventh round). Luckily for the baseball fans of the world, Gibson chose the diamond over the gridiron. And on September 8, 1979, Kirk Gibson made his major-league debut for the Tigers.

Gibson's decision to play professional baseball turned out to be well advised. By the time he concluded his playing career, Gibson was a two-time World Series champion (1984 and 1988), the National League Most Valuable Player (1988), and the American League Championship Series Most Valuable Player (1984). But he will be remembered most for his heroics in the 1988 World Series.

As members of the Los Angeles Dodgers, Gibson and his teammates were the underdogs as they faced the powerful Oakland Athletics in the 1988 World Series. Having injured both legs during the National League Championship Series, and fighting a stomach virus to boot, Gibson was not expected to play.

In Game One, playing in front of their home crowd, the Dodgers were trailing by a run in the bottom of the ninth. Mike Davis was on first, and Los Angeles was down to its final out. It was at this point that Dodgers manager Tommy Lasorda called on the hobbled Gibson to pinch-hit against Oakland's Hall of Fame closer Dennis Eckersley.

Eck quickly got Gibson down in the count, 0–2. Gibson laid off the next two outside pitches. After fouling off a pitch, and then running the count full,

Eckersley was again ready to fire. With the crowd in frenzy, the pitch came in. With an awkward upper body swipe, Kirk took the backdoor slider over the right-field fence, and proceeded with a gimpy trot around the bases, pumping his fist to the jubilation of the crowd. The Dodgers would take the momentum from this 5–4 victory and run away with the title, four games to one.

After his playing career came to an end, Gibson worked as a broadcaster before returning to the dugout to manage and coach. He was named the National League Manager of the Year in 2011, with the Arizona Diamondbacks.

4 JOE CARTER: DREAMS CAN COME TRUE

Joseph Christopher Carter was born on March 7, 1960, in Oklahoma City, Oklahoma. Like many young boys, Carter dreamed of baseball stardom. And perhaps as a foreshadowing of things to come, just months after Carter's birth, Bill Mazeroski hit the first game-winning home run to clinch a World Series.

As the highly talented youngster continued to hone his craft, Carter was finally ready to turn professional after his junior year at Wichita State, when he was selected by the Chicago Cubs as the second overall pick in the 1981 amateur draft.

Two years later, Carter made it to the majors. And before all was said and done, the young man from Middle America would enjoy a decade and a half in both leagues, where he put up some pretty impressive numbers. Need convincing? Carter was a five-time All-Star who ended his career with 396 home runs and 1,145 RBIs. Carter also drove in at least 100 runs in 10 seasons.

But to this day, when the name of Joe Carter is mentioned, there is always the one glorious moment that will forever define the man.

The year was 1993 and the Toronto Blue Jays were vying for their second straight World Series title. Things were looking good for the Jays as they led the Philadelphia Phillies three games to two. Additionally, the Blue Jays were at home playing in front of a packed stadium in Game Six. Although Toronto was in control, there was a reason the Phillies were the National Leagues pennant holders, and when they scored five runs in the seventh inning, and took a 6–5 lead into the ninth inning, the Philly fanatics were tasting a Game Seven. But to quote the great Yogi Berra, "It ain't over 'til it's over."

In the bottom of the ninth, Philadelphia reliever Mitch "Wild Thing" Williams came in from the pen to try to seal the deal. Williams lived up to his name by walking the leadoff batter, Ricky Henderson, on four pitches. After Williams got Devon White to fly out to left, Paul Molitor ripped a single up the middle to put runners on first and second. With the crowd in frenzy, Carter walked to the plate. The slugger had never gotten a hit off Williams in his career, having been retired in all four appearances against the hard-throwing left-hander.

Williams started Carter off with two balls but fought back to even the count at two and two. Williams intended his next pitch to be high and away, but the delivery went down and in. Carter jumped on the mistake, sending the ball into the left field bleachers for a walk-off victory.

Carter's ecstatic dance around the bases mirrored the excitement of the hometown crowd, as there was a collective leap into the air. After the game, Carter was quoted as saying, "I actually dreamed of that moment many times. I dreamed of that moment when I was a little kid. I'd be sitting at my father's garage and daydreaming about that moment. I even wrote it down a few times: 'My dream is to hit a home run to win the World Series.'"

He summarized his sentiments with what the entire baseball world was thinking: "It was the ultimate sports fantasy."

With the blast, Carter became the first person to hit a come-from-behind, game-winning home run to clinch a World Series.

3 HANK AARON: 715

Henry Louis "Hank" Aaron was a Depression-era baby, born on February 5, 1934, in Mobile, Alabama. Affected by the disastrous economy of that era, his parents, Herbert and Estella, struggled to make ends meet, forcing the young Henry and his seven siblings to spend much of their youth picking cotton. But despite their financial woes, the Aaron family loved their baseball. The boys honed their batting skills by hitting bottle caps with sticks, and this unique approach apparently paid dividends as both Henry and his brother Tommie went on to play Major League Baseball. Each established solid reputations, both as players and men of character, but Hank truly left a legacy for the ages.

After a stint playing with the Indianapolis Clowns of the Negro Leagues, Aaron would make his major-league debut on April 13, 1954, with the Milwaukee Braves. In total, Hammerin' Hank played for 23 seasons. And by the time he had retired, he had compiled a staggering list of accomplishments:

- Major-league record for the most career runs batted in (RBIs) with 2,297.
- Major-league record of 1,477 extra-base hits.
- Major-league record of 6,856 total bases.
- 3,771 career hits, placing him third on the all-time list.
- National League's Most Valuable Player in 1957.
- Three Gold Glove Awards.
- The only player in the history of the game to hit 30 home runs in a season at least 15 times.
- 17 consecutive seasons with at least 150 hits, another major-league record.
- All-Star team selection every year from 1955 through 1975.
- And that other thing . . . Hammerin' Hank launched a career total of 755 home runs!

But clearly, Aaron had one dinger that stands apart from the rest. As he began to draw closer to Babe Ruth's "unobtainable" mark of 714 career home runs, he tried to downplay the excitement. But as the sporting world clamored for news of every at-bat, the achievement in the making took on a life of its own.

Unfortunately, there was a sinister element at play in those years. In the early 1970s, racial tension in the United States still ran high. Many fans took offense to the notion that one of the most hallowed milestones in baseball was going to be broken by a black man. To add to the strain, when Aaron ended the 1973 season, he was still sitting on 713 homers, one behind the Babe.

During the ensuing off-season, Aaron received tremendous support, but he received many death threats as well. At one point he publicly wondered if he would survive until the following spring. But as the 1974 season began, Aaron seemed to brush off the overwhelming pressure of the moment, and he dramatically homered off of Jack Billingham in Cincinnati in his first at-bat of the season. This tied him with Babe Ruth at 714.

A few days later, Aaron and the Braves returned home. The date was April 8, 1974. A record crowd of 53,775 came to Atlanta's Fulton County Stadium.

The long-anticipated moment occurred in the fourth inning. To the delight of the roaring crowd, Aaron smacked a pitch from Los Angeles Dodgers hurler Al Downing into the center bullpen. Broadcaster Vin Scully offered an elegant account:

"What a marvelous moment for baseball; what a marvelous moment for Atlanta and the state of Georgia; what a marvelous moment for the country and the world. A black man is getting a standing ovation in the Deep South for breaking a record of an all-time baseball idol. And it is a great moment for all of us, and particularly for Henry Aaron. . . . And for the first time in a long time, that poker face in Aaron shows the tremendous strain and relief of what it must have been like to live with for the past several months."

Aaron would end his career with 755 home runs. Although Barry Bonds has since surpassed the mark, many fans still regard Aaron as the true home run king because of the steroid cloud that hovers over Bonds.

On August 1, 1982, Aaron was enshrined into the Baseball Hall of Fame with 97.8% of the votes, second only to Ty Cobb's 98.2% at the time, and it speaks volumes about the richly deserved respect accorded to one of the classiest gentlemen to ever play the game.

2 BOBBY THOMSON: THE SHOT HEARD 'ROUND THE WORLD

As famous as he became for his legendary home run, many fans don't know that Bobby Thomson was not a native of the United States.

Robert Brown Thomson was born on October 25, 1923, in Glasgow, Scotland. When he was two, little Bobby, his mother, and his five siblings made their way to America to join their father in pursuit of a better life. And for the youngest child, Bobby, what a life it would be.

Thomson quickly acclimated to life in the States, showing early promise as a ballplayer. In 1942, the young man who grew up in Staten Island, New York, must have thought he hit the lottery when he signed a baseball contract with the New York Giants right after graduating from Curtis High School. His signing bonus? $100. But before his professional playing days could begin, Thomson served his country in the army air force, where he trained as a bombardier.

After the conclusion of World War II, he returned to his first love, eventually making it to the big leagues to stay in 1947 after being called up to play 18 games at the end of the previous season. His rookie year proved successful, as he batted .283 with 29 home runs and 85 runs batted in. Just two years later, in 1949, he was even more impressive, posting a .309 batting average with 27 home runs and 109 RBIs.

But in baseball, as in any sport, a single moment can forever define a career. And this has never been more applicable than Bobby Thomson's historic moment in the 1951 National League playoffs.

On August 11, the Giants were trailing their crosstown rival Brooklyn Dodgers by a staggering 13½ games. There seemed little hope for the boys from the Polo Grounds, but that's when they caught fire, winning their next 16 games in a row and 37 of their last 44, tying the Dodgers at season's end. A three-game playoff would ensue for the National League pennant.

Although Brooklyn won the coin toss to determine home field advantage, Dodgers manager Chuck Dressen made the controversial decision to play Game One at home and Game Two and, if necessary, Game Three, on the road. Dressen argued that if his team could take the first game, the club would need only one of the next two to secure the pennant. But the strategy backfired, as the Giants took Game One at Ebbets Field in Brooklyn, with Thomson's two-run blast off of Ralph Branca providing the difference in the Giants 3–1 victory.

The Dodgers fought back and dominated in Game Two at the Polo Grounds behind a six-hit complete-game effort by their rookie hurler Clem Labine, taking the game 10–0 and tying the series at a game apiece. It all came down to Game Three, one game to decide the season and the pennant.

The day was October 3, 1951. Despite the significance of the game, only 34,320 fans attended, due in large part to poor weather. The contest featured a battle of pitching aces, with the Dodgers Don Newcombe facing off against the Giants 23-game winner, Sal Maglie.

The Dodgers got off to a fast start, scoring in the top of the first inning when Jackie Robinson singled to knock in Pee Wee Reese. After that, both pitchers silenced the bats until the bottom of the seventh, when Thomson's sacrifice fly tied the game at one run each. But in the top of the eighth, a fatigued Maglie gave up three runs to Brooklyn, so that when the Giants came to bat in the bottom of the ninth, they trailed by a score of 4–1.

Hope was dim, but there was no quit in the Giants. Alvin Dark singled to start the rally, then Don Mueller followed with a single of his own. With men on first and third, Monte Irvin then popped up for out number one. Next, Whitey Lockman doubled to send Dark home and Mueller to third. Clint Hartung came in to run for Mueller, who injured his ankle sliding into third. The Dodgers pulled an exhausted Newcombe, inserting Ralph Branca in relief. Although Branca had given up several homers to Thomson during the season, as well as a dinger in Game One of the playoff series, Dressen made the decision to bring him in.

With rookie Willie Mays on deck, Thomson stepped into the box. Branca's first pitch was down the middle for a called strike. The second pitch came in high and tight, but Thomson somehow turned on it, sending the ball over the left field wall, and the Giants into the World Series.

In one of the most memorable home run calls of all time, Russ Hodges, who was broadcasting the game on WMCA radio, gave the following account of the action:

> Bobby Thomson . . . up there swingin'. . . . He's had two out of three, a single and a double, and Billy Cox is playing him right on the third-base line. . . . One out, last of the ninth . . . Branca pitches . . . Bobby

> Thomson takes a strike called on the inside corner . . . Bobby hitting at .292. . . . He's had a single and a double and he drove in the Giants first run with a long fly to center . . . Brooklyn leads it 4–2 . . . Hartung down the line at third not taking any chances . . . Lockman with not too big of a lead at second, but he'll be runnin' like the wind if Thomson hits one . . . Branca throws . . . [sound of bat meeting ball] There's a long drive . . . it's gonna be, I believe . . . **THE GIANTS WIN THE PENNANT!! THE GIANTS WIN THE PENNANT! THE GIANTS WIN THE PENNANT! THE GIANTS WIN THE PENNANT!** Bobby Thomson hits into the lower deck of the left field stands! The Giants win the pennant and they're goin' crazy, they're goin' crazy! HEEEY-OH!!! [10-second pause for crowd noise] I don't believe it! I don't believe it! I do not believe it! Bobby Thomson . . . hit a line drive . . . into the lower deck . . . of the left field stands . . . and this . . . place is goin' crazy! The Giants! Horace Stoneham has got a winner! The Giants won it . . . by a score of 5 to 4 . . . and they're pickin' Bobby Thomson up . . . and carryin' him off the field!

Interestingly, the only reason the most famous call in baseball history can be heard today is that a Brooklyn-based fan by the name of Lawrence Goldberg asked his mother to tape the game. For years, an urban legend was promulgated stating that Goldberg had recorded the game to torment a friend, who was a Giants fan, with the hometown broadcaster's call. But in reality, Goldberg was actually a lifelong Giants fan.

Although the Giants went on to lose the Series to the Yankees, four games to two, the glory of Thomson's home run has never diminished. Bobby Thomson passed away on August 16, 2010, but during his charmed life, when asked about his famous clout, he said, "It was the best thing that ever happened to me. It may have been the best thing that ever happened to anybody."

1 BILL MAZEROSKI: MAZ

Although Pittsburgh, Pennsylvania, claims him as its favorite son, William Stanley Mazeroski was actually born on September 5, 1936, in Wheeling, West Virginia. The young man affectionately referred to as "Maz" rose from a Depression-era childhood to become a solid young man, and an excellent two-sport athlete.

At Warren Consolidated High School in Tiltonsville, Ohio, Maz was a standout in both basketball and baseball. He eventually chose the infield over the hardwood, and this decision would set the course for what was arguably the most memorable home run in the history of our national pastime.

Recognized early because of his outstanding talent, Mazeroski was signed by the Pittsburgh Pirates in 1954, when he was just seventeen. Though he initially was a shortstop, the Bucs quickly switched him to second base, another fateful turn in his career, this one ultimately leading to his becoming one of the most valuable defensive players of all time. Maz's first Gold Glove was earned in 1958, and seven more would follow. Over his career he amassed a .983 fielding percentage, and he topped the National League in assists in nine seasons. More than a half century since his professional debut, he still holds the major-league record for double plays by a second baseman. So how good was he? Baseball analyst Bill James wrote that "Bill Mazeroski's defensive statistics are probably the most impressive of any player at any position."

In the 1960 World Series, the Pirates were paired against the powerful New York Yankees, who had just won their 10th pennant in 12 years. Like most second basemen, Maz wasn't considered a power hitter, but in the fourth inning of Game One he launched an offering from Yankees pitcher Jim Coates over the left-field scoreboard. To the delight of the hometown fans, the two-run blast would prove to be the difference in Pittsburgh's 6–4 victory.

Game Two was a different story, however. The Yankees came back with a vengeance, pounding out hit after hit to squash the National League champs by a score of 16–3. Game Three's venue changed to Yankee Stadium, where the outcome was another Yankee rout, this time 10–0. But then the gritty Pirates squeaked out Games Four and Five by the scores of 3–2 and 5–2, respectively.

Now the Pittsburgh club was only one game away from clinching its first championship since 1925, and they were heading home, where they could wrap up the series in Game Six. But nothing doing, said the Yankees, who put on another batting clinic to claim the win by an eye-popping 12–0.

The scene was now set for Game Seven. A crowd of 36,683 packed Forbes Field in Pittsburgh with visions of a home team victory, and the Bucs hopes soared when they scored two runs in the first inning and two more in the second to take a 4–0 lead. It was not to last. New York turned the tables by scoring one run in the fifth and four more in the sixth. The game then seesawed back and forth with Pittsburgh pulling ahead, so that the Yanks were down by two runs going into the top of the ninth. New York came back once again, this time to even the score at 9–9.

The city of Pittsburgh took a deep, anxious breath. It had been decades since their beloved Bucs were even in the Series, let alone in a position to win. And now here they were, bottom of the ninth, tie game, the World Series at stake. Nothing short of high drama, with the hopes and dreams of millions of fans on the line, not to mention all those who wagered on the game.

At this point in the series New York had scored twice as many runs as Pittsburgh, a total of 55 to 26, but the scrappy Bucs had managed to hang on, and now needed to push just one more man across the plate to claim the championship.

Mazeroski led off the bottom of the ninth.

Yankees hurler Ralph Terry glared in and delivered his first offering. Maz laid off the pitch. Ball one. Terry wound up and let fly again, this time over the plate. Maz offered, his bat made contact, and as the world watched, the baseball went deep, *deep*, and soared over the left-field wall.

The delirious Mazeroski hopped and skipped around the bases, waving his hat to thunderous roars and applause from Steel City fans. As the legendary NBC announcer Mel Allen would call it, "There's a drive into deep left field . . . look out now . . . that ball is going, going, gone! And the World Series is over! Mazeroski . . . hits it over the left-field fence, and the Pirates win it 10 to 9 and win the World Series!"

Due in large part to his defensive prowess, Mazeroski was enshrined in the Baseball Hall of Fame in 2001. But it was Maz's legendary swing on October 13, 1960, that resulted in the only home run to win Game Seven of a World Series, and with it a legitimate claim to the title of the greatest home run in baseball history.

So what ever happened to that legendary baseball? A fourteen-year-old boy by the name of Andy Jerpe had the incredible luck of finding it outside the stadium. And to make Jerpe's dream complete, Mazeroski signed it.

So is the baseball in Cooperstown? Is it prominently displayed in Jerpe's home? Did the young man cash in and sell it to a collector for an untold fortune? Actually, none of the above. The prized possession was actually lost in a high patch of weeds when Jerpe used it while playing ball with friends.

You just can't make this stuff up!

EXTRA INNINGS

102 BIG PAPI: SEÑOR OCTUBRE

Dave Roberts.

The Boston Red Sox spare, fleet outfielder who we best remember from Game Four of the 2004 American League Championship Series.

The Boston Red Sox were trailing 4–3 to the New York Yankees in the bottom of the ninth, down three games to none in the series, three outs from elimination and on the brink of another soul-crushing baseball winter.

Kevin Millar opened the ninth by working a walk off New York's future Hall of Fame reliever Mariano Rivera.

Roberts then took Millar's place at first base. Speed was his game, but he hadn't been in one for 11 days. In then an unheralded move, Roberts had been acquired from Los Angeles Dodgers at the July 31 trading deadline for a moment like this—if it would ever come.

"I remember Maury Wills (who stole 586 bases in his career) on the back-field in Vero Beach," said Roberts. "He said, 'DR, one of these days you're going to have to steal an important base when everyone in the ballpark knows you're gonna steal, but you've got to steal that base and you can't be afraid to steal that base.'"

Dave Roberts did—barely.

Hope was alive standing on second base.

Then Bill Mueller singled him home.

The game was tied, but not over.

It wouldn't be until the 12th inning—five hours and 12 minutes after the first pitch. When David Ortiz's left-handed swing golfed Paul Quantrill's 2-1 offering into the Yankees bullpen.

It was the second-most famous play from that game, but Ortiz continues to call it his career-defining moment.

"That hit," Ortiz is happy to repeat through the years, "it put me on the map."

It was a map that traced back to the Dominican Republic, when Ortiz, then known as David Arias, was a seventeen-year-old in a 1992 Seattle Mariners tryout camp.

"David was this big kid who had power," scout Gordon Blakeley told Mike Ashmore of *The Trentonian* after Ortiz was elected to the Hall of Fame. "But he really wasn't very good at anything else; kind of a one-tool guy, and even the was a question mark because it was so pull-oriented.

"I don't know if you remember Oscar Gamble but he pulled off everything and tried to hit towards the right-field foul pole, and I remember David hitting a lot of balls really hard, but foul and out of play. But the area scout said to me, 'He's got a really good makeup,' so I said, 'Well, let's sign him. I think David got maybe $3,500. But of course, when I ran into David years later when he was a star with the Red Sox, he goes, 'You didn't give me enough money. And I said, 'No, but I gave you an opportunity.'"

In 1996, the Mariners would deal Arias to the Minnesota Twins for veteran third baseman Dave Hollins.

That same year he would trade the name Arias for his late mother's last name, Ortiz.

In the Twins system the 6-foot-3, 230-pounder was compared to Hall of Famer Willie McCovey and Dave Parker—big men with big bats.

Ortiz first taste of the big leagues came in 1997.

By 2002, he was the Twins cleanup hitter. Ortiz clubbed a career-high 20 home runs helping the Twins to their first playoff appearance in 11 years. In Minnesota he wasn't called Big Papi, but the Big O, known for being a charismatic, gregarious prankster.

He was twenty-seven.

That December, the Twins had placed Ortiz on waivers. He was trade bait with no nibbles.

Depending on what story you believe, the Twins, then operating on a small budget, didn't want to pay Ortiz, who was eligible for salary arbitration and the chance to potentially double his $950,000 salary, or they believed Matthew LeCroy was a better option.

Neither were considered particularly good defensive first baseman. The two had platooned, splitting designated hitter duties in 2002.

There was also concern in the baseball world about Ortiz staying healthy. He had chronic wrist woes and knee surgery had interrupted his 2002 season.

The Twins also had two up-and-coming left-handed hitting prospects, Joe Mauer and Justin Morneau.

With no potential trade partners, the Twins released David Ortiz.

The Boston Red Sox had no interest in him.

Just like every other team in baseball.

Ortiz's agent had to send faxes to every team in baseball alerting them to the big man's availability.

Part of the Red Sox's off season plan was to upgrade first base and designated hitter.

New general manager Theo Epstein felt he could do better than Tony Clark, Cliff Floyd, and Jose Offerman.

Epstein traded for Jeremy Giambi, not the marquee star like his slugging brother Jason, but he hit left-handed and was considered a walk machine with on-base percentage becoming more and more important in the game.

The Red Sox were also about to purchase Kevin Millar, a right-handed hitting first baseman from the Florida Marlins.

First base was covered. Or so the Red Sox thought.

Then Pedro Martinez called asking the Red Sox to sign his friend, David Ortiz.

Martinez, a Cy Young Award–winning pitcher, a future Hall of Famer, was in contract extension talks with team president Larry Lucchino.

According to the *Boston Globe*'s Alex Speier, the Red Sox decided to have one of their scouts in the Dominican League to work out Ortiz at first base "determine his fit for the roster and how it might be complementary to or redundant with Giambi."

Ortiz was offered a show-me contract but no guarantee.

Giambi was in the Red Sox opening day lineup. Ortiz was not.

Giambi was hitting .125 at the close of April. Ortiz was not much better. His average was .212. He only had two home runs by the time May came and went. Ortiz asked Epstein to trade him to get more playing time somewhere else. Epstein said no.

Giambi's last Red Sox at bat came in early August.

By then David Ortiz was in the midst of building the foundation of his legend.

He finished fifth in the American League Most Valuable Player voting. With good reason—he slugged 31 dingers and knocked in 101 runs.

He was even better in 2004 with 41 homers and 139 RBIs.

Red Sox broadcaster Jerry Remy dubbed him "Big Papi' that year. (Ortiz had the habit of calling teammates and strangers "papi," Spanish for daddy. Remy decided there was no bigger papi than Ortiz.

Nine days before he hit the walk-off against the Yankees, Oritz had delivered a walk-off against the California Angels to advance the Sox in the playoffs. (The irony: Ortiz started his Red Sox postseason career 0-for-16.)

On the same day he delivered the two-run homer that he believed put him on the baseball map, he beat the Yankees with a 14th-inning single, sending the series back to New York where Red Sox completed their epic comeback.

No team in baseball history had been down three games to none to win a series.

In that 2004 postseason, Ortiz went 22-for-55 with five home runs. (He would hit 17 homers and knock in 61 runs in 85 postseason games.)

The Red Sox beat the St. Louis Cardinals in the World Series, the team's first World Championship since 1918.

Ortiz would be part of three Red Sox World Series championships.

In 2009, the *New York Times* reported Ortiz had tested positive for a performance-enhancing substance. (That year he didn't hit his first homer until May 20.) Seven years later, he would be exonerated by the baseball commissioner.

(Ortiz told Tom Verducci of *Sports Illustrated* in 2016: "Let me tell you, there's not one player in baseball, not one player, that has been drug tested more than David Ortiz. I guarantee you that. I never failed a test.")

Ortiz then become a kind of spokesman and symbol for the city after the Boston Marathon bombings in 2013, with an F-bomb laced speech given before an April 20 game against the Kansas City Royals.

In 2016, when Ortiz was forty, he hit 38 home runs—the most by a player in his final season.

His final home run total was 541—including 11 walk-off home runs in the regular season.

His number 34 (which he picked as homage to Twins Hall of Famer Kirby Puckett) was retired a year later.

In 2019, Ortiz survived being shot in the back while visiting in the Dominican Republic.

In 2022, Ortiz was a first-ballot selection for the baseball Hall of Fame.

"Being in the Hall of Fame, I never really never dreamed of it," Ortiz said the evening of his selection, Pedro Martinez by his side. "All I was looking for was the opportunity to be able to be a great player and it came true once I got to the Red Sox."

SOURCES

Books

Appel, Marty. *Pinstripe Empire: The New York Yankees From Before the Babe to After the Boss.* New York: Bloomsbury USA, 2012.

Armour, Mark. *The Great Eight: 1975 Cincinnati Reds.* Lincoln, Nebraska: University of Nebraska, 2014.

Auker, Elden, and Tom Keegan. *Sleeper Cars and Flannel Uniforms: A Lifetime of Memories from Striking Out the Babe to Teeing It Up with the President.* Chicago: Triumph Books, 2006.

Barra, Allen. *Yogi Berra: Eternal Yankee.* New York: W.W. Norton & Company, 2010. *Mickey and Willie: Mantle and Mays, the Parallel Lives of Baseball's Golden Age*. New York: Three Rivers Press, 2014.

Bashe, Philip. *Dog Days: The New York Yankees Fall From Grace and Return to Glory, 1964–1976.* New York: Random House, 1994.

Belth, Alex, ed. *Lasting Yankee Stadium Memories: Unforgettable Tales from the House that Ruth Built.* New York: Skyhorse Publishing Inc., 2010, 2013.

Bench, Johnny. *Catch You Later: The Autobiography of Johnny Bench.* New York: Harper Collins, 1979.

Berkow, Ira. *Hank Greenberg: Hall of Fame Slugger*. Philadelphia: The Jewish Publication Society, 2001.

Bouton, Jim. *Ball Four*. New York: Dell, 1971.

Bradlee, Ben Jr. *The Kid: The Immortal Life of Ted Williams.* New York: Back Bay Books, 2014.

Bryant, Howard. *The Last Hero: A Life of Henry Aaron*. New York: Anchor, 2011.

Cairns, Bob. *Pen Men: Baseball's Greatest Bullpen Stories by the Men Who Brought the Game Relief.* New York: St. Martin's Press, 1993.

Cataneo, David. *Tony C: The Triumph and Tragedy of Tony Conigliaro*. Nashville, Tennessee: Rutledge Hill Press, 1998.

Cramer, Richard Ben. *Joe DiMaggio: The Hero's Life.* Simon & Schuster, 2000. *Babe: The Legend Comes to Life.* New York: Simon & Schuster, 1974.

Creamer, Robert W. *Stengel: His Life and Times*. New York: Simon & Schuster, 1984.

Daniel, W. Harrison. *Jimmie Foxx: The Life and Times of a Baseball Hall of Famer*. Jefferson, North Carolina: McFarland & Co., 2004.

Durocher, Leo, and Ed Linn. *Nice Guys Finish Last*. Chicago: University of Chicago, 2009.

Eig, Jonathan. *Luckiest Man: The Life and Death of Lou Gehrig*. New York: Simon & Schuster, 2005.

Freedman, Lew. *Hard-Luck Harvey Haddix and the Greatest Game Ever Lost*. Jefferson, North Carolina: McFarland, 2009.

Frost, Mark. *Game Six: Cincinnati, Boston, and the 1975 World Series: The Triumph of America's Pastime*. New York: Hyperion, 2009.

Gammons, Peter. *Beyond the Sixth Game: What's Happened to Baseball Since the Greatest Game in World Series History*. New York: Penguin, 1986.

Golenbock, Peter. *Dynasty: The New York Yankees, 1949–1964*. Englewood Cliffs, New Jersey: Prentice Hall, 1975.

Griffey, Ken, and Phil Pepe. *Big Red: Baseball, Fatherhood and My Life in the Big Red Machine*. Chicago: Triumph Books, 2014.

Halberstam, David. *October, 1964*. New York: Ballantine Books, 1995. *Summer of '49*. New York: William Morrow, 2006.

Hamill, Pete, ed. *The Subway Series Reader*. New York: Simon & Schuster, 2000.

Hirsch, James S. *Willie Mays: The Life, the Legend*. New York: Scribner, 2010.

Holtzman, Jerome. *No Cheering in the Press Box*. New York: Holt, Rinehart and Winston, 1974.

Honig, Donald. *Baseball When the Grass Was Real: Baseball from the Twenties to the Forties Told by the Men Who Played It*. Lincoln, Nebraska: Bison Books, 1975. *Baseball Between the Lines*. Lincoln, Nebraska: University of Nebraska, 1993.

James, Bill. *Whatever Happened to the Hall of Fame? Baseball, Cooperstown, and the Politics of Glory*. New York: Free Press, 1995. *The New Bill James Historical Baseball Abstract*. New York: Free Press, 2003.

Johnson, Richard A., and Glenn Stout. *Red Sox Century: The Definitive History of Baseball's Most Storied Franchise*. New York: Houghton Mifflin Harcourt, 2005.

Klima, John. *Bushville Wins!: The Wild Saga of the 1957 Milwaukee Braves and the Screwballs, Sluggers, and Beer Swiggers Who Canned the New York Yankees and Changed Baseball*. New York: Thomas Dunne Books, 2012.

Leavy, Jane. *The Last Boy: Mickey Mantle and the End of America's Childhood.* New York: HarperCollins, 2010.

Lewis, Michael. *Moneyball: The Art of Winning an Unfair Game*. New York: W.W. Norton & Company, 2004.

Kahn, Roger. *The Boys of Summer*. New York: Harper Perennial Modern Classics, 2006.

Kennedy, Kostya. *56: Joe DiMaggio and the Last Magic Number in Sports.* New York: Sports Illustrated Books, 2011.

Mack, Connie. *My 66 Years in the Big Leagues*. New York: Dover Publications, 2009.

Madden, Bill. *1954: The Year Willie Mays and the First Generation of Black Superstars Changed Major League Baseball Forever.* Boston: DaCapo, 2015.

Maraniss, David. *Clemente: The Passion and Grace of Baseball's Last Hero.* New York: Simon & Schuster, 2007.

Marmer, Mel, and Bill Nowlin. *The Year of Blue Snow: the 1964 Philadelphia Phillies*. Phoenix, Arizona: Society for American Baseball Research, 2013.

Montville, Leigh. *Ted Williams: The Biography of an American Hero.* New York: Anchor, 2005. *The Big Bam: The Life and Times of Babe Ruth*. New York: Anchor, 2007.

Okrent, Daniel. *The Ultimate Baseball Book: Expanded and Updated.* New York: Mariner Books, 2000.

Parker, Clifton Blue, and Bill Nowlin. *Sweet '60: The 1960 Pittsburgh Pirates*. Phoenix, Arizona: Society for American Baseball Research, 2013.

Peterson, Richard "Pete". *Pops: The Willie Stargell Story*. Chicago: Triumph Books, 2013.

Piersall, Jim, and Al Hirshberg. *Fear Strikes Out: The Jim Piersall Story*. Lincoln, Nebraska: Bison Books, 1999.

Rampersad, Arnold. *Jackie Robinson: A Biography*. New York: Knopf, 1998.

Ritter, Lawrence. *The Glory of Their Times: The Story of the Early Days of Baseball Told by the Men Who Played It*. New York: Harper Perennial Modern Classics, 2010.

Robinson, Frank, and Dave Anderson. *Frank: The First Year*. New York: Holt, Rinehart and Winston, 1976.

Rosenthal, Harold. *The Ten Best Years of Baseball: An Informal History of the Fifties.* New York: Contemporary Books, 1979.

Sherman, Joel. *Birth of a Dynasty*. Emmaus, Pennsylvania: Rodale, 2006.

Snyder, Brad. *A Well-Paid Slave: Curt Flood's Fight for Free Agency in Professional Sports.* New York: Plume, 2007.

Sowell, Mike. *One Pitch Away: The Players' Stories of the 1986 League Championships and World Series.* New York: Macmillan, 1995.

Stein, Fred. *Mel Ott: The Little Giant of Baseball.* Jefferson, North Carolina: McFarland, 1999.

Stout, Glenn, and Richard A. Johnson. *The Cubs: The Complete Story of Chicago Cubs Baseball.* Boston, Houghton Mifflin Harcourt, 2007.

Vecsey, George. *Stan Musial: An American Life*. New York: ESPN Books, 2012.

Ward, Geoffrey C., and Ken Burns. *Baseball, An Illustrated History*. New York: Knopf, 1994.

Websites

baltimoresun.com
baseballprospectcus.com
baseball-reference.com
bostonglobe.com
bronxbanterblog.com
chicagotribune.com
hardballtimes.com
latimes.com
nydailynews.com
nypost.com
nytimes.com
philly.com
sabr.org
sportingnews.com
washingtonpost.com

Articles

Abraham, Peter. "David Ortiz already had a presence in the Hall of Fame. Now, he'll be immortalized." *Boston Globe*, January 25, 2022.

Ashmore, Mike. "Future Stars Series VP Of Player Personnel l Gordon Blakeley Speaks on Signing HoF'er David Ortiz." January 27, 2022.

Bishop, Bill. "Casey Stengel." SABR Baseball Biography Project. Retrieved January 11, 2016.

Boxerman, Burton. "Ken Boyer." SABR Baseball Biography Project. Retrieved January 11, 2016.

Cahill, Michael. "Al Weis." SABR Baseball Biography Project. Retrieved January 11, 2016.

Crehan, Herb, and Bill Nowlin. "Carl Yastrzemski." SABR Baseball Biography Project. Retrieved January 11, 2016.

Feinsand, Mark. Epstein: Ortiz asked for a trade in 2003, MLB.com, April 24, 2018.

Goldstein, Richard, "Dick Sisler, 78, Whose Homer Won '50 Pennant for Phillies." *New York Times*, November 23, 1998.

Hoffer, Richard. "Mickey Mantle: The Legacy of the Last Great Player on the Last Great Team." *Sports Illustrated*, August 21, 1995.

Johnson, Bill. "Gabby Hartnett." SABR Baseball Biography Project. Retrieved January 11, 2016.

Lapointe, Joe. "Boy Who Helped Yankees Is a Hit Again." *New York Times*, April 14, 2006.

McAdam, Sean. "Former Twins GM Terry Ryan recalls, with candor and remorse, decision to walk away from David Ortiz" *Boston Sports Journal*, January 25, 2022.

McCue, Andy. "Branch Rickey." SABR Baseball Biography Project. Retrieved January 11, 2016.

Miller, Mark. "Harvey Haddix." SABR Baseball Biography Project. Retrieved January 11, 2016.

Neal III, LaVelle. "Before Hall of Fame, before 'Big Papi,' David Ortiz was a fun-loving Twin," *Star Tribune*, January 25, 2022.

Nowlin, Bill. "Tony Conigliaro." SABR Baseball Biography Project. Retrieved January 11, 2016.

———"Johnny Pesky." SABR Baseball Biography Project. Retrieved January 11, 2016.

———"Rick Wise." SABR Baseball Biography Project. Retrieved January 11, 2016.

———"Ted Williams." SABR Baseball Biography Project. Retrieved January 11, 2016.

Reusse, Patrick "While Twins saved money, Ortiz keeps saving Red Sox," October 16, 2013.

Rippel, Joel. "Kent Hrbek." SABR Baseball Biography Project. Retrieved January 11, 2016.

Rosen, Dick. "Hal Smith." SABR Baseball Biography Project. Retrieved January 11, 2016.

Schulman, Henry. "Candlestick Classics #3, Day of Sweet Revenge: Joe Morgan's Clutch Homer Knocked the Dodgers Out of the Pennant Race on the Final Day of the 1982 Season and Made the Braves Champions." *San Francisco Chronicle*, September 7, 1999.

Shaughnessy, Dan "David Ortiz's election seems to be another sign of a shift in Hall of Fame voting philosophy," *Boston Globe*, January 25, 2022.

Speier, Alex, Who is really responsible for David Ortiz landing in Boston?, *Boston Globe*, September 29, 2016.

Stein, Fred. "Mel Ott." SABR Baseball Biography Project. Retrieved January 11, 2016.

Weber, Bruce. "Dusty Rhodes, Star Pinch-Hitter in '54 Series, Dies at 82." *New York Times*, June 18, 2009.

Wolf, Gregory H. "Joe Adcock." SABR Baseball Biography Project. Retrieved January 11, 2016.